1-4

America in the World

America in the World

A Guide to U.S. Foreign Policy

Wallace Irwin, Jr.

PUBLISHED FOR THE
FOREIGN POLICY ASSOCIATION
BY PRAEGER PUBLISHERS

The Foreign Policy Association is a private, nonprofit, nonpartisan educational organization. For 65 years, the Association has worked to stimulate wider interest, greater understanding and more effective participation by American citizens in world affairs. FPA sponsors a wide variety of programs and publications analyzing the problems of American foreign policy. It works closely with many other public and private organizations and with the nation's schools and colleges in its educational effort. The Association strives to air different viewpoints impartially; it advocates none.

Library of Congress Cataloging in Publication Data

Irwin, Wallace.
    America in the world.
    Bibliography: p.
    Includes index.
    1. United States—Foreign relations—1945–
I. Foreign Policy Association.   II. Title.
E744.I69 1983   327.73   83-1154
ISBN 0-03-062874-1
ISBN 0-03-062876-8 (pbk.)

Published in 1983 by Praeger Publishers
CBS Educational and Professional Publishing
a Division of CBS Inc.
521 Fifth Avenue, New York, NY 10175 USA

3456789   052   987654321

Printed in the United States of America
on acid-free paper

In the democratic countries generally, the great body of citizens are refusing to wait until negotiations are over or policies are acted upon or even determined. They demand to know what is going on and to have an opportunity to express their opinions at all stages of diplomatic proceedings....

The usefulness of this new departure is subject to one inevitable condition. That is, that the democracy which is undertaking to direct the business of diplomacy should learn the business.

Elihu Root,
American statesman (1922)

Foreword

Foreign policy has always been a popular topic of discussion and debate in the United States. For two centuries the American-in-the-street has been trading opinions—sometimes even trading blows—with his or her neighbor over whether to lean toward royalist England or republican France; whether to annex Texas or Cuba or Canada; whether to fight in Europe; what to do about Russia, China, Israel, Vietnam, Greece, Poland, El Salvador, nuclear weapons, the United Nations, imported Japanese cars, even the whales of the deep ocean.

To many of us, much of the time, foreign policy means little but trouble. Dean Rusk, who was Secretary of State in the stormy 1960s, used to describe the State Department gloomily as "the department of bad news." The imperturbable George P. Shultz, on being sworn into the same office in 1982, took a more buoyant stance, saying he saw opportunities ahead to do "wonderful things" abroad; but how buoyant he would be after some time in that office remained to be seen. If foreign policy is still a popular topic in the problematical 1980s, one reason may be the simple pleasure most of us get from deciding who is to blame.

But surely there are more serious reasons. America's wide and deep involvement in world affairs, year after year, is obvious to whoever so much as glances at the headlines or the TV news. And that involvement cannot fail to affect our individual lives. For example:

- For security in a world of conflict, this country has over 2 million of its citizens in a permanent and expensive military establishment, much of it posted on foreign soil.
- Wars, insurrections, and palace revolutions keep breaking out in distant countries, and most of them seem to affect American interests, some even threaten to draw Americans into combat again.
- The United States and the Soviet Union are now in the fourth decade of their nuclear arms race, and nobody can be sure it will not end in world catastrophe.
- The nation's compassion is stirred—and its strategic interests are often affected—by popular pressures in many countries for basic human rights and a better material life.

- The ceaseless two-way tide of goods, money, and people flowing across our borders creates ever-changing patterns of gain and loss for American jobholders, investors, consumers, and ethnic groups.

In these and other ways, for better or worse, Americans feel the world's impact. And that is only half the story, for America, in its turn, exerts a tremendous impact on the world:

- Foreign economies depend heavily on exports to this country, the biggest national market on earth.
- The outward flow of American capital, manufactures, farm products, technology, and training is an enormous factor in world economic growth and change.
- The United States is the Western anchor of the world balance of power and a leading participant in most of the main issues on which imminent decisions of war and peace depend.
- American actions will go far to determine in the decades ahead whether a sustainable balance can be struck between humanity's rising population and the earth's resources.
- And American life, despite all its well-advertised faults, still excites admiration and imitation abroad by its dynamism, freedom, tolerance, and material abundance.

All these kinds of interaction may be pretty much taken for granted nowadays, but things have not always been that way. Less than half a century ago, the question of whether the United States could (or should) isolate itself from the world's evils (and also from the world's goods, in both senses of that word) was still being hotly debated. What changed all that was World War II, from which the country emerged as the strongest power on earth and the main adversary of that other superpower, the Soviet Union.

Today America's global supremacy is less than it was, and Americans no longer enjoy that wide margin for error that goes with overwhelming power. Controversy continues on how to meet this changed situation, but there is not much support for the old-fashioned isolationist solution of simply slamming the door on the world. America's need for physical security, its economic interests, its bonds of kinship and affection with foreign peoples, its commitment to universal ideals—all these things pull us irresistibly toward continued deep involvement in the world and its problems.

The Citizen's Role

Granted all that, do we as citizens really need more than a casual awareness of the foreign policy problems our leaders are hired to cope with? Can anything good result when you or I, armed with a few scraps of information, lobby in Washington or demonstrate in the streets for the foreign policy we think we want?

There is a respectable school of thought that says no. A little learning, said the poet Alexander Pope, is a dangerous thing. Involvement of a sketchily informed electorate in foreign policy, we are often told, only leads to disjointed policies based on narrow interests and popular illusions. Therefore, this field of policy above all should be left to the professionals. After all, we don't perform heart transplants by majority vote; why use that method to make foreign policy, which is just as intricate, and is dangerous not to one person but to millions?

Obviously, this book would not have been written if the author agreed with that point of view. Policy-makers are not always wise, and citizen-critics are not always foolish. Anyway, whether we, the people, ought to be involved in foreign policy or not, we *are* involved. Foreign policy issues are a main feature of America's political landscape. Politicians regularly disagree on them and so do the professional experts; and elections often turn on those disagreements. Particular issues, ranging from the future of Israel to import competition, are of overriding importance to large and influential groups. Now and then, an issue like the Vietnam War or the Iranian hostage crisis arouses almost the whole nation. No President can halt the tide of popular pressure when citizens, ignorant or not, become strongly concerned over some foreign policy question. Where the people feel their interests to be at stake, no leader can succeed in a policy that they oppose.

All the more reason, then, why we who do involve ourselves with matters of foreign policy should do so with knowledge and intelligence. That is the first and simplest reason why *studying* foreign policy, not just talking casually about it, is worthwhile. A further reason is that, in our society, the few thousand leaders and professionals in government and private life who largely determine the nation's foreign relations year in and year out—those who are called the "foreign policy establishment"—are recruited mostly from among those of us who keep informed in this field. The more you know about foreign policy, or about certain aspects of it, the more likely it is that you will become influential in making it.

Finally, there is a reason which has a touch of idealism in it. Most of us feel some curiosity about, and concern for, the human family to which we belong. That famous line of the ancient Roman dramatist Terence still reverberates: "I am a man, and nothing that is human do I consider foreign to me." To feel that kinship in the abstract is not difficult; to clothe it with reality, and to do anything useful about even a small part of it, requires knowledge.

The aim of this small book, then, is to help satisfy that need for knowledge. It is not "all you need to know"; its aim is not to be an end of the journey but an aid to exploration, something like a road map. Nor does it attempt to convert anybody to this or that opinion on disputed issues; rather, it assumes that readers want to weigh the facts and arguments and form opinions of their own.

The Scope of Foreign Policy

The term "foreign policy" is used in so many ways that a working definition may be useful. Does the United States actually have *a* foreign policy—some master list of dos and don'ts to guide the nation's conduct abroad, either written down or carried around in the policy-makers' heads? No, it does not. A sufficient definition of U.S. foreign policy as the term is used in this book is simply this: *the sum of everything the United States government* does or says that affects the nation's foreign relations.* Foreign policy evolves from day to day, usually in small details, sometimes by sudden leaps. There is some coherence and continuity in it but there is also much confusion, contradiction, and accident. Some policies, like the Atlantic Alliance or the reduction of trade barriers, have proved to be remarkably durable, standing out like mountain peaks as events move along (although even mountains change and erode with time). Others, like support for human rights or U.S.-Soviet détente, appear and disappear as bafflingly as the smile on the Cheshire cat. Still others, like avoidance of "entangling alliances," have vanished, seemingly forever, with changes in this nation's world position. If there is one thread running through the whole story, it is the ceaseless effort to assess and define American interests

---

*As later chapters emphasize, there are in the United States and elsewhere many influential actors on the international scene besides governments: business firms, churches, news media, nonprofit associations, etc. They may conduct their own "foreign policies," but the term as used here does not refer to them.

in a complex and fast-moving world, and to promote those interests by the use of this nation's great, but not limitless, power and influence.

Any account of U.S. foreign policy would be pretty pale stuff without some description of "the world out there" with which the policy deals. The emphasis in this book is on the United States as a major actor on the world scene, but there is attention throughout to the scene itself and to the other actors in the drama—their history, character, and aims, as well as their interactions with this country, especially since World War II.

Politics, like all studies of human behavior, is an inexact science at best. The vast effects of the actions of nations—armies on the march, mass migrations, great wealth and great misery arise—in the final analysis, from the workings of human minds, no two of which are the same and whose secrets nobody fully understands. A competent chemist can tell you precisely what will happen when two known compounds are combined under given conditions. But no expert on diplomacy or power politics can say without a tremor of doubt that, if the United States offers a foreign government inducement A, or threatens it with penalty B, desired result C can be obtained.

Thus, even the profoundest study of past and present cannot reveal the future. But even a little study, such as this, may help us to understand better what forces are at work in world affairs, and what kinds of futures may be possible. And that should enable us to act a little more intelligently in shaping the future we hope to see.

Acknowledgments

First on the list of those to whom thanks are due are my old colleagues at the Foreign Policy Association, for it was in conversation with them that the idea of this book arose. Our thought was that students and adults alike, in tackling any subject related to U.S. foreign policy—such as one of the topics in FPA's annual *Great Decisions*—could find valuable background in a short book summing up the whole range of this immense subject. We had no illusion of competing with the numerous excellent full-sized textbooks on the subject—still less with the countless scholarly works on every conceivable aspect of international affairs. Our modest aim was, and is, to open a small window from which, without too laborious an effort, an attentive reader can view the entire foreign policy panorama in a reasonably clear perspective. Having surveyed the view, some might be encouraged to venture more deeply into this fascinating, bewildering, and immensely important field of knowledge.

A simple idea becomes complicated the minute you proceed to carry it out. The task, indeed, has required far more knowledge and judgment than this one writer can lay claim to. I am greatly indebted to those who read and criticized all or parts of the manuscript in its various revisions: L. Dean Brown, Giuliano M. Galloratti, Nancy L. Hoepli, David C. King, Christopher A. Kojm, Ralph B. Levering, Cecilia M. Lynch, and William E. Schaufele, Jr. Their comments have saved the book from many errors and greatly improved its treatment of issues and events. Needless to say, whatever mistakes remain are the author's responsibility.

To Nancy Hoepli, my successor in the FPA editorial chair, I am especially grateful for her resourceful support and confidence during a longer struggle than either of us had expected. Thanks are also due to Betsy Norman Brown and Gordon Powell, editors at Praeger Publishers, for encouragement, guidance, and suggestions at critical points.

Special acknowledgment is due to the Exxon Education Foundation, whose grant to FPA was a key event in making this project a reality.

I am also mindful of other debts that have waited long and patiently, and for which this is a small payment on account. They are owed to the many, living and dead, who were my teachers—at home, in school and college, and during three decades of labor in the foreign policy vineyard. And they are owed to my wife, son, and daughter, who put up with me and sustained me through many a year when, without knowing it, I was learning how to write this book; and to them it is dedicated in love and gratitude.

Contents

America in the World

Part I
The World and the Nation

I cannot say that I am in the slightest degree impressed by your bigness, or your material resources, as such. Size is not grandeur, and territory does not make a nation. The great issue, about which hangs a true sublimity, and the terror of overhanging fate, is what are you going to do with all these things? What is to be the end to which these are to be the means?

Thomas Henry Huxley,
English scientist and educator,
to an American audience (1876)

The World of Nations

If you look at a political map of the world, one fact that may strike you is how unevenly its land area is divided. About 170 independent countries* share the planet's land surface of some 57 million square miles (not counting virtually uninhabited Antarctica, which belongs to no nation). But more than half of that area belongs to the largest six: the Soviet Union, Canada, China, the United States, Brazil, and Australia. At the other extreme are a score of tiny states whose areas add up to less than that of Connecticut.

Look at a population table and you will find an inequality that is even more extreme. The five most populous countries (with China and India far in the lead followed by the U.S.S.R., the United States, and Indonesia) contain over half the world's people. The ranking is quite different from that for land area: India, smaller than Canada, supports 27 times as many people. And if you look at a ranking of the world's biggest economies, the list changes yet again, with the United States, the Soviet Union, Japan, and West Germany accounting for over half the economic production of the world. China, with nearly nine times Japan's population, produces less than half as much as Japan. India produces less than Australia but supports 47 times as many people. Significantly, the two superpowers—the United States and the Soviet Union—are among the top four on all three lists.

With all their extreme differences of size, wealth, population, and

---

*Country, nation, and state all mean roughly the same thing in ordinary American writing on international affairs, but there are important shades of difference. See Glossary, page 217, for discussion of these and other terms.

culture, it is these 170 states, each with its own people, government, flag, and territorial boundaries, that make up the *nation-state system* (it is pretty disorderly, but it is a system) by which humanity in our age is governed. The system has thousands of years of history behind it. Sometimes many small states have been fused into one great one, usually by conquest: imperial Russia and Germany are examples. At other times—as in the decades since World War II—great states or empires have dissolved into many small successor states.

It is a safe bet that these convulsive changes, like earthquakes or volcanic eruptions, are not over yet. In our century, whole states in Europe have appeared and disappeared, and the borders of others have been drastically redrawn in response to conflicting territorial claims and the fortunes of war. (Exclaimed an exasperated President Woodrow Wilson at the Versailles peace conference in 1919: "Bring me maps that do not overlap.") And over 80 new states have arisen from former colonial empires in Asia, Africa, and the Caribbean.

Still today, international territorial disputes abound, as the wars of the early 1980s between Iran and Iraq and between Britain and Argentina sharply remind us. As of 1982, the roll of nations with unsolved territorial disputes included: Israel, Syria, and Jordan; the Soviet Union and Japan; the Soviet Union and China; China and India; China and Vietnam; Vietnam and Cambodia (Kampuchea); India and Pakistan; Pakistan and Afghanistan; Iran and Iraq; Albania and Yugoslavia; Albania and Greece; Greece and Turkey; Cyprus and Turkey; Spain and Britain; Argentina and Britain; Argentina and Chile; Guatemala and Belize; Peru, Chile, and Bolivia; Nicaragua and Colombia; Venezuela and Guyana; Venezuela and Brazil; Morocco and Spain; Morocco, Algeria, and Mauritania; and Ethiopia and Somalia. In addition, the unique conflict between South Africa's white rulers and its black majority shows signs of some day evolving into a struggle over territory.

It is a mixed story of great good and great evil—the long political evolution that has brought the nation-state system to where it is today. On one side of the ledger is a record of spectacular advances in the arts, sciences, technology, and the breadth and quality of daily life, in which the rise of large states and empires, supplanting smaller tribal or feudal units, has played a decisive part. On the darker side are long chronicles of war, tyranny, and blundering leadership that have produced human suffering and tragedy on a colossal scale. How much longer the system will last is anybody's guess. Whether it may some day be succeeded by some kind of world-state, with power to enforce its will on quarreling nations—and whether this would be a good or a bad solution—these, too, are questions to which we will return in a later chapter.

But today, like it or not, the nation-state system is still very much alive, and is the main political framework of the world. Nationalism—the shared loyalty of the citizens to their country, its language, and culture against all others—is perhaps the strongest and most nearly universal political emotion in the modern world. The armed forces and economic resources of nation-states are the main instruments of power. The governments of states, with their elaborate diplomatic machinery, are the accepted authorities for sorting out international disputes and common interests, negotiating agreements, attending international conferences, and determining the uses of power that decide world events.

Sometimes in periods of conflict and crisis a state loses this authority as a result of civil dissension or foreign domination or both. Consider, for example, the history of China from about 1850 to 1949, or Haiti and the Dominican Republic in the early twentieth century, or Lebanon since 1976, or Poland since 1980. In such cases a state with its laws and institutions does not cease to exist, but its ability to make and enforce its own decisions not seriously impaired.

True, the nation-state is not alone on the world stage. There are other important actors, some constructive and some not. But the state with its power and authority towers above them all. So our exploration begins with a closer look at this remarkable institution.

The National Interest

Two words to keep in mind are *interest* and *power*. Since there is no all-powerful world government, every state uses its own power to defend and promote what it considers to be its own interests. Its power, compared with that of its competitors, may be great or small, and if its leaders are wise they will pursue only those interests that they have the power to pursue successfully. The United States, for instance, can assert an interest in the outcome of the revolutionary conflicts going on in Central America, and with its great power and influence in this nearby region it can at least make a good try at achieving the outcome it desires. So too can lesser states—nearby Cuba, Venezuela, Mexico, even distant France and Spain—whose leaders have asserted an interest in the same situation and have enough power and influence to stand some chance of affecting the course of events. By contrast, Belize, a tiny new state next door to Guatemala, lacks even enough power to defind itself without British help, and can do very little about these struggles even though its own vital interests are involved. And a small and distant state like Sri Lanka or Finland would be most unlikely to squander any of its limited power on events so remote from its own interests.

What does this term national interest really mean? Is there some scientific way of defining the national interests of, say, the United States, or Britain, or Sweden, or India? There is not. All that can be said with any certainty is that, as a practical matter, the national interest of any nation is what that nation decides it is, wisely or not, by its own decision-making process. The decision is subject to change. Leaders may be forced by foreign circumstances, or by public opinion, to change their minds; or they may be turned out of office and their successors may have quite different ideas.

Nevertheless, a few points can be set down which apply fairly generally to the national interests of all states:

1. In foreign policy as in all public policy, defining the national interest on any great question is a complex sorting process. Leaders have to reconcile, or else choose between, many different and conflicting interests *within* the nation. Especially in a society as pluralistic as the United States, countless organizations—business groups, unions, farmers, soldiers, bureaucrats, churches, veterans, ethnic groups, etc.—compete for governmental favor and urge that their interests and values be recognized as central to the national interest and be reflected accordingly in the nation's foreign policy. Every policy-maker, as part of the job, must be a broker or a referee among all these pressures. But high officials may also feel that it is their duty to lead and educate the public, for they are in a far better position to know the world situation and how it affects the nation as a whole. Events may prove them wrong, but they have the last word on the subject as long as they are in power. Chapter 3 will consider how this process works in the complex American constitutional system.

2. A nation's interests are not all equally important. The term *vital interests* is overused, but some interests certainly are vital—meaning that the nation would fight, if necessary, to defend them. The physical survival of the nation, obviously, heads the list. Secure possession of the national territory is near the top—although in dire necessity a nation may trade territory for survival, as Finland did after the "winter war" with the Soviet Union in 1940. Independence—a nation's freedom to live according to its own cherished values and to make its own decisions without dictation from abroad—that, too, although hard to define exactly, is a very great if not a vital interest. Secure access to essential supplies abroad may

sometimes be considered a vital interest: Western Europe's need for Middle East oil is an example. Indeed, nations have sometimes fought wars to serve foreign economic interests they considered "vital," not to their survival but to their prosperity.

Other interests, less than vital but highly important for many nations, include an advantageous foreign trade balance, protection of traveling citizens and foreign investments, and control of migration across national borders. Highly important to many nations is the vigor of whatever foreign alliances they depend on for their security. Less tangible, but in its way just as important, is the nation's prestige—its reputation for power, for achievement, for keeping its word, for fidelity to its ideals and beliefs, and for serving the well-being of others. Countless smaller interests, from sharing radio frequencies to the return of fugitive criminals, are left to the give-and-take of negotiation.

Obviously, a nation cannot hope to maintain all its interests against the claims of others. Where two nations' interests conflict sharply and both conclude that the interests at stake are less than vital, the obvious solution is peaceful compromise; for the destructiveness of modern war may, in some cases, raise peace itself to the level of a vital interest.

3. Between the interests of different countries there is much conflict, but there is also much harmony. A great part of a nation's foreign policy serves interests that are the same as—or at least compatible with—those of other nations. To put the matter in the jargon of game theory: while conflict situations are *zero-sum* games (A can win only what B, the adversary, loses), cooperative situations are *positive-sum* games in which all players can win. Innumerable common or compatible interests tie the world's nations together in a dense web of cooperation: fostering science, technology, and the arts, promoting trade, relieving hunger and poverty, delivering international mail, controlling arms races, settling disputes without war, holding Olympic games, aiding refugees and disaster victims, fighting terrorism and the drug traffic, quarantining communicable diseases—the list is long and growing longer. To be sure, nations argue constantly over the terms of cooperation; but cooperate they do, and civilization could not even limp along if they didn't. The most important means by which they arrange to cooperate is diplomacy, which includes the intricate—and all too fallible—art of negotiation. Better means could surely be found if only nations were more vividly aware of the interests they hold in common. Without the growth of that awareness through experience and education, the hope for future peace and world order would be dim indeed.

4. Finally, the fact must be faced that power itself is an underlying interest of every state. Some states seek to increase their power even at the risk of war; others are content to keep the power they have; but none, large or small, would willingly see its power reduced, especially in relation to potential enemies.

And, sad to say, the interests that most nations are apt to pursue most energetically are not the great common interests of mankind, but rather their separate and disputed interests—for the defense of which the ultimate recourse is national power. We had better look a little more closely, therefore, at the nature and role of power in international life.

National Power

Political power is the capacity of a government to control events. Both at home and abroad, it is vital to any nation's existence. Countless nations in ages past, having lost power, have fallen victim to internal chaos or foreign conquest or both. Domestically, power is necessary to enforce rules and restraints against wrongdoing, to collect taxes and finance and carry through costly public programs, and to discourage would-be political challengers. Internationally, power is necessary, above all, to uphold the nation's interests against foreign pressure.

Unfortunately, there is another side to the coin. Some holders of power are incompetent. Others are born tyrants, or are easily seduced by the pleasure, pomp, prestige, and privilege—and all too often the plunder—that go with wielding power. And even rulers who can resist these temptations may be driven to tyrannical acts as they struggle against domestic disorder.

Morally, therefore, political power is neutral. Like fire, it can create or destroy. Some nations in their domestic life do their best to prevent the abuse of power by surrounding it with legal restraints. But internationally the problem is more difficult. To be sure, when national purposes clash, most governments most of the time prefer peace with compromise to the enormous hazards of war. Thus the simple rule of self-interest is usually enough to keep the system functioning peacefully. But what rule applies when the clash involves interests that are deemed vital and violence threatens to mushroom into war? Is there some universal rule, or some universally accepted authority, that can authorize a nation to make war in one situation and forbid it in another? Unfortunately, although there are universal rules laid down in the United Nations Charter, they are extremely general; nations (including the great powers) regularly differ on how to apply them to particular cases; and there is no supreme world power to act when the great powers disagree. Thus, legal restraint on war-making between nations has yet to prove really effective.

For example: the UN Charter's rule concerning "collective self-defense" (Article 51) has been widely construed as meaning that country A may send military aid, or even combat forces, to help country B—at the latter's request—defeat an armed challenge to its authority, perhaps instigated or supported by unfriendly country C. Article 51, or its equivalent, has been cited as justification for British and U.S. military aid to Greece and Turkey after World War II; for sending U.S. forces to fight in Korea (1950–1953) and Vietnam (1964–1973); for the more recent entry of Vietnamese forces into Cambodia; Cubans into Angola and Ethiopia; Russians into Afghanistan; the French into Chad—to name a few cases. But what if, as often happens, the leaders of the armed challenge claim that *they* are the lawful government, and that the government that invited country A's troops in is a mere puppet of country A? All too often, the legal arguments get swallowed up in such controversies over the facts; and then it is now law put power—in the political arena, or in battle, or at the negotiating table, or in all these ways—that decides the outcome.

Power takes various forms. Military power is the most drastic of all, and the mere possession of armed forces strong enough to impress an adversary is a key factor in a nation's ability to defend its interests. But economic and technological power is also basic; indeed, only a stern dictatorship, or large infusions of foreign aid, can build military strength on a weak economic basis. Besides, a strong economic power can extend aid, trading privileges, and other benefits to friendly countries and deny these things to unfriendly ones. A nation that ranks high in these two kinds of power can also exert great diplomatic influence, for other governments are inclined to follow its lead. And the words it utters—its presidential speeches, statements to reporters, overseas broadcasts, etc.—carry extra weight because of the power behind them.

What makes a country rank high or low among the powers of the world? Some obvious factors are its size, its population, and the strength of its armed forces. Physical geography is also important: especially helpful are abundant natural resources (strategic minerals, fuels, fertile soils), a seacoast with good harbors, and a temperate climate. All these factors enter into a nation's economic and political power.

No less important are other, less tangible factors. What of the nation's economic system: does it make effective use of its geographical, techno-logical, and human resources? Can it organize and carry out large-scale undertakings? What of the quality of the people? How many are well-educated and competent in different trades and professions? How healthy, well-fed, disciplined, and enterprising are they? Have they a strong enough sense of nationhood to overcome any religious or caste or ethnic divisions among them? Do they work well with peoples of other countries? How stable, honest, and competent is the government? Do the people accept their government as legitimate—as having a right to rule—or are there major factions sharpening their knives somewhere for a revolutionary coup? Finally, how wise and skillful are the nation's leaders in shaping its foreign policies, attracting friends, and discouraging enemies?

But—no matter how complex its roots may be—power in the last resort is simple, raw, and cruel: physical coercion, the power of force. A government that does not have the weapons on its side (if not its own, then those of a stronger friend)—that is overawed by a hostile neighbor, or has armed rebels or private armies roaming the countryside—has failed to answer the very first question of politics: who is the ruler?

Military power, however, has serious drawbacks and limitations. It can be extremely costly, for one thing. One respected authority, Ruth Leger Sivard, places military expenditures by all nations in 1981 at about $550 billion*, which is between 5 and 6 percent of the world's economic product and over half of what all nations spend on education and health combined. And, although military spending in industrialized countries stimulates some technologies, it also diverts major resources and techno-logical talent from more constructive uses. The great stimulus to military spending is tension in regions of sharp power rivalry—often leading to massive financial aid from interested outside powers. Thus a number of Arab countries, as well as Israel, aided respectively by Arab oil states and by the United States, spend 15 to 20 percent of their economic product on armed forces; and impoverished Vietnam, still at war in Cambodia and aided by the Soviet Union, is thought by some authorities to be spending as much as half. The cost is also heightened by constant competition in more sophisticated—and costly—weapons systems.

What can be said against weapons as such can be said many times over against what they are designed for—war. Aside from its great human and economic costs, war is an extremely uncertain method of pursuing national purposes. This is true enough of war fought with "conventional"

---

*Ruth Leger Sivard, *World Military and Social Expenditures 1981* (Leesburg, Va.: World Priorities, 1981).

weapons; it is infinitely more true of any war that might be fought with the colossally destructive power of nuclear weapons.

It is little wonder that, in an age of such immensely potent military technology, the rulers of nations generally strive to avoid war, or at least to limit its extent. The preferred use of military power, in fact, is as an implied threat, to strengthen the nation's hand in the diplomatic poker game. That is what President Theodore Roosevelt had in mind in his famous advice to "speak softly and carry a big stick." Much of the statesman's art consists in combining the threat of the military "stick," not brandished too openly, with various tempting "carrots," such as promises of friendship, economic aid, diplomatic support, etc., so as to gain the nation's vital objectives without war. But this approach is not free of risks, for when a threat is defied it must either be carried out or be exposed as a bluff.

National power, then, can be exerted either negatively (force) or positively (cooperation). In one extremely important case, military alliance, it is a mixture; for military allies cooperate with each other against a common adversary, either to fight a war or to ensure their survival in case of attack. It has happened many times in history, from ancient Greece to modern Europe, that relatively weak states menaced by a superior power have had little choice but either to come under the big power's domination or to join an alliance against it. If two opposing powers, or alliances, show restraint; if both make roughly the same estimate of their relative power and correctly read each other's intentions; and if both are willing to settle for less than their maximum aims—then the result may be a more or less stable and peaceful *balance of power*. Two or more rival states or groups of states, each dominant within its own sphere, can then coexist—not without tension, but without war. But, as the history of our century tragically shows, these "ifs" do not always come true.

Indeed, ideas like "vital interest" and "national power" seem to be rather dim lights by which to conduct a nation's foreign policy. Gross miscalculations of power, or of the other side's intentions, have led many a nation to catastrophe. Adolf Hitler, for example, convinced himself that the anti-Communist United States would never make war on him, especially after his 1941 invasion of the Soviet Union.

As for vital interests—true enough, some nations' grievances or dangers have been great enough to justify resort to war, most of us would agree. But many wars have served no interest more vital than the obsessive ambition of one ruler, or a nation's claim to more territory for security or "living space," or a declining power's desire to hang on to its traditional sphere of influence, or a religious commitment to a holy war, or the hope that a patriotic foreign war will unite a quarrelsome people, or loyalty to a rashly embattled ally—or merely a new outbreak of some ancient, deep-rooted hatred between two peoples. Neither rulers nor peoples are always reasonable. War is the heaviest price we pay for this defect. War, indeed, is the gravest disease of the state system, and modern weapons have made it graver still. Whether it will prove fatal, or will transform the system into something else, remains to be seen.

International Organizations

Inevitably, the patterns of common interest among nations have produced a large and increasing number of international (or, more precisely, intergovernmental) organizations.

The *Political Handbook of the World: 1981* lists 115 international organizations. They deal with every human activity that interests governments: military defense, international trade, transport, communications, agriculture, health, tourism, police work, human rights, labor standards, science, education, the arts, aid to refugees, environmental protection— among other things. In membership they range from two neighboring countries to virtually every state in the world. The names or initials of some—the United Nations, NATO, UNICEF, the World Health Organization, the Arab League, to mention a few—are well known to the public; others, such as the World Intellectual Property Organization or the International Olive Oil Council, are known mainly to specialists. The United States belongs to nearly all of those that are worldwide in scope and to a number of regional ones as well.

Of all international organizations, the **United Nations** is the most universal, both in its membership (nearly all the world's states are now members) and in the great breadth of its purposes and concerns. Its highest purposes, in the words of its Charter, are "to maintain international peace and security" and "to be a center for harmonizing the actions of nations" in the pursuit of peace, human rights, economic and social progress, and other common aims.

These are the broadest and most difficult tasks that the nations of the world have ever undertaken together. In pursuing them, the members have bound themselves legally to something that looks at least like the shadow of a universal law, overriding mere calculations of national interest. The Charter, which has the legal force of a treaty, obliges all UN members to "settle their international disputes by peaceful means"; to "refrain . . . from the threat or use of force" against each other's territory or independence; to carry out the decisions of the Security Council; and—not a trivial matter—to pay their assigned shares of the UN's annual budget. These rules are often grossly violated and seldom enforced, and their meaning is constantly disputed in particular cases. Still, they stand as basic norms of national conduct—guideposts, perhaps, to a better world order of the future.

Many observers have judged the UN—perhaps too soon and too sweepingly—as a failure. It is certainly less successful than many specialized agencies and programs associated with it, which were created for less ambitious purposes, such as fighting epidemic disease, improving labor standards, or coordinating postal services: after all, it is harder to high-jump seven feet than four feet. Anyway, justified or not, complaints of failure aimed at the UN are sent to the wrong address, for the UN has very little existence apart from the 157 member states whose flags fly so brightly outside its headquarters in New York. Credit for its successes and blame for its failures belong to them—in proportion to their power and influence—and above all to its chief founder, permanent host, and most influential member, the United States. At the heart of the UN's troubles are its members' unyielding conflicts—between the Soviet Union and the industrial democracies, between rich nations and poor nations, and between regional enemies in the Middle East and elsewhere.

Measured against the UN's enormous purposes, the means that its members have given it are very modest. That part of its budget which the UN Charter legally obliges the members to pay comes to about $700 million a year—roughly the budget of the state of Delaware. Its "voluntary" programs—the UN Development Program, the World Food Program, and a long list of others—add up to an additional $2 billion a year. Its international secretariat numbers about 12,300, fewer than the New York City fire department; and despite what the official rules say, the prime consideration in appointing secretariat officials is usually not merit (though many are extremely able) but pressure from member governments to get as many jobs for their nationals as possible.

As for the UN's powers of decision, the General Assembly can debate and recommend, but cannot command any state to do anything. The Security Council has the legal power to use force against states that violate or threaten international peace; but no armed forces have ever been put at its service for such a purpose. Any such step—even economic or diplomatic sanctions against an offending state—can be vetoed by any of the five permanent Council members (the United States, the Soviet

Union, Britain, France, and China). The Secretary-General is a world figure, and undoubtedly, had it not been for the quiet diplomacy of successive holders of that office and their able lieutenants, there would have been still more wars. But the Secretary-General has no power of his own to override the will of even the smallest state.

Despite such limitations, the UN's members, on their good days, have managed to do a good deal of harmonizing. During its first 36 years the UN issued a highly influential Universal Declaration of Human Rights; helped defend South Korea against aggression; posted international peacekeeping forces in trouble spots in the Middle East, Cyprus, and elsewhere; helped save the chaotic Congo, after that big Belgian colony had been hastily thrust into independence in 1960, from being recolonized or torn to pieces; created technical aid programs for developing countries; mobilized international aid for refugees; sponsored world treaties on arms control, outer space, and the law of the sea; held pioneering world conferences on the human environment, population problems, women's rights, and other emerging issues. And, year in and year out, it has served as a sounding board, a safety valve, and a diplomatic switchboard for dealing with disputes among nations. The frantic bargaining for votes on key UN resolutions shows that governments attach real importance to what the UN says. Far short of the extravagant hopes that attended its founding, the UN has nonetheless compiled a notable record.

Just as significant in a different way is the regional body known as the **European Communities (EC)**. The heart of this ten-nation group, the European Economic Community (EEC), is as near to being a super-government as any international organization in our time—although its ruling council of ministers can act only if no member objects. The EC includes all the major countries of Western Europe except Spain and Portugal, which are candidates for membership. It has a staff of some 9,000 in Brussels and an annual budget of $21 billion—about 1 percent of its members' combined economic product. It includes a European Court of Justice and a Parliament—the latter elected by popular vote, though possessing little legislative power. The EEC has abolished tariffs on trade among its members, has a common tariff on imports from outside the community, and accords special trading preferences to 61 developing nations in Africa, Asia, and the Caribbean. Most of its budget goes to support farm prices—a sore point for Britain and West Germany, which pay most and get least from that program. The EEC's rules protect many inefficient industries, but its overall success in stimulating the region's economy has been spectacular. "The ten" have also entered the diplomatic realm, often taking common positions on issues such as the Arab-Israeli dispute.

In quite different ways, the UN and the European Communities mark the outer limits of international organization in our era. Despite their achievements and those of other world and regional bodies, the fundamental problem of how humanity can build a safer and more livable world remains unsolved.

The Other Actors

The sovereign governments of the world, with their military power, flags, anthems, pomp, and machinery of diplomacy, obviously dominate the international stage, but they do not monopolize it.* This chapter ends with a glance at some nongovernmental actors that—despite frequent efforts of governments to use, restrict, or destroy them—exert, in their different ways, enormous influence.

1. International business.   The flow of international trade and investment is a vital element in the economies of most nations. In 1981 foreign trade accounted for 17 percent of all U.S. economic transactions—slightly more than twice as large a share as in 1970. The corresponding figure for some countries goes as high as 40 percent. The vast bulk of trade is carried on by private firms, and only a minor proportion by state trading monopolies such as those of the Soviet Union and China.

Moreover, foreign direct investment—business controlled by a multinational company located abroad—accounts for much of the economic activity within countries. Multinational firms headquartered in the United States, which leads the world in this respect, controlled $168 billion worth of businesses in other countries in 1978. Other countries are also prominently represented in the multinational list: in 1979, for instance, European, Japanese, and other foreign firms controlled some $52 billion worth of business in this country.

Still another dimension of private international economic activity is international banking. Banks in all industrial countries and in many of the more advanced developing countries do much of their business through

---

*Among their minor competitors, especially in the United States, are lower units of government—state or municipal—which often operate abroad to promote trade and investment, and sometimes set up their own offices in foreign capitals.

foreign branches. Dollars held in banks abroad—called *Eurodollars*—run into the hundreds of billions and play a major part in the world economy. No less significant, both economically and politically, are the large loans that Western banks have made to governments in the developing world and in Eastern Europe since the mid-1970s. Poland's unpaid Western debts of over $27 billion have been a significant element in the interdependence between Poland and the West during the recent troubles in that country.

Some of the largest multinational firms make the smallest countries look like dwarfs. A few years ago a study showed that if nations and private firms were ranked on one list according to the size of their annual product, 54 of the first 100 names on the list would be those of private firms.

The interests of a foreign business and the interests of the country in which it operates are not the same, but they are compatible or the business would not be there. A business, whether it is the corner drugstore or the largest multinational, exists primarily to make money by providing something people want and can pay for. Its chief aims are not to abolish poverty or defeat communism or promote peace, although all those purposes are often (not always) served as a by-product of its activity. Business has earned worldwide respect as the most successful generator of wealth, jobs, technological know-how, and tax revenues. It keeps vital goods moving between nations, including those whose governments are not even on speaking terms. Among its leaders are individuals of extraordinary managerial talent and broad knowledge. The impact of private business enterprise on world civilization, both in raising living standards (though very unevenly) and in changing people's tastes and aspirations, is incalculable.

Even nations with the most tightly controlled economies deal with foreign businesses to some extent. But none—not even those most strongly committed to free enterprise—gives the business firm an entirely free hand. Everywhere it must pay taxes. Often, law or no law, custom obliges or encourages it to pay bribes. If it exports or imports, state-imposed trade barriers may put it at a disadvantage. If it deals in weapons or other military items, the state may forbid it to sell to countries that the state considers unfriendly. If it operates in a developing country, the host government may require it to hire and train local people, reinvest its profits locally, or avoid competing with favored local firms.

Businesses may bargain with a government for relief from such curbs, but in the end they either accept what it decides or go elsewhere. Generally they steer clear of politics and diplomacy unless an important business interest is at stake. As a U.S. oil executive in Libya said in 1981, when U.S.-Libyan relations were at an all-time low: "We have nothing to do with the politics of this place. We're just trying to make a buck." In some cases the politics of developing countries have led to angry seizures of U.S.-owned oil, mining, and other businesses. Executives see such catastrophes as part of the risk of doing business abroad, and try to minimize the risk by staying on the good side of those who hold, or may attain, political power.

2. **Mass information media.** In a world of spreading literacy and high-technology mass communications—where continents converse via satellite and scarcely the remotest hamlet in the poorest country is without a transistor radio—the influence of mass media on international affairs would be hard to exaggerate. Much of the flow of information, images, and ideas is controlled by governments; in fact, one-party states like the Soviet Union, China, and many developing countries regard the mass media as a vital instrument of political control at home and of influence abroad and do their best to monopolize publishing and broadcasting within their territories. But a great proportion of the international flow of news, commentary, and idea-laden entertainment remains in private hands. And, with few exceptions, private news agencies, newspapers, magazine and book publishers, broadcasters, and film producers jealously guard their right to publish or present what they choose, whether it makes this or that government look good or not. Western governments generally support this position, and have resisted recent attempts in the UN Educational, Scientific, and Cultural Organization (UNESCO) to strengthen government information services, especially in developing countries, at the expense of private news media.

The quality of what the private media publish about world affairs varies widely. The best is scrupulously accurate, balanced, and thoughtful—and often courageous in exposing wrongdoing. The worst is superficial, sensational, and slanted toward the opinions of the publisher or the particular public to which it caters. With a few commendable exceptions, the highly competitive mass media give little space to the long-term trends and underlying forces that shape events—and a great deal to violence, war, threats of war, and the doings of famous or infamous individuals. But whatever their defects, the alternative is worse. No government, not even the most democratic, can be expected to speak the whole truth on matters affecting its own interests. The independent media with their tactless revelations and frequent inaccuracies often make diplomacy more difficult, but they are a vital corrective for governmental bias and a necessity for all who want to make up their own minds about world events.

3. Nonprofit organizations. Science, technology, the arts, literature, education, medicine, labor, religion, sports, the relief of suffering, the defense of human rights, the protection of the environment—there is no limit to the variety of constructive activities which private, nonprofit associations (in UN jargon, *nongovernmental organizations* or NGOs) carry on across national lines. Some are based in one country and operate internationally; others have affiliated groups in many countries. Many have done pioneering work in their fields, and governments and UN agencies have followed where they led. If we have today anything remotely resembling a world civilization, the fact is due in great measure to the work of these nonprofit groups.

Not surprisingly, NGOs have prospered best in open societies, chiefly in North America and Western Europe, where the power of the state is limited. There, religious bodies, universities, and philanthropies have wide scope. Often NGOs work closely with—and are partly financed by—governments, especially in humanitarian and scientific work. But many take stands independent of, or even directly opposed to, governments on issues ranging from human rights (Amnesty International, the American labor movement, and several Catholic organizations in Central and South America and South Africa) to the conservation of whales (the World Wildlife Fund, among others, against the governments of Japan and the Soviet Union). Such opposition is a difficult and sometimes risky business in countries where all organizations function under the suspicious eye of the state, but some Western-based NGOs have done useful work even in those circumstances.

4. Private individuals. Singly and in the mass, the impact of private individuals on international life is enormous. Highly creative, dynamic, persuasive, or merely popular leaders in religion, science, sports, the arts and other fields—from Karl Marx to Harriet Beecher Stowe and John D. Rockefeller, from Albert Einstein to Mother Teresa—have exerted an influence far beyond their own countries and even their own lifetimes. Less conspicuous, but just as real, is the influence of the tens of thousands of teachers and other professionals who work abroad from year to year and of young people who study abroad. A recent survey, for example, showed that 35 heads of foreign governments had been students or academic exchangees in the United States.

At a humbler level but on a far more massive scale, the migration of millions of people fleeing from war, oppression, disaster, or poverty is constantly changing the societies and politics of nations and creating new links—as well as new problems—between them. And the millions who cross international borders as migrant laborers, tourists, soldiers, or employees of private firms or NGOs not only exert an economic effect but also contribute, for better or worse, to the impressions that peoples have of one another.

Although all these kinds of contacts across national lines are essentially nongovernmental, they can be of great interest to governments. Dictatorships regularly foster and exploit private cultural, intellectual, and other international contacts for their own political purposes, or else do their best to prevent them. Democratic governments often do the same, but less heavy-handedly.

In other cases, especially migration, governments intervene mainly for defensive purposes. Most countries use a visa system to control the influx of visitors and immigrants—not always successfully, since many borders are easily crossed by stealth. The United States, an especially attractive destination, has a complex, cumbersome, and still-evolving immigration policy. Conversely, the Soviet Union and other countries in the Soviet bloc impose strict controls over emigration.

5. Criminals. Many kinds of criminal activity cross national borders every day. Most of it is traffic in contraband goods—drugs, black-market weapons, stolen jewelry and art works, hides of protected animals, or goods smuggled in to avoid paying tariff. Sometimes the contraband is people—illegal border-crossers looking for work, or in some cases slaves or prostitutes. Often, too, a person accused of a crime in one country takes refuge in another.

All governments declare themselves against crime of all kinds. More than 100 national police forces belong to Interpol, a world police organization that exchanges data on criminals. Numerous treaties and international programs are aimed at various kinds of crime, notably the highly profitable drug traffic. And there is a wide, though incomplete, pattern of extradition treaties requiring that accused persons be returned for trial in the country where the crime took place. But all governments do not define crimes in the same way, and their cooperation in suppressing it leaves much to be desired. Political and economic interests often interfere. Where opium is a profitable cash crop, or where an international gunrunner has political connections in his own country, suppression may prove difficult or impossible.

6. The would-be states. Unique among the "other actors"

are the groups that want to become states. The world is dotted with movements whose aim is some kind of political self-determination—to take over the state that rules over them, or to achieve autonomy within a part of it, or to break away and become independent. In widely varying strength, such movements exist among Palestinians in the Middle East, Kurds in Iran and Iraq, Basques in northern Spain, Croatians in Yugoslavia, Muslims in the southern Philippines, Catholics in Northern Ireland, native Taiwanese in Taiwan, the black majority in South Africa, Puerto Ricans in the United States, anti-Castro exiles from Cuba—to name just a few cases.*

The methods of such groups often include violence against innocent bystanders—in a word, terrorism, the low-budget warfare of the poor and weak. If the group gains enough strength, the violence may escalate to full-scale war with sophisticated weapons. A number of the states in existence today were helped to power by terrorist tactics, including Indonesia, Israel, Kenya, Algeria, Vietnam, Angola, Mozambique, and Zimbabwe—and long ago, lest we forget, the United States. Other challengers, such as the Chinese in Malaya (present-day Malaysia) and the Biafrans in Nigeria, tried and failed. Some of the "terrorist gangs" of today will probably become recognized governments some day; others will be defeated by, or reconciled to, the states they now challenge.

Often these internal struggles have international repercussions—the challengers seeking support abroad and the governments trying to head them off. There are few international rules in this field, although a recent treaty to discourage one common tactic, aircraft hijacking, has had some success. All governments declare themselves to be opposed to terrorists, but generally reserve that term for the insurgents they oppose, while calling those they approve of "freedom fighters" or "liberation movements." The Soviet Union has openly backed many insurgent movements fighting Western rule, while Western and Islamic governments are reported to have been doing the same for the anti-Soviet Afghans. There have been numerous reports of covert backing by Communist or radical Arab governments, among others, for acts of political terrorism in Western

---

*The small terrorist bands in the industrial democracies, such as the Baader-Meinhof gang in West Germany, the Red Brigades in Italy, the Japanese Red Army, or the Weather Underground in the United States, do not really belong in this category, for they have no real political program beyond demoralizing established governments. Despite the anguish and worldwide publicity their assassinations and other violent acts sometimes produce, none of them has yet succeeded even in this limited sense.

countries. Washington has—in the past at least—covertly backed UNITA, the faction fighting the Marxist government in Angola; and in 1981–1982 it would not deny published reports of U.S. backing for rebels against the left-wing government of Nicaragua. The United States seldom supports such movements openly, but the diverse American population includes influential friends and financial backers of insurgent movements ranging from Northern Ireland and Cuba to the Middle East and South Africa.

Such, then, in the barest outline, is a picture of the nations of the world and of the other actors that participate along with them in the nation-state system.

2

From "United Colonies" to Superpower

"What is past is prologue," says an inscription at the entrance to the National Archives in Washington. What our country is today in world affairs can be better understood if we recall how it has developed over two centuries, both as a national society and as an actor on the international scene. In this chapter, spanning the 170 years from the American Revolution through World War II, we will see how changing conditions have affected the way Americans perceived their interests at different times; have increased or diminished the power and influence the United States could exert upon other countries in support of those interests; and thus have shaped and reshaped, through much trial and error, the nation's foreign policies.

Independence

Like a young person breaking away from the family, the people whose representatives declared on July 4, 1776 "that these United Colonies are, and of Right ought to be, Free and Independent States," bore a strong resemblance to their mother country. They were predominantly British by birth or ancestry, and their leaders almost entirely so. Their grievance, simply stated, was that a king and parliament in distant London had infringed their English rights of self-government and saddled them with taxes, trading restrictions, and other burdensome laws that they had had no part in framing. When negotiation—and beginning in 1775, open insurrection—failed to wring satisfactory redress from the government in

London, they took the revolutionary step of declaring themselves an independent nation.

In time, the American offspring became profoundly different in many ways from the English parent. There were clashes of interest and periods of severe strain—once even renewed war. But the dominant theme became friendship—based partly on a common commitment to freedom and partly on unique ties of ancestry, language, culture, and affection. In fact, even at the outset those ties of sentiment—reinforced by commercial interest— were so strong that many colonists opposed independence. Some even fought for King George III against the rebels; others moved to England or to Canada.

The first urgent need of U.S. foreign policy was for foreign help in winning the war. Even before independence was declared and hope for a reconciliation given up, leaders of the 13 embattled colonies joined in sending secret agents to several European countries. Not surprisingly France, England's main rival, offered the most help. In 1778, on its own initiative, it became the first military ally of the United States. Some trade and financial backing also came from Spain and the Netherlands. The defeat of Britain demonstrated what imperial Rome had found out ages before, and what the superpower United States was to learn two centuries later in Indochina: that a small but determined power, fighting on its own home ground and aided by its enemy's enemies, can defeat the greatest power on earth when the latter is distracted by other commitments, is divided at home as to the wisdom and justice of a war so far away, and wearies of the fight.

The outcome also vividly demonstrated the force of ideas—or ideology, to use a modern term—in the affairs of nations. Perhaps never since the rise of the great world religions had emerging ideas about human nature and destiny so stirred up the world's political tides as the ideas of liberty and equal rights expressed in the preamble to the Declaration of Independence. These ideas had been nurtured in Europe, but they were raised to dramatic height by the successful American struggle. They have worked like yeast ever since in the politics of the world. The fact that America was, in Lincoln's phrase, "conceived in liberty," and despite many lapses has shown an ever-widening commitment to it in its domestic life, remains even now a main source of this country's world influence.

Early Foreign Entanglements

Having won their war, the new nation's leaders were determined not to squander its energies on foreign adventures. In 1793 France, having deposed its monarchy in its own revolution, sought American support in its new war against royalist England. Many followers of Thomas Jefferson, forming what would later become the Democratic party, were eager to respond. The Federalists led by Alexander Hamilton, and the merchant class generally, favored the English side. But President Washington's policy of "no entangling alliances" prevailed, supported by both Hamilton and Jefferson as his top cabinet officers; and the French alliance of 1778 became a dead letter. For two decades Washington and his successors saw the national interest as requiring a neutral course (today we might call it "nonaligned") between Britain and Napoleonic France, which were almost continuously at war until 1815.

The most difficult problem raised by this policy was how to protect American trading ships—which did a thriving business at the expense of the two warring powers—from seizure by one side or the other; also, how to stop a notorious British practice of seizing American seamen on the high seas and "impressing" them into the British Navy. A three-year undeclared sea war with France (1798–1801) brought some relief in that quarter, but the problem would not go away. Beginning in 1807 an exasperated Jefferson Administration enacted a series of embargo laws forbidding trade with either of the offending powers. Still the trouble continued. In 1812 the quarrel with Britain, embittered by the impressment issue, escalated into a war that sputtered along for three years.

Thus the young republic learned that even if it could avoid military alliances, there were other kinds of entanglement—especially trading interests—that made it impossible to insulate America from the world's quarrels.

This episode was also an early instance of the policy-maker's eternal problem of ends and means. Were the costly means adopted—embargo and finally war—necessary in the long run to secure American neutral rights on the high seas? Some historians doubt it. But others have called the War of 1812 our "second war of independence," noting that British governments thereafter treated their former American subjects with new respect. In a similar vein, there is wide agreement that the sporadic wars (1801–1815) fought by the U.S. Navy against the piratical Barbary states that then ruled North Africa were both justified and effective in helping to end those states' centuries-old plunder of commercial shipping.

Continental Expansion

An even more basic American drive during those early decades, and for a long time thereafter, was the westward and southward expansion of the nation's territory into the near-wilderness of North America. The scores of Indian tribes west of the Appalachians, many of them ferocious in battle but all of them hopelessly inferior in strength and seldom able to unite, were relentlessly expelled from one hunting ground after another. Much more formidable were the Europeans, still in possession of most of the continent. Yet within half a century the self-confident republic, using both diplomacy and military force, had extended its sway all the way to the Pacific.

Westward expansion was already an issue during the colonial era. Hunters, trappers, and land speculators from the English colonies became increasingly active in the disputed lands between the Alleghenies and the Mississippi. It was in that region, as well as in Canada, that British forces fought a successful war (the North American phase of the Seven Years' War, 1756–1763) against France and its Indian allies. Several of the colonies, which asserted overlapping claims to huge areas in the West, bitterly resented a British ordinance of 1763 forbidding the colonists to enter these lands lest there be further trouble with the Indians.

That restriction ended with the peace treaty of 1783, under which Britain ceded to the new republic all its lands from New England to Georgia and from the Atlantic to the Mississippi. By 1802 all the western lands claimed by the states had been ceded to the U.S. government and were being prepared for eventual statehood.

Thus the great westward expansion began. In 1803 it took another giant leap, this time beyond the Mississippi, with President Jefferson's purchase of the Louisiana Territory from Napoleonic France. Some 828,000 square miles, stretching north and west from the Mississippi delta to the headwaters of the Missouri in what is now Montana, were bought for a paltry $15 million—about 3 cents an acre.

This amazing windfall for American diplomacy was far more than what Jefferson had had in mind. His main concern had been to get possession of the port of New Orleans, thereby freeing American traders to ship their exports down the Mississippi without risk of European interference. Luckily for the United States, at that moment Napoleon Bonaparte, who had regained French sovereignty over the territory after an interval of Spanish rule, was anxious to cut back on France's imperial commitments in North America. So he surprised the American negotiators by offering a deal which doubled the size of the United States at a single stroke.

Thus began a succession of annexations, fulfilling what would later be called by imperial-minded Americans the *manifest destiny* of the United

States to occupy the continent. In 1819 came the purchase of Florida from the battered empire of Spain. In 1836 the sparsely populated province of Texas, already dominated by American settlers, seceded from the young republic of Mexico; nine years later it accepted annexation by the United States. In 1848, after a two-year war against Mexico, the United States gained all of Mexico's remaining northern provinces from western Colorado to California. Meanwhile to the north, smoldering boundary disputes involving Maine, Oregon, and the intervening border with Canada were settled by peaceful Anglo-American negotiation in 1842 and 1846.

How did the new American republic manage to spread itself, in the span of a single lifetime, from its Atlantic coastal birthplace clear to the Pacific? Pioneering courage and individual ambition, to say nothing of a fierce and jingoistic concept of the national interest, had much to do with it. But the opportunity to exert these qualities to the full arose largely from the foreign policy setting of the time. For decades after American independence, North America remained a theater of struggle between the powers of Europe. The same quarrels among Britain, France, and Spain that had aided the fight for independence were still helping the young republic long afterward. Most of the American gains were at the expense of the big loser in Europe's wars, Spain, nearly all of whose empire in the West dissolved into weak and quarreling republics after Spain's humiliating defeat by Napoleon.

Several decades were to pass before the United States could digest its vast new territories and begin to exert its power on the world stage. In the early nineteenth century, American diplomatic skill had to achieve what American power could not. Ironically, the most useful diplomatic relationship of that time was with the former arch-foe, Britain. In 1823 Britain's wish to exclude its rivals, especially France, from taking advantage of Spain's colonial losses led a shrewd British foreign secretary, George Canning, to suggest a joint Anglo-American declaration against transfer of Spain's ex-colonies "to any other power." Secretary of State John Quincy Adams opposed the idea as barring future U.S. acquisition of, for example, Cuba—and as likely to leave Britain, the great naval power, dominant in the whole region. Instead, President Monroe decided to issue a purely American "doctrine" opposing new *European* colonial acquisitions in the hemisphere, and promising, in return, to stay out of purely European quarrels. Canning was thus only partly successful; but for decades afterward the only real enforcement of the Monroe Doctrine was by the British Navy, and that mainly against France. Only much later was

American power sufficient to confront European powers—Britain itself among others—seeking to expand their influence in the Caribbean and Central America.

Trade, Slavery, Civil War, and Internal Growth

To that far-sighted observer, Alexis de Tocqueville of France, it was apparent even in the 1830s that the United States was destined to become a world power. But for 50 years after the conquests of the Mexican War, only the great windfall purchase of Alaska in 1867 significantly extended the nation's territory. Nor did the United States play any important part, militarily or diplomatically, in the wars of Europe, Asia, or Latin America during that period. Even in the Caribbean, Washington was unable to prevent Britain from expanding earlier toeholds in eastern Guatemala (now Belize) and along the Mosquito Coast of Nicaragua as it maneuvered to control a hoped-for canal route to the Pacific.

Only commercially was the United States increasingly active abroad, including the Far East. In 1844 American diplomacy achieved something of a coup—obtaining peacefully from imperial China essentially the same trading privileges for which Britain had just fought a three-year war. This was possible because China was wary of a British trading monopoly and welcomed the American connection. This pact paved the way for the lucrative trade of the famous American China clippers. It was also the start of a century of American good feeling toward China, strongly reinforced by the influence of American missionaries in that country.

Then in 1854, in somewhat similar fashion, the antiquated and reclusive island empire of Japan was opened to American—and European—trade and contacts. This was achieved partly through a show of force—the famous visit of a naval squadron under Commodore Matthew Perry—and partly by American diplomatic skill in convincing the Japanese that an American connection was the only way to fend off more menacing powers, meaning Britain and Russia. Thus began Japan's rapid, at times explosive, entrance into the modern world.

Increasingly, however, what shaped and distorted U.S. foreign policy in that era was the gathering domestic struggle over Negro slavery. Beginning in the 1830s, some Southern champions of slavery sought to tilt the political balance not only by extending slavery into existing U.S. territories but also by promoting the annexation of new lands to the south. This impulse weighed heavily in the annexation of Texas and in the conquest of Mexico's other northern provinces. It also underlay much of the American interest in that Caribbean storm center, Cuba.

There were, to be sure, many reasons for U.S. interest in Cuba. American statesmen had long worried lest a powerful Britain or France seize the island, so close to U.S. shores, from enfeebled Spain. This fear had been a factor in the Monroe Doctrine. But by the 1840s, American policy and action concerning Cuba were dominated by the slavery interest. Cuba's white ruling class, large-scale slaveholders, were in chronic rebellion against Spanish misrule. What if Spain, in desperation, should emanicipate Cuba's half million black slaves? With such arguments fanning fears of a slave uprising, leaders in the American South advocated annexation of Cuba as a slave state. Twice in the 1840s Democratic presidents offered to buy Cuba from Spain but were rebuffed. Twice private armies, recruited by proslavery adventurers in Louisiana, invaded Cuba but were crushed. In the 1850s the Democratic party, then dominated by the proslavery faction, explicitly supported annexation of Cuba.

There were similar activities elsewhere in the region, but they too came to nothing, or not much. An American freebooter, one William Walker, briefly made himself dictator of Nicaragua, dreaming of making it a slave state and a center for a renewed African slave trade. Other slavery advocates talked of taking another big bite out of Mexico. The most they got was the Gadsden Purchase of 1853. That small addition to the American Southwest was conceived as part of a far-south route for the planned transcontinental railroad, the idea being to discourage free-soil settlement to the north.

All such maneuvers—as well as illegal smuggling of slaves into the South in violation of the ban dating from 1808—came to a halt in 1861 when the sectional struggle erupted at last in civil war. For four years there was diplomatic war as well—the seceding Confederacy seeking foreign recognition and material support, and the Union striving to isolate the rebellious states and enforce its naval blockade. At first the Lincoln Administration faced an uphill fight. Europe's ruling classes, importers of Southern cotton and no lovers of democracy, generally leaned toward the Confederacy. The British government accorded to Jefferson Davis's regime in Richmond the rights of a belligerent power and, most damaging of all, allowed British shipyards to build and equip Confederate warships.

The Union's troubles also presented opportunities to the European powers elsewhere in the hemisphere, Monroe Doctrine or no. In 1861 the turbulent Dominican Republic became once again a Spanish province, but the venture was a disaster and Spain again withdrew in 1865. The mercurial emperor of France, Napoleon III, had grander ideas. In 1863 he sent an invading army into Mexico, which was then gripped by civil war, ousted the popular nationalist Benito Juárez, and installed Archduke Maximilian of Austria to rule Mexico as France's puppet. The venture, foolish in concept and ineptly handled, was a four-year fiasco. Whatever hopes it might have had were dashed by the rising fortunes of the Union armies against the Confederacy. Lincoln's military successes began to impress European governments, and his proclamation of January 1863 emancipating the slaves powerfully impressed public opinion everywhere. In 1865 Britain, whose pro-Confederate tilt had offended much if not most of the British public, was quick to restore good relations with Washington. And in 1867, France liquidated its Mexican misadventure without the United States having done more than send vaguely menacing notes to Paris.

In the decades following the Civil War, American attention was seldom on foreign policy. The turbulent "reconstruction" of the war-torn South, the first steps of millions of ex-slaves into freedom, the development of the American West, the rapid industrialization of the Northeast and Midwest—these were the priorities around which political issues centered. In that generation America laid the foundation of industrial might and technological prowess that was soon to make it a world power; but few Americans were thinking about that future role. Indeed, so indifferent to foreign expansion had the public become that a succession of postwar attempts by the Andrew Johnson and Grant administrations to acquire Hawaii, Samoa, Cuba, Santo Domingo, and the Virgin Islands all died in Congress. Some politicians even fancied that Canada would welcome annexation by the United States, but this illusion was soon dispelled.

One great acquisition did go through, however: the vast northern province of Alaska, sold in 1867 for $7.2 million by an overextended Russian empire. Generations later Alaska, only 50 miles from Soviet territory, would emerge as a key element in U.S. Pacific strategy.

Preoccupied as they were with domestic matters, American statesmen found it convenient to settle many issues of that time, especially with Britain, by peaceful means. In the Treaty of Washington (1871), a long list of accumulated Anglo-American disputes was taken care of by submitting them to impartial arbitration or to mixed commissions of the two powers. On the list were highly emotional U.S. claims for the depredations of British-built Confederate sea raiders; a disputed U.S.-Canadian boundary near Vancouver Island; and numerous quarrels over fishing, navigating, and trading rights between this country and Canada. Arbitration, indeed, was in the air. Two presidents of that era, Hayes and Cleveland, served as impartial arbitrators in South American boundary disputes. The quest for "world peace through world law" has been a recurrent theme, though seldom a dominant one, in U.S. foreign policy ever since.

America's Imperial Age

The generation of comparative quiet in U.S. foreign relations could not last forever. Many circumstances—notably the rising interest in foreign markets for booming American manufactures—converged in the 1890s to stir the nation toward greater involvement, both peaceful and warlike, abroad.

Washington's main attention was on two regions. One was the Caribbean, where Spain's hold on rebellious Cuba was growing still weaker and Cuban revolutionaries were agitating for U.S. support. The other was the Far East, not only an increasingly important area of American trade—with China, Japan and, after 1882, Korea—but also an area of increasing turbulence as Japan, its population and industrial power growing rapidly, began to push beyond its island realm.

The two far-distant regions were linked, especially in American minds, by that momentous idea that was later to become the Panama Canal. It was a time when influential writers like Alfred Thayer Mahan, a U.S. naval officer with a flair for strategy, were calling for a big navy as the key to U.S. world influence and access to world markets. In this scheme of things a U.S.-controlled canal across the Central American isthmus was seen as vital to the American position both in the Caribbean and in Asia. And conversely, acquisition of key bases in the Caribbean would be necessary to protect the canal.

These elements came dramatically to the fore in the Spanish-American War of 1898. Some historians have blamed the war on American jingoism whipped up by sensation-seeking mass-circulation newspapers, but there was more to it than that. By 1897 Spanish repression in Cuba had aroused American public opinion and had also damaged U.S. trade and investment in the island. Moreover, there was fear that a show of American weakness might tempt other European powers, especially Germany, to intervene in the Caribbean.

In this situation President McKinley became convinced that only Cuban independence, which Spain would not consider, could solve the problem. In February 1898, in the midst of intricate negotiations, news arrived of the shocking explosion of the U.S. battleship *Maine* in Havana harbor, with heavy casualties. The incident has never been explained, but press and public blamed Spain and, in a blaze of emotion, demanded and got a declaration of war. When war came it was immensely popular, all the more so because Spain was quickly and crushingly defeated. Under the peace treaty, Cuba became independent under U.S. protection, and Puerto Rico, the Philippine Islands, and Guam were ceded outright to the United States.

Also in 1898, on the same wave of enthusiasm, the island kingdom of Hawaii, already a U.S. economic dependency, was formally annexed by act of Congress. Five years later, having created what was then a virtual puppet republic in Panama, the United States acquired sole control of the Canal Zone, and by 1914 the canal was a reality. United States military and naval facilities were built—and still exist today—in the Canal Zone, in Puerto Rico, at Guantánamo Bay in Cuba, and in the Virgin Islands (the last-named was purchased from Denmark in 1917). In the same era, other islands in the Pacific also came under the American flag: Midway, American Samoa, and Wake—all of which, half a century later, would figure in a great war no one could then foresee.

Thus the age of American imperial grandeur began—combining, much as Europe's did, strategic and commercial interests with the loftier aims of Christian missionaries and educators. But the enthusiasm was by no means unanimous. Many Americans, mindful of our own country's colonial origins, felt uneasy about the Stars and Stripes flying over subject peoples abroad. It was this anticolonial sentiment that prevented the annexation of Cuba. The same sentiment, plus complex economic interests, soon shaped U.S. policy in the Philippines—after a rough start against a nationalist insurrection—toward an enlightened program of education and development in preparation for the islands' independence. Eventually it also led to a unique constitutional evolution in Puerto Rico, and in 1977 to agreement to return the Canal Zone to Panamanian control.

On a far larger scale were the turbulent events in Asia. Japan's easy military victory over China in 1895 not only made China's island province of Taiwan a Japanese colony; it also set off a new scramble between Japan and the European powers for exclusive spheres of influence in China. This trend was opposed not only by Britain, which saw its uniquely privileged position in China threatened, but also by the United States, which was more interested than ever in the China trade since acquiring the

Philippines. In 1899, with British encouragement, the United States proposed that all the powers with spheres of influence in China agree to equal treatment in their spheres for the trade of all nations. One year later this U.S. "Open Door" policy assumed an additional political dimension—insistence on foreign respect for China's "territorial and administrative entity." Threatening that entity at that moment was a foreign punitive expedition against the Chinese patriots of the Boxer Rebellion, who had rashly made hostages of several hundred Western nationals in Peking. The U.S. intercession staved off a wider conflict and was duly appreciated by the Chinese.

The Open Door policy was hailed in the United States as a success for American ideals—as well as American commerce—and was given lip service by most of the interested powers; but it could not long forestall the collapse of imperial China or the struggles of other powers over China's body. Soon the United States—which, after all, had staked out something very like a sphere of influence of its own in the Caribbean—saw no alternative to quietly accepting China's steady slide into the sphere of influence of Japan. Only much later would a series of still greater convulsions shake China out of the Japanese grasp and make the United States the dominant Pacific power.

Immigrants, Minorities, and American Pluralism

All through those decades of rising U.S. power, a force was at work profoundly reshaping American society and its relations with the outside world. This was the coming of scores of millions of people to these shores in wave after wave of immigration.

Since earliest colonial times America had been Europe's fabled land of opportunity and of refuge—from war, poverty, religious persecution, and political oppression. Immigration from the time of U.S. independence to 1820 averaged less than 10,000 a year; but it increased steadily thereafter until, between 1840 and 1850, some 1.5 million—mostly Irish and Germans—arrived as workers to build the new canals and railroads linking the Atlantic seaboard to the Midwest.

But a bigger flood was yet to come. After the Civil War the rapid industrialization of the Northeast and Midwest, plus the opening of vast new farmlands, created a huge job market and brought hundreds of thousands a year to these shores from northern Europe and later, increasingly, from Russia, Poland, Italy, Greece, and other countries of Eastern Europe and the Mediterranean. The peak decade was 1901–1910, when 8.8 million immigrated. Then the flow tapered off, stopped almost entirely during the Great Depression of the 1930s—and resumed, in a much altered pattern, after World War II.

On both sides of the water, the main interests at work in those high-immigration decades after 1880 continued to be economic. An overpopulated and underfed Europe was moving its poor and aspiring lower classes to a still underpopulated, booming, and far less class-conscious United States where industry and agriculture were hungry for cheap labor. Religious and political persecution of Jews, Poles, Czechs, Hungarians, Armenians, and others in the Russian, Austrian, and Turkish empires played their part—as did the dread of something new in European life, compulsory military service. Immigrants driven by such conditions were generally content to accept low-wage, heavy manual labor against which Irish-Americans had begun to rebel. And owners of mines, mills, and railroads were glad to use this new labor supply as a way to hold wages down and discourage unions.

For many decades the U.S. government played little part in either promoting or controlling the volume of immigration. It did not even require immigration visas. Most major immigration acts passed between 1875 and 1920 were aimed at excluding the sick, the criminal, or those with unacceptble morals or politics. The main promoters of immigration in the early peak decades were private American railroad and shipping companies, which sent hordes of recruiting agents to Ireland and Southern and Eastern Europe. The main foe of immigration by the end of the century was organized labor, which feared job competition.

True, it was U.S. governmental action in the years before 1918 that ended the mass importation of cheap labor from China and Japan to California—a response to both racial prejudice and the economic self-interest of American labor. The Chinese were excluded in 1882; in 1917 the exclusion was extended to all Asians. But not until the severe economic recession after World War I did Congress act to limit the numbers of immigrants from all countries. National origins quota acts, adopted in 1921 and 1924, discriminated especially against Southern and Eastern Europe and other areas deemed "undesirable" by an electorate of largely Northern European ancestry. This discrimination did not end until the 1960s.

What have two centuries of immigration contributed to the foreign relations of the United States? These things, among others:

- The human brain and muscle needed to conquer a continent and make this country a world power.
- A wealth of intellectual, scientific, and artistic talent—a priceless gift to America from the world.
- Potent reinforcement for this nation's founding idea that "all men," not just Englishmen or Northern Europeans, "are created equal" and have equal rights.
- Lasting bonds of affection and culture with the "old country"—creating pressure on Washington to support the aims of particular nations and peoples even when a wider view of U.S. interests might argue for a different course.

To complete the picture of America's minorities, we must remember two categories of people who cannot be called immigrants, but who have suffered the worst disabilities in our society. In both cases racial difference is a factor.

One category consists of those who were already there when the conquerors came. These include the American Indians, Mexicans whose land was annexed in 1845 and 1848, Eskimos and Aleuts in Alaska, Polynesians and Micronesians in the Pacific, and Puerto Ricans in the Caribbean. Many individuals from nearly all these minorities have made their way into the American mainstream; thus far the majority have not. Economically and socially, in varying degrees, they are still second-class citizens, almost like immigrants in their own country. National policy toward them has sometimes been cruel, sometimes magnanimous, often merely confused and absentminded.

The other category—over 26 million Americans who have African ancestors and are classified as black—has posed the most harrowing moral dilemma in American history. Millions of Africans came to the Western Hemisphere not as immigrants but as property. In the United States, their emancipation was bought with the blood of our only civil war. Their long struggle for full equality of opportunity is far from over.

This country's treatment of its racial minorities takes on added political significance abroad because of the rise of the largely nonwhite third world since World War II. Only in recent years have most white Americans realized that the great majority of the world's people belong to other races and deeply resent white dominance. As a superpower and an open society, the United States has to expect its performance toward its own nonwhite citizens to be watched with especially critical eyes.

The positive side of the coin is the still vigorous American tradition of pluralism, tolerance, and equal opportunity among peoples of many backgrounds. Such openness is not the general condition in today's world, but it can be an example to others.

There is, then, a global significance in these American efforts. Harold R. Isaacs, an authority on the world's many conflicts of race, religion, and tribe, has summed it up in these words: "We [in the United States] are engaged in trying to see whether . . . different kinds of people can coexist with some decent mutual respect and acceptance instead of tearing each other limb from limb, to see, in short, whether we finally can create a *one* that will preserve the *many*. . . . Limited and qualified as its achievement might still be, the American society has come closer to realizing these goals than any other has yet managed to do . . . . The shape of much of the rest of the world's politics will be influenced in critical measure by what we make of ours."*

World War I: The New World and the Old

Until World War I, the expanding foreign policy of the United States stayed almost entirely clear of the power struggles in what was still the power center of the world, Europe. America had acquired its own sphere of influence, the Caribbean, which Europe generally respected. American statesmen, in keeping with the other half of the Monroe Doctrine—and with public sentiment as well—generally left Europe's quarrels to the Europeans. And Europe itself, ever since the defeat of Napoleon in 1815, had managed to keep its quarrels within bounds—there were wars, but they were short and limited in scope—by an informal system known as the Concert of Europe. All the leading European powers in that system respected the need for a balance of power among them, and none tried to push its luck too far.

Beginning around 1890, however, a new situation arose that fundamentally threatened this tranquil situation. Germany, already united and well on the way to great industrial power under the leadership of Prince Otto von Bismarck, started building a first-class navy and challenging Britain and France for what today would be called superpower status. Rival alliances formed; arms races gathered speed; disputes and miniwars broke out over African colonies and later in the Balkan states.

---

*Harold R. Isaacs, *Power and Identity: Tribalism and World Politics.* Headline Series, 246 (New York: Foreign Policy Association, 1979), pp. 59–60.

Finally in August 1914, with all Europe in a war of nerves over a quarrel in Serbia, a sequence of miscalculations on both sides led to the great explosion. Both alliances—Britain, France, imperial Russia, and Japan on one side, Germany, Austria-Hungary, and Turkey on the other—cheerfully predicted a quick victory. Both were wrong, for the war, employing weapons far more destructive than any known before, settled down to year after year of mass slaughter in the trenches of eastern France and along the Russo-German front.

For more than two years after 1914 a doggedly neutral United States found itself being pulled step by step into the war on the side of the British and French allies. Three factors led to this result. One was the increasingly important American interest in trade with Europe, an interest that was menaced by the warring powers' navies. Second was Britain's double advantage in naval power and in geography. Britain could easily bottle up Germany's North Sea and Baltic ports with an effective blockade that neutral ships could not challenge; but Germany, unable to blockade the British Isles, resorted instead to a more violent method—submarine warfare on the high seas.

The third factor was psychological. Old ties of language and tradition caused American popular sympathies, except among the German-American and Irish-American minorities, to lean heavily toward Britain and France. Germany's invasion of neutral Belgium at the outset of the war, and the ineptness of German propaganda in this country, made the pro-allied tilt all the stronger.

All these factors worked together in Britain's favor. So strong were President Woodrow Wilson's own sympathies for the British side that he as much as told the British government in the first months of the war that it could go on violating U.S. neutral rights, as generally defined in maritime law, without risking more than paper protests. By contrast, indignation was high when German U-boats, launching torpedoes without warning, destroyed American cargoes and, in some cases, American lives. The worst shock was the sinking of the passenger liner *Lusitania* in 1915. Among more than 1100 civilians drowned were 128 Americans, including 37 women and 21 children. American exporters to Germany might fume at the British Navy's blockade, but as one senator remarked, the drowning of American women and children was more moving than the sight of American cotton sitting on a wharf.

Still, the high-minded Wilson strove hard to keep the nation out of the war and to shorten the war by negotiation. "Peace without victory" was his plea in 1916—in vain, for the terrible sacrifices of both sides had already made this psychologically impossible. But Wilson persisted, foreseeing—as he later confided to a friend—that the American people, once in the war, would "go war-mad, quit thinking and devote their energies to destruction . . . and the spirit of ruthless brutality will enter into every fibre of our national life." His prophecy was not far off the mark. In February 1917 the hard-pressed German general staff started a campaign of unrestricted submarine warfare which by April—only five months after Wilson's reelection as the man who had "kept us out of war"—led inexorably to the U.S. declaration of war. The nationwide war mobilization that followed included an officially orchestrated campaign of hate propaganda against Germany and a fever of amateur spy hunting and suppression of dissent. But it also produced a U.S. war effort beyond all expectations—a vast outpouring of munitions and an American expeditionary force of 2 million men landed in Europe.

Eighteen more months of heavy fighting lay ahead. In 1917 imperial Russia, tottering under German blows, collapsed in revolution. V.I. Lenin's Bolshevik party soon dominated the Russian scene and promptly made a separate peace with Germany, leaving the Western allies to fight on. In 1918, despite a final series of furious German offensives, the injection of massive and highly effective American fighting forces on the Western front proved decisive. On November 11, Germany, continental Europe's greatest military power since Napoleonic France, surrendered.

"I called the New World into existence to redress the balance of the Old"—so wrote Britain's George Canning in the 1820s, referring to his country's influence in shaping the Monroe Doctrine. The boast was exaggerated then, but in 1917–1918 it came true.

Peace—and U.S. Isolation

Early in 1917 Wilson, unable to bring either side to talk peace, announced to the world in the famous "Fourteen Points" his own idea of a peace settlement. It should be "a peace between equals," not one imposed by the winner on the loser. It should provide for self-determination of the subject peoples still under Austrian and Turkish rule. And, to replace the balance-of-power system from whose failure the war had sprung, it should create "a general association of nations" to guarantee the territory and independence of all states, great and small.

As sheer war propaganda, the call for self-determination was a master stroke, adding to unrest among Czechs, Hungarians, and other minorities on the enemy side. And when the peace conference met in 1919 at

Versailles outside of Paris, with Wilson himself leading the U.S. delegation, self-determination was widely agreed on by the victorious powers. This is not strange, for the consequent price was paid entirely by the losers of the war and by Communist Russia, whose new government was seen in the West as implacably hostile and was not present at—nor, in fact, invited to—Versailles. Under the Treaty of Versailles and related treaties signed in 1919–1920, the old Austro-Hungarian Empire was dissected into its national parts, bringing independence to Czechoslovakia and Hungary and leaving Austria as a remnant republic. Russia's provinces of Finland, Lithuania, Latvia, and Estonia became independent republics. Poland's long-lost independence was restored. In the Balkans, once part of Turkey's empire, Albania became independent whereas Serbia and several other small nationalities were combined in the new federation of Yugoslavia.

Self-determination, then, had done well. But for Wilson's ideal of "peace without victory" there was no hope. Britain and France, having suffered grievous losses in the war, wanted Germany punished, and much of the war-indoctrinated American public agreed—just as Wilson had feared. Germany and Turkey were stripped of their colonies in Africa, the Middle East, and elsewhere, which were then parceled out among the European victors either as outright colonies or as "mandates" under the loose supervision of the League of Nations. The shaky new German republic was reduced in territory, disarmed, required to accept responsibility for all the war damage and loss (the so-called "war guilt" clause), and saddled with heavy financial reparations—which its shattered economy soon proved unable to pay. Wilson's warning of January 1917—that an imposed peace would leave "a sting, a resentment, a bitter memory upon which terms of peace would rest, not permanently, but only as upon quicksand"—was ignored, and it was to prove tragically prophetic.*

To guarantee and secure all the provisions of the peace, good or bad, the Versailles Treaty included as an integral part the basic statute, or covenant, of Wilson's most ambitious conception, the League of Nations. The League's council of major powers, to include the United States, was to be responsible for the security and territorial integrity of all states, large and small. The term *collective security* came into use to describe this bold concept. Britain's David Lloyd George and France's Georges Clemenceau

---

*There was a sting for Japan, too. Its proposal that the League Covenant include a clause affirming the equalilty of all races was rejected by the Western leaders—including Wilson, who felt obliged to defer to racial prejudice in the United States.

were unenthusiastic about the League, but both accepted it as the price of U.S. support for the rest of the treaty.

Then came one of the bitter ironies of history. Wilson, the chief advocate of the League, and therefore of the treaty in which it was implanted, could not sell it to his own Senate. Some senators thought the treaty too hard on Germany; others, too soft. Irish-Americans, inflamed by British treatment of Ireland, resented anything Britain had a hand in. Italian-Americans resented Wilson's failure to back certain territorial claims of Italy, which had fought on the Allied side. And transcending all these objections was opposition to the League itself. A group of Senate "irreconcilables," led by Henry Cabot Lodge of Massachusetts, denounced the League covenant as false to the hallowed American tradition of "no entangling alliances" and likely to commit this country to defend distant lands of no importance to U.S. interests.

Moderate backers of the League urged Wilson to accept certain Senate reservations which they believed would not be fatal to the League—chiefly, reaffirming U.S. sovereign rights on various matters—in order to muster the needed two-thirds vote. Wilson, who had already done a lot of conceding at Versailles, dug in his heels and refused. He then "went to the people" on a nationwide speaking tour. The tour failed; an exhausted Wilson collapsed and soon afterward suffered a crippling stroke. In November the treaty, laden with reservations, was rejected in the Senate by the combined votes of Lodge diehards and Wilson loyalists.

In the presidential election of 1920 the Democrats, still championing Wilson's League, lost in a landslide to Republican Warren G. Harding. On taking office in 1921 Harding declared the League of Nations "deceased."

Would U.S. membership in the League have changed the course of events that led to World War II? No sure answer to such a question is possible, but there are strong reasons to doubt it. Ironically, after the League got under way the United States gradually changed from frosty abstention to extensive cooperation with it, though it never joined. A U.S. office for League affairs was set up at the League headquarters in Geneva. The United States participated in League efforts not only on technical and humanitarian matters but on political issues as well—including attempts to restrain Japanese encroachment in China (1932), Italian aggression against Ethiopia (1935), German, Italian, and Soviet intervention in the Spanish civil war (1936–1939).

Unfortunately, all those political efforts were either grossly inadequate or wrongly conceived; and against the menace of the age, Hitler's

Nazi Germany, the League achieved nothing at all. What doomed the League and the peace it was supposed to preserve was not U.S. nonmembership as such, but the aggressiveness and brutality of some powers and the failure of will of others, whether through the League or otherwise, to resist aggression in its early stages. As we have learned once again in the United Nations, an international organization is as good as, and no better than, the will and wisdom of the powers on which it depends.

Isolation, Depression, Aggression, War

Whatever the final verdict on the League, there was a simpler meaning in the Senate's rejection of it. Most Americans were fed up with the world and its problems. Feeling secure once again behind their two great oceans—except for a period of anti-Communist hysteria just after the war—and enjoying by the mid-1920s a new wave of prosperity, they chose isolation. "We are so snug here," remarked President Calvin Coolidge to a foreign visitor. It took nearly two decades for Americans to learn that a great power cannot be snug for long in a highly inflammable world.

The truth, still little realized, was that the Europe-centered balance of power that had kept most of the world more or less at peace from 1815 to 1914 had not just been interrupted—still less restored—by the great war; it had been destroyed altogether. What had destroyed it was the expanding industrial and military power of Germany, too great for a purely European alliance to balance. The four years of war had not changed that strategic fact, for the European victors were as exhausted and demoralized as the losers; moreover, their punitive peace had given the Germans a rallying cry for revenge. From that time onward, if Germany were once again to reach for hegemony over Europe, one of two countries, the United States or the Soviet Union—or both of them—would have to stop it. But all that, in the Washington of the 1920s, lay in the unseen future.

A lowered U.S. profile abroad, to be sure, was not necessarily a bad idea in all cases. In Mexico and the Caribbean, the U.S. posture ever since 1898 had been one of repeated political, military, and even administrative intervention, chiefly to safeguard U.S. commercial or strategic interests against local political turmoil. But often the U.S. presence itself added to the turmoil by offering an obvious target to patriots; and besides, a policy with such strong colonial connotations could not go unchallenged in American politics. In the 1920s the policy began to change. United States Marines were evacuated from the Dominican Republic in 1924, from

Nicaragua in 1933, and from Haiti in 1934. Theodore Roosevelt's assertion that the Monroe Doctrine implied a U.S. right to intervene in the area—the "Roosevelt corollary" to the Monroe Doctrine—was publicly disavowed by the State Department in 1930 and, with greater finality, by Franklin D. Roosevelt in 1934. Simultaneously, the United States worked to reinforce the multilateral, hemisphere-wide Pan-American conference system, which was to evolve later into the Organization of American States (OAS).

A comparable change took place in U.S. relations with Mexico. There the overthrow of the dictator Porfirio Díaz in 1910 was followed by decades of revolutionary violence and sheer banditry, much of it directed against Americans and American-owned firms. There were repeated U.S. military interventions during the Wilson Administration. Legal controversies raged over American rights to oil and other properties. Anti-American feeling remained intense until 1928, when President Coolidge appointed as U.S. ambassador Dwight W. Morrow, a master of conciliation and of friendly gestures. Even after 1938, when Mexico nationalized the U.S. oil companies, the highly contentious issue of payment to the expropriated owners was settled without any use or threat of force.

All these conciliatory moves in Latin America were accelerated as war clouds gathered over Europe. Both Nazi Germany and the Soviet Union were politically active in the region during the 1930s. Washington's answer was the Roosevelt Good Neighbor policy and the stress on Pan-American solidarity. Except in distant Argentina, which through most of World War II was neutral with an inclination toward Germany, the policy worked. In the Mexican case, for example, the final settlement of the oil claims came in 1941, on the eve of U.S. entrance into the war; and, simultaneously, Mexico joined in an agreement for cooperation with the United States in the war emergency. By March 1945 all the Latin American states had formally declared war on Germany, thereby qualifying for original membership in the postwar United Nations organization then being planned.

Unfortunately, during the decades between the wars U.S. policy in Europe and Asia—and, it must be said, the policies of the European democracies as well—showed only intermittent awareness of the approaching danger. Toward the struggling Weimar Republic in Germany, American statesmen in the 1920s could think of nothing more important than the payment of German reparations to the Allies so that the latter, in turn, could pay their war debts to the United States. Toward Japan's step-by-step encroachment against China, the U.S. response until 1940 was little more than a battle of diplomatic notes while American oil and steel were sold without interruption to supply the Japanese war machine. Toward the new Soviet regime in Russia, the first U.S. reaction, in 1918–1920, was to contribute troops to a series of small, half-hearted, confused, and futile Allied military interventions. Then came massive U.S. food relief during the Russian famine of 1921–1922. There was no U.S. diplomatic recognition until 1933, when President Roosevelt, alarmed at Japanese aggression in northern China, decided to mend America's diplomatic fences with China's Russian neighbor; but the move had little effect in restraining aggression anywhere.

And meanwhile, in the vital matter of international trade, after a hopeful start in the early 1920s on reciprocal trade agreements with Latin America, U.S. policy was written unilaterally, and disastrously, in Congress. The Smoot-Hawley Tariff Act of 1930 was the high tide of U.S. protectionism. It set off a predictable wave of retaliatory trading curbs by other nations against U.S. exports. The result was a deepening and lengthening of the world economic depression, mass unemployment and social unrest which had already begun—a fertile seedbed in Germany and Italy for hate propaganda, rearmament, and aggression.

Had American leaders and their constituents been willing to face the political facts in Asia and Europe during the interwar decades, they might have given more attention to U.S. military power. But policy on questions of international security was cast in a more optimistic mold. In 1921 the U.S.-sponsored Washington Naval Disarmament Conference agreed on a "5-5-3" formula to govern the relative size of the American, British, and Japanese battleship fleets, and on the scrapping of excess warships. It looked like a good start, but Japan kept its promise only so long as convenient, and by the mid-1930s, despite more such conferences, a full-scale naval arms race was on.

Peace by negotiation was also a popular theme. It found a famous expression in the Kellogg-Briand Pact of 1928, whose parties pledged to renounce war forever as an instrument of national policy and to settle all their disputes by peaceful means. The pact, initiated by the United States and France, gained no less than 63 adherents, but without any means of enforcement it had no practical effect. A more useful step was the creation of a Permanent Court of International Justice, designed in part by an American jurist, Elihu Root. Presidents from Harding to Franklin Roosevelt all sought Senate ratification of the court's statute, going so far as to concede a proviso that no case involving the United States could come before the court without prior U.S. consent; but even this cautious formula was rejected by the Senate after much dillydallying in 1935. (Finally in 1945, the United States joined the successor body, the International Court of Justice, which is the judicial arm of the United Nations—but only with crippling reservations attached by the Senate.)

Meanwhile in 1933, in the distress of the depression, Germany's experiment in democracy collapsed and Adolf Hitler, leader of the National Socialist (Nazi) party and apostle of the German "master race," came to power. Within a year he denounced the Versailles ban on German rearmament, and in 1936 defiantly marched his new army into the demilitarized Rhineland. Yet all through the 1930s, the decade of bloody Japanese and bloodless German aggression, the West, including the United States, showed little stomach for resistance; indeed, Hitler's pose as savior of the West from communism was widely credited.

As in earlier European crises, the main American response was isolationism—a determination not to get involved. From 1935 to 1937— while Hitler and his Italian Fascist partner, Benito Mussolini, were rearming, invading, or threatening other countries, and helping General Francisco Franco overthrow the Spanish Republic—Congress passed a series of neutrality acts, outlawing the transfer of American-made arms to belligerents, or the shipment of any arms to belligerents in American ships, and empowering the President to ban travel by U.S. citizens on belligerent ships. When Roosevelt made a speech in 1937 calling for an international "quarantine" of aggressors—a rather vague idea, but clearly unneutral in its implications—the public outcry was so strong that he dropped the issue. There was no resistance when Austria was forcibly united with Germany in March 1938. In September 1938, when Britain and France made their notorious pact with Hitler at Munich, ratifying German seizure of part of Czechoslovakia, Roosevelt himself publicly agreed with them that Czechoslovakia was not worth a war. What he knew all too well was that America was in no condition to fight even if the people had wanted to: as late as 1940 the U.S. Army numbered only 267,000. In the next five years that number would be multiplied by 30.

The alarm bells did not ring loudly in Washington until September 1939 when Hitler and the Soviet dictator Josef Stalin, eight days after signing their famous (and, as it turned out, short-lived) nonaggression pact, jointly invaded Poland and partitioned it between their two countries. Britain, having made clear that it would honor its alliance with Poland, kept its promise, and World War II was on.

The United States immediately showed where its sympathies lay by amending the neutrality law so that Britain and France could buy military goods—for cash only. In 1940, with France invaded and defeated and a German invasion of defiant Britain seemingly imminent, Congress voted funds for the first two-ocean navy; tens of thousands of military aircraft were ordered; and military conscription was enacted for the first time since the Civil War. Roosevelt, without even seeking Congressional consent, "loaned" Britain 50 over-age U.S. destroyers for U-boat patrol duty in exchange for a lease on British naval bases in the Caribbean. And in March 1941, when Allied cash reserves were running low, Congress, after much debate, passed the Lend-Lease Act. Under its terms the United States, the "arsenal of democracy" in the sloganeers' phrase, provided for the next four years a vast stream of supplies for the war effort—including that of the Soviet Union, massively invaded in June 1941 by Germany.

These steps were taken only over heavy political resistance from isolationist forces, still strong nationwide and especially in the Midwest. Isolationism at that time was an odd mixture—part admiration for, or fear of, German power; part pacifism; part old-fashioned antiforeignism; part the traditional American notion that our democratic ideals must not be sullied by foreign entanglements. The political champion of these views was Republican Senator Robert A. Taft of Ohio, who made a strong bid for his party's presidential nomination in 1940. But Taft was fighting a losing battle against the facts: Hitler's pact with Communist Russia and his brazen aggression against Poland, France, and the Low Countries; and Britain's inspiring stand under the eloquent Winston Churchill. It was this tide of events that caused the Republicans to reject Taft as their nominee in favor of Wendell L. Willkie, an internationalist backed by the party's Europe-minded Eastern wing. Still, isolationism, centered in the America First Committee, remained strong even after Roosevelt's reelection, resisting his increasingly pro-British policy until, a year later, the United States itself was drawn into the war.

The trigger that put the United States in the war was pulled in Asia, not Europe. In 1940 Japan—now formally allied with Nazi Germany and Fascist Italy—was pressing beyond China into Indochina, the colonial realm of defeated France, and was threatening the adjacent empires of Britain and the Netherlands. The U.S. response was increasingly firm. By July 1941 the export of U.S. scrap iron to Japan was stopped; then Japanese assets in this country were frozen, thus ending Japanese-American trade including the export of U.S. oil and steel to Japan. The oil embargo was especially damaging to Japan's plans; Roosevelt, knowing this, held to it inflexibly. On December 7, 1941 the Japanese blow fell—not on the Netherlands' oil-rich empire in Indonesia, as some had predicted, but on the U.S. fleet at anchor in Pearl Harbor, Hawaii. Within four days the United States was at war with Germany, Italy, and Japan.

Victory was to come nearly four years later, in mid-1945, at the price of tens of millions of war dead including over 400,000 Americans. Although U.S. war sacrifices were dwarfed by the stupendous losses of China, Russia, Japan, and Germany, the U.S. contribution to victory was far greater than it had been in World War I. American generals and admirals commanded the Allied forces in both Europe and Asia; American economic sinews armed the whole war effort. And the United States, ending the war at the height of its power, was in a position to influence decisively the shape of the postwar world.

Roosevelt had known in a broad way what shape he wanted that to be. He stressed two basic principles. One was an extension of human freedom—his famous formula of the "four freedoms," freedom of speech and religion, freedom from want and fear—"everywhere in the world." The other principle was cooperation among the great powers to deter aggression and keep the peace, working through a world organization to which all nations would belong—and in which, this time, the United States would play a leading part. He even thought up its name: the United Nations.

International planning for the new organization went forward while the war was still on, culminating in the signing of the UN Charter in San Francisco in June 1945. Responding to Washington's lead, a host of influential citizens and voluntary organizations joined to rally public support for the UN and, more broadly, for constructive U.S. leadership in the postwar world. Isolationism was in retreat, and American hopes were high for an era of peace to redeem the tragedy of war.

Roosevelt died on the eve of victory in Europe. He did not live to see which of his hopes would be realized and which would not. In the second part of this book we will see how the United States, a superpower in a greatly altered world, has fared since 1945 in its attempts to put its new-found power and influence at the service of the national interest—and, at times, the common interest of all.

3

The Process: Making U.S. Foreign Policy

When Thomas Jefferson took office as the first U.S. Secretary of State in 1790, one of his tasks was to arrange for permanent U.S. diplomatic representation abroad. By 1791 the young republic had ministers or lesser-ranking diplomats (the rank of ambassador was shunned as being too extravagant and smacking of royalist pomp) in five countries: Britain, France, Spain, the Netherlands, and Portugal. To assist Secretary Jefferson in instructing these envoys and in shaping U.S. policy on such burning issues as western border troubles with Britain and Spain and neutral rights on the high seas (and also in running a patent office and handling other domestic functions for which the new department was then the administrative catchall) a frugal Congress had provided a staff of five clerks, a part-time translator, and two custodians who doubled as messengers.

Small-scale it certainly was, but foreign policy already had its frustrations. Jefferson, laboring to extract concessions from Britain, was repeatedly undercut by the pro-British Alexander Hamilton, Secretary of the Treasury, who was closer to President Washington than he was. It was over this issue that Jefferson resigned in 1794. Meanwhile Washington, noting that the new Constitution entitled the Senate to give the President "advice" on treaties, visited the Senate one day to seek its advice on certain pending treaty negotiations with Indian tribes. He was so incensed when the Senate delayed the matter by referring it to a committee that he never went back. Thus, at the beginning, we can see in miniature some typical headaches that have plagued the makers of U.S. foreign policy for two centuries.

But if there is some continuity, there is much more change. The rise of the American republic to world power; the spread of the European state system to virtually the entire world; the changes in human life wrought by modern war, science, technology, mass production and marketing, urbanization, rapid transportation and instant communication; and the vastly increased complexity of political life in the United States itself—all these factors combined have transformed and complicated almost beyond recognition not only the substance of U.S. foreign policy but also the process by which it is made.

Some crude numbers suggest the extent of the change. Jefferson's State Department of five clerks has grown to 24,000 employees, two-thirds of them abroad. Career Foreign Service officers alone now number some 3,400. Those five American legations in Europe that reported to Jefferson in the 1790s have become 134 U.S. embassies and other diplomatic missions spread out over every region of the globe. In addition, 116 U.S. consulates represent American commercial and other private interests, and perform various diplomatic duties, in major foreign cities.

Other departments of the government have spawned whole bureaus to deal with international aspects of their work and to help stir the foreign policy pot. Intelligence-gathering—and countering hostile snooping by other powers—is the main function of two agencies and a big part of the workload of several others. There are separate bureaucracies for foreign aid, trade, international information, arms control, and—a fact that long ago ceased to be even a pretended secret—covert political operations in foreign countries. To help the President manage all this, an elaborate structure of coordination and command has arisen in the White House. And Congress, to strengthen its overseeing of the whole process, has passed mountains of laws and hired whole platoons of foreign policy specialists.

This sprawling machinery came into being, of course, in response to specific problems facing the United States as a world power. The most important of these problems are discussed in later chapters. The focus in this chapter is on the foreign policy machine—the seemingly chaotic process by which it functions, and the main instruments by which foreign policy decisions are carried into action.

THE INSTRUMENTS OF FOREIGN POLICY

As we have already noted, there are various instruments of national power and influence—chiefly diplomatic, economic, and military—by which nations seek to promote their interests on the world scene. Although they are discussed here separately, they are most often used in combination. The manager of foreign policy, like an orchestrator of music, has to know what each instrument can and cannot do and what part it can play in particular situations.

The Diplomatic Art

Of all the instruments, diplomacy must head the list. It is mainly by diplomatic contact with other nations that the United States settles or eases disputes and joins with like-minded governments to promote common interests.

Diplomacy is the primary function of the State Department and its embassies and other diplomatic missions, located in the capitals of all but the smallest countries, as well as at the headquarters of the United Nations, NATO, and a few other major international bodies. The ambassador and his top staff of Foreign Service officers in each embassy are expected to be expert communicators and negotiators. Their job is to work out agreements, clear up misunderstandings, explain America and its policies to the host government and people, soothe hurt feelings, and brief visiting U.S. officials on the local scene—among other things. Equally important, they keep up a steady flow of reports to Washington on whatever affects U.S. interests, and recommend actions they think the United States should take. Thus they contribute to policy, although while serving in the field they seldom make it; and the skill with which they work goes far to determine whether a given policy succeeds or fails. They are, in short, the highly trained brains, eyes, ears, and voices of the United States in the countries where they are assigned.

It is recorded that in 1828 the State Department received a dispatch from the American consul in Barcelona, Spain, complaining that he had last heard from the department in 1816. Things move faster in Washington now. Telegraphic traffic to and from the field runs to well over 1,000 messages a day for the State Department alone. Washington is permanent

The State Department—
Crew of the Ship of State

If the President, in his foreign policy role, can be likened to the captain on the bridge of the ship of state (and Congress, perhaps, to the board of directors of the shipping company), then the ship's crew would be those 24,000 employees of the Department of State.

The State Department is head-quartered (appropriately, according to Washington's amateur humorists) in a section of northwest Washington known as Foggy Bottom. The communications center in its sprawling sandstone office building processes about a million words a day of telegraphic traffic, much of it coded—outgoing instructions and "info" messages to, and reports from, diplomatic posts and consulates around the world.

State (as it is called in the federal bureaucracy) is the main day-to-day source of information for the U.S. government on what foreign governments are up to. It is also the normal channel when the United States has something to discuss or settle with a foreign government. It negotiates treaties and agreements; consults and maneuvers among other governments to promote U.S. interests and objectives, win and keep friends, frustrate enemies, and keep the lid on explosive situations. It attempts to give guidance to other government agencies on countless aspects of their work involving foreign policy. Through its consular offices it looks after U.S. commer-cial and other private interests abroad, protects U.S. citizens in danger, and issues (or denies) visas to foreigners wishing to enter this country.

State is the nation's main center of expertise on the international relations of foreign countries, especially their relations with the United States. Its professional staff, including the career Foreign Service, is, for the most part, exceptionally qualified. Gone are the days when wealthy gentlemen, graduates of Ivy League colleges, some of them brilliant and others of very moderate ability, dominated the U.S. career diplomatic service and lent it an air of patrician finesse. Examinations for the Foreign Service are stiff, and only a small minority of applicants are accepted. Most career FSOs master the language, history, and culture of at least one—sometimes several—of the areas in which they serve. The few veteran FSOs who make it to the top permanent grade of career minister are men—and, in a few cases, women—of rare ability and broad experience in different regions and functions.

Under the Constitution, the President appoints all U.S. ambassadors. Frequently he and his staff confer with—and sometimes even instruct—an ambassador who is involved in a key policy issue, although this function normally falls to the State Department. Most ambassadorships go to senior Foreign Service officers whom the Secretary of State recommends, but a considerable number in every administration are filled by noncareer appointments from private life. These "political" appointees vary greatly in fitness for the work. Some are appointed chiefly because they have performed outstandingly in some related field; others chiefly because they have been big contributors to party campaign finances. Many of the best have proved highly effective as diplomats.

The limitations most often found among State Department and Foreign Service professionals are those common to most bureaucrats: overspecialization and excessive caution—a reluctance to do or say anything that might rock the boat. These qualities, indeed, are almost built into the system, although many able Foreign Service officers transcend them. Many State Department or embassy desk officers are apt to feel uncomfortable about high-level decisions that may complicate or strain relations with the particular government they deal with every day, and are somewhat out of their element in discussions of broad strategy or of relations with Congress and the public. There has been some progress in enabling FSOs to reacquaint themselves with their own country between tours of duty abroad, but this too remains a problem.

These bureaucratic tendencies have contributed to the distrust which presidents have often shown for the State Department's experts as sources of foreign policy advice. They also add to the difficulty of coordination in a department whose business, because of the fragmentation of world politics, is hard enough to coordinate anyway. To make matters worse, some otherwise able secretaries of state have been bored by administrative problems and have contributed to State's reputation as an administrative mare's nest.

Whoever aspires to help straighten out State's problems should be warned: many able people have tried. Beyond a reasonable point, making a tidy arrangement out of the whole range of U.S. relations with 170 foreign countries is inherently impossible. But, tidy or not, the wealth of foreign policy expertise and competence in the State Department and Foreign Service is an immense national resource, probably unsurpassed in any other country.

host to 142 foreign embassies and is a mecca for visiting presidents, kings, prime ministers, and other potentates. The Secretary of State and other high officials fly to conferences and negotiations abroad whenever important interests are at stake. Members of Congress also travel frequently to countries in which they take a political or foreign policy interest—usually, but not always, after comparing notes with the State Department. And the President himself—and often, at his request, the Vice President—conduct what are sometimes the most important foreign policy discussions of all; for only they can speak with the authority that comes from having been elected by the whole nation, and can meet on a basis of formal equality with the top leaders of other countries.

So frequent are these high-level travels, in fact, that ambassadors sometimes complain of being reduced to the status of messengers and travel agents—and about the confusion that comes from so many cooks stirring the foreign policy broth. However, it can be useful for different officials to deal with the foreign leaders they happen to know best, provided they coordinate with each other.

The typical end products of diplomacy are agreements. Some agreements are legally binding treaties, but most are less formal working papers or even unwritten understandings. Important agreements are often published as communiqués—for example, the Shanghai Communiqué of 1972 on resumption of relations with China, or the NATO communiqué of January 1982 on Allied reaction to the Polish crisis. The vast bulk of agreements are on workaday matters—trade, immigration, conference arrangements, etc.—and make few or no headlines.

On highly sensitive matters where full agreement proves impossible for years or even decades, such as the future of Taiwan or of Israeli-occupied Arab territories, diplomacy plays a different role: muffling the sounds of discord in careful ambiguities, while maintaining communication so that tempers won't explode, conflict will be minimized, and the hope of agreement kept alive. Diplomats can, and are sometimes instructed to, deliver blunt warnings: "Look out; if you push us on this issue there will be trouble." But their characteristic style is more like this: "Let's see if we can't work this out."

Like anybody "in the middle," embassy negotiators spend at least half their negotiating time arguing not with the foreign adversary but with their own government: "How do you expect me to get them to buy the U.S. position on point A unless you authorize me to give some ground on point B?"

The negotiator may then give Washington an analysis of what the other side really wants and what sort of common ground looks possible. Having studied the embassy's views on such questions, the decision-makers in Washington write the confidential instructions.

But the diplomat in the field is no automaton. The embassy officer must know how to couch Washington's instructions in words that will spare the host country's pride and cultural sensitivities or cater to the whims of a key figure in the host government. It is his or her job to be acquainted with all those facets of diplomacy, for success in negotiation depends on them.

Linkage in Negotiation

The matter of linkage raises some of the trickiest questions in foreign policy. In any genuine negotiation, the side that demands something must expect to give something equivalent in return. But equivalents in diplomacy are hard to measure. For example, was the Carter Administration right to defer Senate debate on the strategic arms control treaty (SALT II) of 1979 in part because of its disapproval of Soviet actions in Afghanistan and Africa? Yes, said some Americans; Moscow needs a strategic arms pact worse than we do and we can restrain it politically by imposing this linkage. No, said others; the arms treaty is in our interest as much as theirs, and they know it; therefore the linkage won't work.

There is another kind of linkage, which is more strategic and long-range: a policy of involving the other side in so many useful relationships that it will be obliged to "behave" lest the valued links be severed. This was a key aspect of Henry Kissinger's Soviet policy during the détente period of the early 1970s. In 1972 a long list of U.S.-Soviet trade, technical, and other cooperative programs was launched. In a separate political agreement both sides undertook to "exercise restraint" in their foreign policies. But before long there was wide complaint by the Americans, including Kissinger himself, that the Soviets had not acted with restraint in various third-world conflicts.

What went wrong? In part, the Russians merely took advantage of the disarray in U.S. policy after the disaster in Vietnam and the Watergate scandal. But they also seem to have calculated that the United States, and still more Western Europe, had developed as strong an interest in East-West trade as they had and would be loath to cut it off. This judgment proved right. President Jimmy Carter's curbs on U.S. grain sales to the

Soviets, a retaliation for the Afghanistan invasion, raised louder cries of pain in Washington than in Moscow and were rescinded a little more than a year later by President Reagan. And in 1982 the Reagan Administration's effort to prevent fulfillment of a huge gas pipeline project between Western Europe and the Soviet Union failed in the face of a wrathful reaction from the Europeans and from the American companies that were involved. Little credence was given to Washington's charge that European trade with the East was helping to build Soviet military power.

Linkage, in sum, is a raising of the stakes in a diplomatic negotiation to achieve more than one aim. It has no magic beyond whatever power and persuasion the government that does the linking can put behind it. Successful linkage requires especially astute judgment as to what various governments and publics want, and what they will pay. It also frequently requires a polite public denial that the link exists—otherwise some other government, having quietly agreed to it, may be attacked at home for surrendering the nation's sovereignty and back out of the deal. Critics have said, for example, that quiet diplomacy might have induced the Soviet Union to grant more exit permits to Soviet Jews in exchange for the U.S.-Soviet trade agreement of 1972. But when Congress in 1974 publicly tied its approval of the agreement to Soviet cooperation on emigration, Moscow indignantly cancelled the pact—and Jewish emigration permits went down, not up.

Diplomacy in a Revolutionary World

Diplomacy, with its time-honored procedures, reasonableness, and restraint, often works under severe handicaps in this turbulent world. The diplomat's working assumption is that the government with which he or she talks and negotiates is stable, legitimate, and can keep its promises. Anything that challenges that assumption, such as a weak central authority or revolutionary violence, hampers the work—and may sometimes even threaten the diplomat's life, for diplomats have lately been favorite targets for terrorists. Yet it is part of the embassy officer's job to report on such matters. That can be difficult, especially in a dictatorship, which might expel a foreigner caught in secret contact with opposition groups. The result may be failure to learn about revolutionary storms brewing—as happened in Iran before the shah's ouster in 1978. And if the revolution succeeds, the United States will be vilified for having backed the oppressor.

Sometimes a revolution brings a withdrawal of ambassadors or even a complete break in diplomatic relations between the new regime and the United States. The break with Iran has lasted since November 1979, but that is far from being a record. There was no U.S. diplomatic mission in Moscow for 16 years (1917–1933) or in Beijing for 23 years (1949–1972). As of 1982, there were no formal diplomatic relations between this country and Albania, Angola, Cuba, Grenada, Iran, Iraq, Cambodia (Kampuchea), Mongolia, Mozambique, or Southern Yemen. The hope of some advocates of such diplomatic boycotts that the ostracized government would disappear has generally proved forlorn. Meanwhile, essential diplomatic business between the estranged countries is carried on through third countries, discreet contacts between their delegations at the UN, or other private intermediaries. The history of diplomatic breaks shows that even the most emotion-charged of them do not last forever. It is hard to "stay mad" when new problems and common interests pile up and demand to be discussed.

Economic Diplomacy

In the foreign policy of the world's biggest economic power, economic instruments have many uses. Most commonly, U.S. financial or technical aid, or trading benefits are granted in exchange for—or at least in the hope of—equivalent economic benefits, such as wider foreign markets and investment opportunities for U.S. business. Economic aid can also be used to strengthen a political or strategic relationship with a key country such as China, Egypt, Israel, or South Korea. But long-term development assistance—as well as humanitarian aid in emergencies—is given with no expectation of any immediate benefit except goodwill.

Some policy-makers, as noted above, have promoted exports to the Soviet Union on the theory that its growing dependence on Western products and technology would make it more cautious about offending Western interests. Others, taking the opposite view, cite a remark attributed to Lenin—that in trading with capitalists the Soviet Union is merely selling them the rope to hang themselves. Holding out an economic carrot to a sworn adversary, say these critics, will not improve his behavior; and attempts to punish him by withdrawing the carrot, or by beating him with the stick of economic sanctions, are equally futile.

Which view is right? The evidence is inconclusive. The economic carrot can be effective when the country in question feels itself to be in serious need, as Russia did in the early 1920s and China apparently did in the 1970s; but when the need grows less acute the carrot tends to lose its effect. As for the economic stick, the record suggests that it works only in somewhat exceptional circumstances. In one famous but unique case, the Iranian hostage crisis of 1980–1981, heavy U.S. economic leverage, aided by highly skilled diplomacy, produced the desired result in spite of the Khomeini government's seemingly bottomless hostility. In another, more momentous case, the cutoff of critical U.S. exports to Japan in 1941 produced a dramatic result Washington had not planned for—the attack on Pearl Harbor. In both of these cases Washington held a fistful of powerful economic cards—not the usual situation. More commonly, cooperation among several trading nations is essential, and politically hard to arrange; for the countries that cooperate simply lose business to those that do not. That lesson was learned by the League of Nations in the 1930s when its economic sanctions failed to stop Italy from seizing Ethiopia, and again by the UN when its thirteen-year sanctions failed to bring white-ruled Rhodesia to its knees. A quarter of a century of U.S. economic boycott of Cuba has merely tightened Cuba's economic links to Moscow. And, as will be seen in Chapter 9, Western economic sanctions against the Soviet Union have had small success.

Moreover, even if full compliance with a sanctions program is arranged, it still may not work. In war, a highly mobilized country under economic blockade may let its people approach starvation before its army goes hungry, and will manufacture substitutes for what it used to import. Even in peacetime, governments hate to be seen yielding under pressure, and are unlikely to do so unless the pressure is truly painful.

The basic problem with all economic sanctions is that the author of the program, when a normal transaction is cancelled, loses as much as the intended victim. The smaller the monetary value of the goods involved, and the fewer the countries trading in those goods, and the more desperate the target country's need, the more likely it is that a sanctions program will work. Efforts to weaken an adversary or hamper its policies by broader sanctions, aimed at wide segments of its economy and involving many rival trading countries, are extremely difficult to sustain. These considerations may help to explain why the Arab countries' experiment with oil sanctions against the United States in October 1973 was brief—and has not been repeated.

Such hostile actions, in which economic power is used for political ends, are but one part—and by no means the most important part—of the vast field of economic diplomacy. Bulking far larger are the economic relations among essentially friendly countries, involving an enormous, unceasing flow of goods, capital, and technology without which modern civilization could not survive.

Ideally, if private transactions everywhere and always were of equal benefit to buyer and seller, governments might be glad to leave economic decisions strictly to the free market; and, indeed, there are powerful arguments in the economic field for governmental restraint. But, as will be seen in Chapter 9, there are countless forces that impel governments, wisely or not, to intervene in the market. Unavoidably, the sorting out of common and conflicting economic and political interests among nations must always occupy a leading place in the U.S. foreign policy agenda.

In general, foreign economic policy is a two-way street, in which the United States must expect to pay for what it gets. The same is true of other nonpolitical functions that involve foreign policy: immigration, travel, tax law, environmental and energy programs, and a host of scientific, cultural, athletic, medical, technological activities, and exchanges that call for cooperation among governments. Operating responsibility for such activities is scattered among dozens of U.S. government agencies, with the State Department doing its best to coordinate any political aspects they may have. As a rule, State is content to let such programs proceed on their own merits, without linking them to questions of ideology or power politics, and has resisted attempts by other governments to introduce such linkages. But there are many exceptions. For example, of the many projects of U.S.-Soviet technical cooperation launched in 1972 in the name of détente, in fields ranging from heart disease research to outer space, most were dropped or cut back after détente began to erode.

The Military Arm

Military power—whether used in battle or maintained as an implied threat—is in some ways the most potent foreign policy instrument of all. The German soldier-scholar Karl von Clausewitz, in a famous understatement, called war "a continuation of politics by other means." The trouble is that in the nuclear age the "other means," at their destructive maximum, have become unusable except as a threat that no national leader in his or her right mind would carry out. Even war below the nuclear level, using weapons no newer than those of World War I, can prove more costly than any likely gains could justify. Each side, when that war began, expected to win, and quickly. As things turned out, both sides lost—so agonizingly and so heavily that world power relations were permanently changed.

Moreover, in modern political life war has to be justified not merely to the rulers but to the people. Gone is the age when kings could send feudal or mercenary armies into battle to avenge an insult or seize a throne for a royal relative. In the TV age, military censorship cannot conceal the horrors of war as easily as it did—on all sides—in the two world wars. War today, especially for a rich democracy whose people have a great deal to lose, is a possible option only when the people believe their nation's vital interests demand this drastic step—and only as long as that belief holds up against the grim facts of battle as seen on the TV screen. As Shimon Peres, an Israeli political leader, said in 1982 arguing for Israeli restraint in Lebanon: "War in our day is war that is photographed. In the battlefield are not only tanks but television cameras, the eye of the entire world, and pictures are stronger than words."

Yet the *capacity* to wage war successfully—to wreak frightful destruction if push comes to shove—can still be a decisive political and diplomatic weapon. One of every American statesman's most difficult tasks is to apply the nation's enormous military power to its foreign policy aims with precision and with the least risk of disaster.

To maintain its military capacity the United States keeps over 2 million men and women in uniform, plus some 800,000 in the reserves, and spent in 1982 over $200 billion, or about 6 percent of the gross national product. The Secretary of Defense, the Joint Chiefs of Staff, and the three service secretaries (Army, Navy, and Air Force), who administer this establishment, are traditionally strong advocates of a big military budget, the most advanced weapons systems, and better pay and training for military personnel. But to call them trigger-happy, as some do, is a mistake. In 1950 the U.S. military were unprepared to stop the invasion of South Korea; and, once the tide of that war turned, successfully opposed proposals to widen the war by bombing China. And among the strongest pleaders for U.S. military withdrawal from Vietnam in 1969–1970 was President Nixon's Secretary of Defense, Melvin R. Laird, a former Congressman sensitive to public opinion. Pentagon views on involving U.S. forces in El Salvador (1981) and in Lebanon (1982) were reported to be of the same kind.

Closely related to military power is the capacity to produce and export weapons. This capacity has become a major instrument of political influence abroad—almost inevitably so as developing countries shop around for ever more advanced weaponry to serve their security, ambition, or prestige. But converting this kind of hardware into lasting political relationships is a tricky business, for local conflicts do not fit neatly into global designs, and the weapon that will shoot in only one direction has yet to be invented.

Cloak-and-Dagger Warfare

Covert operations—actions against foreign adversaries in which the instigator's hand is concealed—are a unique and highly problematical instrument of foreign policy. Covert action resembles war in that it too is a kind of hostile action—and is sometimes violent as well. Indeed, the Central Intelligence Agency (CIA)—which was created in 1947 primarily to take charge of collecting and analyzing foreign intelligence—inherited its covert operations division from a World War II agency, the famous Office of Strategic Services (OSS).

The wartime operations of the OSS, including sabotage, murder, "black" propaganda, and organizing underground resistance behind enemy lines, were aimed against the nation's declared enemies and have seldom been questioned on either moral or pragmatic grounds. The CIA, however, was the first U.S. agency to use such methods systematically against countries with which the United States was not officially at war. Its exploits, revealed in bits and pieces to the world, have created great controversy.

CIA covert operations helped the political center and free trade unions, and opposed Communist efforts to gain power, in Italy and France in the years after World War II. They helped overthrow unfriendly governments, and install and uphold more friendly ones, in—among other places—Iran (1953), Guatemala (1954), the Congo (Zaire) (1960), and Chile (1973). In Cuba (1961) and Angola (1975) similar operations failed. It is a fair guess that they have succeeded at times, and failed at other times, in cases not publicly known.

Successful or not, whether this kind of activity is morally or even pragmatically justifiable, except against a declared enemy in wartime, is still a hotly debated question. Some, like the 1961 attack on Cuba in the Bay of Pigs, have been embarrassing public failures; others have been revealed in painful detail in Congressional investigations, exposés by disaffected ex-agents, etc. One result is that it has become virtually impossible to maintain a tactful silence about the existence—and sometimes even the details—of a major covert operation such as those in Angola in 1975 and in Central America in the early 1980s. The consequent cost to the good name and credibility of the United States in many quarters—and to the CIA's covert capabilities—has been substantial. Yet those who oppose all covert action on principle have not demonstrated that the ends sought can never justify such means, or that the United States can prudently deny itself an instrument of policy which, with little public attention to the fact, is widely used by other powers, notably the Soviet Union.

Public Relations

Finally, public relations—in the broadest sense of the term—is a uniquely important instrument of foreign policy. Under this heading come not only all words and pictures, but all actions originated by the U.S. government that are aimed at shaping favorable public attitudes, both at home and abroad, toward the United States and its policies. (*Propaganda* once meant much the same thing, but because of its use and abuse in World War I it soon came to mean "lies" in common usage—something "our" side doesn't do but "the enemy" does.)

The most potent public relations office in the world is the American presidency. The President's words in speeches and news conferences, his itinerary when he travels abroad, the people he meets or declines to meet, his smiles, frowns, and gestures—all these, magnified by the world news media, can be a tremendous force for articulating U.S. foreign policy goals, enlisting popular support, and deflecting criticism.

When Dwight D. Eisenhower, a famous general portrayed in Soviet propaganda as a militarist, went to the United Nations in the first year of his presidency and called for an international "atoms-for-peace" program, he identified himself and his country with peaceful ideals in the eyes of the world. Eisenhower's successor, John F. Kennedy, dramatized American concern for the emerging nations of the third world—and countered the glamour of Cuba's defiant Fidel Castro—by putting his personal stamp on two new U.S. programs of high visibility, the Alliance for Progress in Latin America and the highly successful United States Peace Corps. Without Kennedy's personal prestige it is safe to say neither program would have amounted to much. The presidency is not only the "bully pulpit" Theodore Roosevelt called it—a place to enunciate American ideals and purposes—but a bully theater too. Its audience is the world and its main performer has the glamorous distinction of being the world's most powerful human being.

In a free country, of course—and in this respect none is freer than the United States—the news media jealously guard their right to cast doubt on the official line when they don't believe it, to poke fun at the President or any other public official, to publicize interagency quarrels over policy or bureaucratic turf, and to ferret out from one official, always on a "don't quote me" basis, inside facts that some other official has been trying to keep secret for reasons of diplomatic or bureaucratic maneuvering or merely because they are embarrassing. Relations between policy-maker and reporter are part mutual need and part cat-and-mouse game, and will never be tranquil. Officials complain that the media focus on violence, public quarrels, and "what's new," to the exclusion of what's important; and that reporters get things wrong through individual bias or incompetence or sheer haste to score a beat on their competitors. Reporters complain that many officials either take a "public be damned" attitude, refusing to inform the media, or else try to use them to float self-serving versions of the facts. Such complaints on both sides are often justified, but a better system has not yet been invented.

To compensate partly for their inability to control the private news media, the President and his staff have at their command the U.S. Information Agency (USIA) with its famous broadcasting service, the Voice of America. In addition, the government-financed Radio Free Europe and Radio Liberty broadcast to Eastern Europe and the Soviet Union and specialize in local news, especially that which the Communist media suppress or distort. The work of these agencies is especially important in those countries—the Soviet bloc above all—whose own news media are tightly controlled and present a highly distorted picture of the outside world. The USIA, particularly through the "Voice," transmits to the world a continuous flow of American news and features in many languages. It has long taken pride in giving the news, good or bad, with balance and without distortion, and in presenting a variety of views, not always favorable to U.S. policy. Its "policy guidance" comes from the State Department but, in order to guard the agency's cherished credibility, has generally been administered with a light hand.

In the long run, no less important than the news media to the nation's world image are the international exchange programs—educational, scholarly, scientific, and artistic—that the U.S. government has conducted or subsidized for many years. Tens of thousands of foreign scholars, teachers, creative artists, and young leaders from all regions of the world have taught and studied in the United States, as have their American counterparts abroad, under the Fulbright and other exchange programs financed by the U.S. government. The goodwill and mutual understanding thus generated may be hard to measure, but their cumulative importance to the national interest—and to the common interest of many nations—is certainly great.

No amount of public relations effort, of course, can compensate for a bad foreign policy. But even the best policy will fail without public consent. Influencing both domestic and world opinion—in keen competition with rival governments—is a fundamental task of American leadership.

THE PROCESS: KNOWLEDGE AND ACTION

Now comes a particularly baffling, yet fascinating, question: By what process does the U.S. government manage all those instruments of foreign policy—diplomacy, economic policy, etc.—and bring them to bear on the foreign policy problems that arise? How are U.S. foreign policy decisions made and carried out?

In real life, the policy process is extremely complex and hard to follow—a confusing cycle in which the flow of incoming intelligence, analysis, clashing of interests and bureaucracies, decisions, actions, and still more public argument, all go on at once. For clarity, however, it is useful to strip the process down to two simple, everyday elements: knowledge and action. A good place to begin, therefore, is the gathering and interpretation of foreign intelligence.

The allure of spy stories has led us to think of intelligence as a business of snooping for secrets in a shadow world of double agents, code-breaking, disinformation, and the like. That world does exist, and always will as long as nations keep secrets from each other. The bits of information governments acquire by such means can sometimes be of crucial importance, but their quantity is small compared to the flood of publicly available information that analysts in the CIA, the State Department, and the Pentagon wade through every day. Much of it comes from minute reading of the world press and monitoring of foreign government broadcasts, in which a small change in phraseology or the omission of a name from an official list can sometimes reveal to the analyst a new turn in the policy of a secretive foreign power. Other bits come from reports by U.S. diplomats and military attachés abroad, from examining satellite photographs, and from a vast number of other sources both open and secret. The skilled intelligence officer can piece these bits together into a meaningful picture.

To be really useful, the intelligence officer has to ask the right questions—things the policy-makers will need to know. Sometimes this means a sharp focus on an immediate policy problem. What U.S. economic reprisals for the Soviet-backed crackdown in Poland would hurt the Soviet economy most? What stand will the new strong man of a certain country probably take on pending negotiations for a civil aviation pact? An obscure foreign politician has just been made his country's ambassador in Washington: what sort of man is he? But intelligence also produces a constant flow of broader estimates on, for example, the changing military and economic strength of major countries, or on internal developments that may affect their international behavior. Such studies can help to alert U.S. policy-makers to emerging problems before they become crises.

The most difficult intelligence problems are faced by the policy-makers. It is sometimes said, for example, that the need for a risky military or political action abroad cannot be explained to Congress and the public without revealing sensitive intelligence, thereby perhaps "blowing the cover" or even costing the life of a valued informant. But if the key evidence is withheld, how can critics of the policy know whether it is convincing or not? A case in point arose in early 1982 when the Reagan Administration sought to justify a menacing U.S. posture toward the leftist government of Nicaragua by charging Nicaraguan interference in El Salvador—but said that much of the intelligence to support that charge was too sensitive to reveal. Congressional and public reactions were wary.

A still more basic problem for the policy-maker is how to keep an open mind to unwelcome facts without becoming irresolute. When action is urgent and the evidence is ambiguous (as it usually is), the commander must assess the risks and make a decision without waiting till all the facts are in. But what if new evidence begins to pile up that the original judgment and decisions were wrong? President Lyndon B. Johnson, it is said, became so allergic to bad news from Vietnam that his staff learned not to give it to him. And senior officials have been known to revise professional estimates by their own intelligence staffs that seemed to reflect badly on established policy or on their own agencies' interests.

The problem is not easy. A leader must not be easily rattled by stray items of bad news. But at what point does perseverance become blind stubbornness? In the joining of intelligence to policy, there is no substitute for honesty, good judgment, and good luck.

Intelligence, in a broader perspective, is one part of a still larger flow of knowledge—a feedback system by which policy guides itself just as the eye guides the hand. Intelligence tells the commander what "they," the outside world, are doing. But the commander also has to know what "we"—his troops, diplomats, bureaucracts of all kinds—are doing to carry out his decisions. This operational feedback suffers from the same bias as intelligence: everybody likes to tell the boss things are going fine. The boss has to be astute enough and tough enough to learn the bad news, and to weed out those who sabotage or simply botch his policy. In a bureaucracy as complex as Washington's, that is no small job. Near the end of 1952 President Truman, about to leave office and anticipating the frustrations of his West Point-trained successor, remarked sardonically: "He'll sit here and he'll say: 'Do this. Do that.' And nothing will happen." Truman's prophecy was not quite on the mark, for Eisenhower as President retained his military style of crisp command and knew how to control the generals and admirals; but neither he nor any other modern President has been free of the frustrations that go with sitting at the apex of a huge bureaucracy.

President and Congress

It is the President, then, who commands this vast, unceasing cycle of information, analysis, conclusion, recommendation, decision, action, information feedback, and still more action—the sum total of which is U.S. foreign policy. But that is only the beginning of the story. The President is at the center of what is probably the most complex and frustrating foreign policy-making system any nation has ever had. And if you could ask any President what makes it so complex and frustrating, you would probably get another short, true, but incomplete answer: Congress.

The essential roles of President and Congress in foreign policy—indeed, in all public policy—were laid down in 1789 when the U.S. Constitution was adopted. Until then, during more than a decade of independence, the Continental Congress had appointed and instructed ambassadors, made treaties, and handled all other foreign policy matters through its appointed officers. In foreign affairs as in all other fields of policy, the lack of a single strong executive had been a glaring defect of the newborn nation. But the framers of the Constitution, after fighting a war to get rid of a British tyrant, had no wish to put a home-grown tyrant in his place.

Hence the careful separation of powers between President and Congress. A treaty negotiated by the President or his agents does not become binding on the United States until it is voted on by the Senate and approved by two-thirds of the Senators present at the vote, and then signed by the President. Major presidential appointments, including ambassadorships, are subject to Senate confirmation. More important still, virtually all programs, foreign or domestic, that the President administers are subject to laws enacted by Congress and to financial limits set by congressional appropriation. Sometimes a big appropriation bill or other important piece of legislation includes one or more amendments, inserted over the President's objections by a group in the House or Senate in exchange for their votes. The President may then veto the whole bill (subject to an overriding vote by two-thirds of both houses), but he has no power to veto the parts he objects to and sign the rest. So, to get the money or the law he wants, he must often accept, and obey—or somehow circumvent—policy decisions by Congress that he didn't want. Many restrictions on U.S. foreign economic aid programs and on the sale of U.S. weapons abroad have originated in this way. Foreign trade, immigration, and military procurement are among numerous other subjects of legislation with strong foreign policy implications over which Congress and the President often clash.

The President can sometimes escape congressional control by various devices, as long as public opinion is with him. An agreement with a foreign country, for example, can be called an "executive agreement," not a treaty, and be exempted from the constitutional requirement for Senate approval. Since 1934 the President has had statutory authority to negotiate reciprocal reductions of trade barriers by executive agreement. This was also the device Franklin D. Roosevelt used in the "destroyers for bases" deal with Britain in September 1940, a moment of high public admiration for Britain's courage under German bombing (see Chapter 2); and Congress, although not even consulted, did not object. Similarly, in the heyday of U.S.-Soviet détente in 1972, President Nixon was able to exempt the five-year "interim agreement" limiting strategic offensive weapons on both sides—a key part of the SALT I package—from the

Senate ratification requirement. But later public misgivings about the SALT process, and about détente itself, were such that the SALT II pact of 1979 had to be written and presented to the Senate as a treaty even though President Carter knew it would be hard to muster a two-thirds vote for it.

The balance between President and Congress has swung back and forth many times. The abilities of a particular President affect it; much also depends on whether the two houses of Congress are dominated by the President's party by the opposition, and on the quality of congressional leadership.

Wider events also strongly affect the balance. Great emergencies—a war or a national economic crisis—strengthen the President's hand as long as his policy is seen to be working reasonably well. During World War II and, to a great extent, during the cold war that followed, congressional criticism of foreign policy was muted and bipartisan harmony prevailed. The watchword was that "politics stops at the water's edge."

But when things go wrong and presidential leadership falters, as it did after the Civil War, or during the Vietnam War and the Watergate scandal, Congress may move into the vacuum. In the 1970s, for example, Congress inserted "legislative veto" clauses into numerous laws on both domestic and foreign subjects. Laws so written—for example, on the transfer of sophisticated weapons to foreign countries—give the President general authority but give Congress power to block, by a majority vote of one or both houses, a specific use of that authority.

The mere threat of a legislative veto has proved a strong lever in the hands of Congress, particularly in monitoring the laws that govern U.S. arms sales abroad. Such a threat forced President Carter, for instance, to delay the sale in 1979 of M-60 tanks to Jordan; and in 1981 President Reagan was obliged by the same means to restrict the types and uses of the controversial AWACs reconnaissance and control aircraft to be sold to Saudi Arabia. The legislative veto device has been challenged in the federal courts as a violation of the constitutional separation of powers, but the Supreme Court has not yet ruled on the question.

Even when the presidency is at its strongest, the congressional checkrein imposes a potent restraint on the foreign policy process. Generally the reins are not held by Congress as a whole but by particular committees—Foreign Relations (called Foreign Affairs in the House), Armed Services, Appropriations for all spending bills, Judiciary for immigration matters—and many others, for foreign policy ramifies as widely through the committees and subcommittees of Congress as it does through the departments and agencies of the executive branch. The chairman is the key, for his or her views can carry great weight both in committee and on the House or Senate floor.

Some of the executive branch's worst agonies occur when key chairmanships are held, sometimes for many years at a stretch, by members who are reelected again and again and who delight in catering to antiforeign sentiments among their constituents. Some senators in this category such as the late Styles Bridges of New Hampshire in the 1950s, and currently Jesse Helms of North Carolina, have managed to get their own men appointed to key jobs in the State Department. The late Representative John J. Rooney, of Brooklyn, N.Y., when he chaired the subcommittee charged with appropriations for the State Department, was famous for cutting State's diplomatic entertainment allowances, which he derided as "booze funds." On the other hand, such senators as the late Arthur H. Vandenberg of Michigan, who was chairman of the Foreign Relations Committee in the late 1940s, and J. William Fulbright, Democrat of Arkansas, who held the same office from 1959 to 1974, were notably studious and thoughtful about the complexities of foreign policy— although they often disagreed sharply with the President.

Thus individual personalities, as well as the swings of the political pendulum, strongly affect the balance of foreign policy power between the President and the Congress. A long-term trend, however, may be moving the balance toward the President, particularly when danger of military conflict arises. The accelerating pace of transport, communications, and data processing strongly favors a single command center that can move fast and decisively in crisis. The Constitution gives Congress sole power to declare war; but the wars in Korea and Vietnam were both fought without a formal declaration. Congress felt obliged to rally around the President in both wars after he had committed U.S. forces to combat. The War Powers Act of 1973—enacted when the President was in deep trouble domestically and the Vietnam War had become intensely unpopular—placed strict curbs on presidential power to send U.S. forces into combat, but such curbs have yet to be tested in a real military emergency.

Many devices exist to reduce friction between the President and the Congress. There are congressional relations staffs in the White House and in all of the executive departments; expert professional staffs—greatly increased in recent years—serving members and committees of Congress; and endless consultations between the two branches. Still, the relationship is not smooth. Sometimes a member of congress, planning to vote "No" because that is how his or her constituents feel, prefers not to be consulted or even informed on the point at issue. Often a strong-minded Secretary of State or other official grows weary of congressional ignorance of the complicated world of foreign policy, or exasperated by congressional leaks to the news media, and resolves to tell Congress as little as possible.

Fundamentally, the tension between President and Congress is in the nature of their constituencies. The view from the White House, national in scope, and the view from any congressional office, responsive to pressures from one district or one state, can never be the same. And almost any member of Congress is likely to disagree with the President on how the control of foreign policy should be divided between the two branches.

Thus a question arises: with this perpetual tug-of-war going on, is a coherent foreign policy possible? Foreign negotiators have been known to complain, in effect: "What good does it do for me to negotiate with you when you can't assure me that your Congress won't reject the result?" Many foreign governments, when an important issue is under negotiation with Washington, take care to stay in touch with key members of Congress who might later hold the power of life and death over the hoped-for agreement.

There is another side to the coin. An astute American negotiator can sometimes squeeze extra concessions out of his foreign negotiating partner by raising the threat of rejection by Congress. Thus, on the whole, congressional involvement probably tends to stiffen the U.S. negotiating position. Whether this is always in the American interest, however, is doubtful. A case in point is a recent U.S.-Canadian draft treaty, negotiated in 1978, on the perpetual issue of fishing rights along the Atlantic coast. The negotiators reached a compromise by which the fish catch would be shared between Americans and Canadians, without overfishing lest the fish populations of the region be endangered. But the treaty could not clear the Senate, which often defers in such matters to the interest group most directly affected—in this case, New England fishermen. The early outlook was for no agreement at all—an outcome that would not serve the interest of either country.

President and Bureaucracy

No less strenuous is the President's perpetual effort—in foreign policy as in all policy—to govern the huge federal bureaucracy. Although the

Constitution places solely on him the duty to "faithfully execute the laws," his power to do so if far from absolute. For one thing, it is hedged about by the laws themselves, which give Congress great influence over how the laws are administered. The congressional power of the purse decides, for example, whether the law requiring the Immigration and Naturalization Service to patrol the Mexican border against illegal border-crossers will be administered by a large, well-trained, and well-equipped force or by a small and ill-equipped one. (In recent times the latter has usually been the case—a situation welcomed by Mexico, by the border-crossers themselves, and by employers in the Southwest who use unskilled labor, but not by competing American workers.) And for another thing, the President, even with a White House staff of several hundred, cannot always impose his will on entrenched and wily bureaucrats who know the details (although not always the broad implications) of their work much better than he does and can often summon powerful congressional influence to their side of the argument.

Among the many agencies in the Washington bureaucracy that have something to do with foreign policy, the central position is that of the Department of State. Under the Secretary of State, it is chiefly responsible for the day-to-day conduct of U.S. relations with foreign governments—above all *political* relations, the kind that can raise questions of power, conflict, war and peace. The Secretary of State is also—officially, though not always in fact—the President's principal adviser on broad foreign policy issues.

The outward signs of the Secretary of State's senior status are imposing. He ranks first in the President's cabinet. Under the law of 1789 creating the State Department (it is the oldest in the U.S. government) he is the only department head whose duties are defined and performed entirely as the President, not Congress, directs. Under the Presidential Succession Act, if the President, the Vice-President, and the two top leaders of Congress were all to die or be disqualified, he would be President. He stands third, just after the President and Vice-President, on the protocol list—Washington's social and diplomatic pecking order

Despite all this, and despite the unique resources of his department (see box, page 50), there are basic reasons why the Secretary of State cannot hope to be the President's sole repository of wisdom on foreign policy. To begin with, the President is under no compulsion to rely on him. Many a President has gone over the head of his State Department by sending his own trusted emissary abroad to deal with, and be his own eyes and ears on, relationships and problems that he considered especially important. Woodrow Wilson had his Colonel E. M. House and Franklin Roosevelt his Harry Hopkins—and what passed between them and foreign governments was often not even told to the State Department. Recent presidents have appointed their own special ambassadors on the politically sensitive Arab-Israeli conflict, and have given major diplomatic assignments to their Vice-Presidents and their national security advisers. And Congress long ago created special agencies, reporting to the White House, to negotiate on international trade and on arms control.

Even without such competition from above, State's control of foreign policy would be limited by the sheer immensity of the subject matter with which today's foreign policy has to deal. In addition to military matters, arms control, and trade agreements, its concerns include—and its harried staff struggles to keep up with—economic development assistance; foreign information, education and cultural programs; and scores of agricultural, environmental, scientific, technological, disaster relief, refugee, health, transportation, communications, and other programs established over the decades, most of them by Act of Congress. Each has its niche in one or more federal agencies. Some are represented in embassies abroad by military, commercial, scientific, cultural, agricultural, labor, and other specialized attachés. And each embassy also has its staff for public information programs, for aid programs where appropriate, and, presumably, for the undercover work of the CIA.

Officially, the U.S. ambassador in each country is supposed to control all these activities as one "country team." But in real life the main lines of communication flow to the relevant agencies in Washington, where State, none too effectively, tries to coordinate. In theory this should enable the U.S. ambassador in country X, for example, to use the promise of a new program of U.S. cooperation—perhaps in space research or insect control or the like—to induce the reluctant government of that country to be helpful on some matter of diplomatic importance to Washington, such as a key UN vote or nonrecognition of a Soviet-backed junta that has just seized power in a nearby country. In practice, State may well find out belatedly that the Washington agency handling the program in question has already made the agreement, and so must hunt for some other diplomatic carrot.

Such coordination can be a grinding task, especially when the program State is trying to "coordinate" happens to be popular with constituents of important congressmen. Moreover, the heads of technical cooperation programs understandably view their work as too important in its own right to be bandied about as political bargaining chips with foreign potentates.

Still more difficult is the perennial struggle of the Secretary of State to be actually, not just officially, the President's chief adviser on the broad lines of foreign policy. On issues with military or economic aspects—for example, arms sales to Taiwan, or U.S. policy on the Soviet-West European gas pipeline—he and his staff normally consult with their opposite numbers in Defense, Treasury, Commerce, and other agencies concerned, hoping to present to the President either a coordinated recommendation or a set of options among which the President can choose. But what if the strong-minded head of an embattled department, while the options paper is on the President's desk, learns through the bureaucratic grapevine that the White House or National Security Council staff is advising the President to decide against him? He may suspect that the staff has not conveyed his views clearly and fairly to the President, but he doesn't want to wear out his welcome by calling the President direct. In such a case, he is likely to ignore the official rules of the game and leak his side of the story (in person or through a subordinate or a friendly senator) to a favorite reporter or columnist. The controversy then explodes into the headlines, and the news media are deluged with special pleading from every politician or interest group with a stake in the outcome. The identity of the source of the leak—by a time-honored journalistic tradition—is never made public; and bureaucratic manhunts to identify and punish the malefactor are seldom successful. Little wonder, because high-level officials are among the main practitioners of this method.

In this highly competitive Washington environment, a Secretary of State will be the President's chief foreign policy adviser in fact only if he has the mental powers, masterful character, bureaucratic maneuvering skill, and physical stamina to outdo his rivals; and—at least as important—if he has the personal confidence of, and regular face-to-face access to, the President. Only four of the fourteen secretaries of state since World War II have had these assets in outstanding degree: George C. Marshall and Dean Acheson under Harry S Truman; John Foster Dulles under Dwight D. Eisenhower; and Henry A. Kissinger under Richard M. Nixon and Gerald R. Ford. Whether George P. Shultz will join that short list remains to be seen. Other holders of the office—Cordell Hull under Franklin D. Roosevelt, Dean Rusk under John F. Kennedy and Lyndon B. Johnson, and William P. Rogers during Richard Nixon's first term—were never close to their chiefs and were primarily executors, not shapers of policy. James F. Byrnes under Truman, Cyrus R. Vance under Jimmy Carter, and Alexander M. Haig, Jr. during a year and a half under Ronald Reagan, all failed to establish their primacy in foreign policy. All resigned after major decisions went against their strongly held views.

The President in the Middle

No matter how masterful the Secretary of State may be, or how persistently Congress intervenes, the heaviest burdens of shaping and guiding a foreign policy that will serve the national interest fall in the end on one man: the President. He may be an activist like both Roosevelts, Kennedy, Johnson, and Nixon—or, like Eisenhower and Reagan, he may stand aloof from the foreign policy arena except when issues are brought to him for decision, then hear all views and render his decision like a court of last resort. He may or may not be highly knowledgeable about international affairs. But whatever his style or his qualifications, when difficult issues come to him for decision he must do the deciding. (Even doing nothing, stalling for time, is a kind of decision—and sometimes the wisest.)

Whom is the President to consult before deciding a thorny question on, say, the deployment or control of nuclear weapons, or what to do next in the Middle East? All the relevant department and agency heads will give him their views. Leading senators and congressmen will shower him with advice, especially if the issue has aroused the public. Heads of key foreign governments may write to him or call him on the phone. Leaders of major interest groups with a stake in the matter will try to get in to see him. His staff will summarize the results of national opinion polls on the issue and brief him on the volume and general thrust of thousands of letters and messages from plain citizens. He may pick and choose among the nation's top authorities on the subject. He may talk the matter over with his wife, a friendly newsman, or members of a "kitchen cabinet" whose names are not on any organization chart. If he is a religious man he may pray for divine guidance.

There is always some element of play-acting in all this, for even if a President's mind is made up he must not be perceived as unwilling to listen. But there is genuine consultation too; for he cannot afford to ignore the aims and desires of important power centers, both foreign and domestic, whose reactions can spell success or failure for his policy.

Indeed, if we look at the foreign policy process through a very wide-angle lens, what we see is the President and his White House staff standing in the middle of an enormous web of interactions—so enormous that some participants in it seem barely to realize each other's existence. At one edge of the web are the American people pursuing their various interests and forming in their heads a wide variety of notions, more or less inaccurate and more or less strongly believed, about the great world beyond their borders. Mediating between the people and Washington are their elected representatives in Congress, who generally know more than the average citizen about that great world but, with a few exceptions, are too busy with other matters to become experts on it. Supplementing this congressional link between Washington and the public are other kinds of links: business, professional, and civic organizations, the news media, opinion polls, and knowledgeable individuals in the foreign policy establishment—many of them former government officials—in universities and elsewhere.

At the opposite edge of the web are the peoples of all the other countries of the world—individuals and groups with *their* lives and concerns. The governments that rule over them consult with the U.S. embassies in their capitals, and with key officials in our government through their embassies in Washington or on high-level visits abroad. The sum total of their relations with the United States is supposed to be brought to a focus—as nearly as humanly possible—in the State Department.

So the President finds himself midway between a State Department that is deeply concerned about the nations of the world and their effect on U.S. interests, and a Congress whose members are just as deeply concerned about the views of their constituents back home. The constituents may be ignorant of what is happening in Germany or Guatemala or the Middle East, but they are experts on one thing: their own desires. And they are the uncrowned rulers of the United States, for their votes make or break Presidents and congressmen. On the other hand, the State Department and embassy professionals—together with their colleagues in other internationally oriented government agencies—may be rather ignorant about the voters' desires, but they are the nation's most knowledgeable contacts with that other great and diverse reality, the world.

A part of the President's nearly impossible job is to reconcile those two jarring forces. If he is to do this even tolerably well, the views he forms must take into account all the conflicting advice that he gets from so many quarters, but must be broader and more "national" than any of it. For systematic, in-house support in this task, he can turn to an official whose job has been much in the news in recent years: the national security adviser.

The office of Assistant to the President for National Security Affairs (that is the official title) started as one thing and gradually became another. As a result of World War II, the government found itself with a growing complex of diplomatic, military, economic, intelligence, and other functions bearing on the nation's interests abroad. To improve coordination among these, Congress in 1947 created a National Security Council headed by the President and including the secretaries of State and Defense. The Vice-President and a few other high officials, notably the Chairman of the Joint Chiefs of Staff and the Director of Central Intelligence, were added later. Different presidents have used the NSC and its professional staff pretty much as they saw fit. In 1961 President Kennedy greatly increased the importance of the staff and of its chief, the National Security Adviser. Two subsequent holders of that job, Henry A. Kissinger (for over four years before he became Secretary of State) under President Nixon and, in a lesser degree, Zbigniew Brzezinski under President Carter, have wielded substantial power in the making of foreign policy, overshadowing the Secretary of State.

The famous arguments between those two offices are interesting not just as Washington gossip but as further proof of the built-in difference of perspective between the White House and State. The difference in many cases reflects the conflict between global and regional approaches to foreign policy that will be discussed in Chapter 6. The State Department, especially since the politics of the third world began to complicate foreign policy around 1960, has shown an essentially regional or local bias. The national security adviser, by contrast, has been more inclined to take a global, superpower-oriented view, emphasizing the strategic conflict with the Soviet Union. There seem to be two reasons for this. First, his boss is commander in chief of the armed forces and has to think not only about diplomacy but also about military power, especially that of the superpowers. Second, his boss is also the nation's highest *elected* official, and is necessarily more sensitive than the career diplomats to what the voters think and feel. And it has been a truism ever since the cold war began that the greatest single foreign policy theme to which most Americans respond—the objective for which they are most willing to pay taxes and accept risks—is resistance to the power of Soviet communism and the support of American interests and values in opposition to that power. That was the heart of the "national consensus" that began to rule U.S. foreign policy, regardless of party divisions, during and after World War II. The consensus was rudely shaken by the war in Vietnam, but even today, this simple fact of public psychology still shapes the responses of the President and his close advisers, as well as of the Congress, as they try to translate for the American public, in the most familiar and easily grasped terms, the complex realities of the wide world.

The Active Foreign Policy Public

To the maker of foreign policy, "the people" are more than a distant national abstraction; the most active of them are a conspicuous daily reality in Washington. Most Americans, to be sure, know little about world affairs and often act as if they cared even less. Only in a moment of national crisis, such as the climactic years of the war in Vietnam, is foreign policy truly made "in the streets" by millions of demonstrators who, by sheer numbers and intensity of emotion, can shape events of which they may have little understanding.

Far more influential in the long run is the minority, running into the millions, of Americans who are regularly involved in foreign policy to one degree or another, either as individuals or as members of influential organizations. Some are specialists on the innumerable subjects that arise in foreign policy, who testify before congressional committees or act as consultants to executive departments. More influential still are a wide variety of organizations—business groups, churches, labor unions, veterans' groups, professional societies, and groups representing economic, ethnic, or public-interest causes. Many of these organizations maintain permanent offices in Washington. Most have some expertise on some aspect of foreign policy; some consult their national memberships on key issues and take formal positions on them; and many are skilled in the art of lobbying in Congress and among executive departments.

When an organization's leader, or its salaried lobbyist, knows which senator is willing to sponsor a small amendment to a pending bill, of no great interest to the general public but important to his or her group—and knows whether the cause would be helped by letters from back home, or by a phone call from some powerful constituent, and knows how to bring about these desired actions—then that individual has a good chance to play a part in making a small piece of U.S. foreign policy.

Are all these public influences, taken as a whole, good or bad for U.S. foreign policy? There will never be a clear answer to that. The crucial amendment our imaginary lobbyist is working on reflects one organization's priorities—not necessarily something that the general public, let alone the State Department or the White House, would consider helpful to the national interest. Many observers deplore what they consider the excessive influence of the milk lobby, or the gun lobby, or the lobbies supporting Israel or Greece, or the oil industry, or other particular interests, however legitimate; or, for that matter, what some regard as the excessive lobbying power of intellectuals and "do-gooders." But those who are not satisfied with the results have an equal right to lobby for what *they* believe in, and to try for a result nearer to their heart's desire.

"The Worst" . . . Except for All the Others

Sir Winston Churchill once wryly remarked that democracy is "the worst form of government except all those other forms that have been tried from time to time." His words could well apply to the way Americans go about making foreign policy. Some go even further and say that when it comes to making foreign policy the American system is *the* worst, period. The Frenchman Alexis de Tocqueville, in his admiring yet critical study *Democracy in America*, written in 1834, said this:

> It is especially in the conduct of their foreign relations that democracies appear to me decidedly inferior to other governments . . . . Foreign politics demand scarcely any of those qualities which are peculiar to a democracy; they require, on the contrary, the perfect use of almost all those in which it is deficient . . . . [A] democracy can only with great difficulty regulate the details of an important undertaking, persevere in a fixed design, and work out its execution in spite of serious obstacles. It cannot combine its measures with secrecy or await their consequences with patience.

That much-quoted comment must often occur to foreign ambassadors in our midst. Again and again they witness the lurches of policy between President and Congress, between the White House and the departments of State and Defense. They see agreements they have confidently negotiated with one arm of the American government revised or rejected by another.

And those who have served many years in Washington must wearily note how a newly elected President often feels obliged to repudiate the policies of his predecessor and wipe the slate clean—then must painfully reinvent by trial and error the same foreign policy he had denounced. (But continuity becomes a curse when the policy is wrong. There is something to be said for a system that enables a new President to toss overboard time-honored policies that have failed—as when Franklin Roosevelt abandoned the high-tariff policy, or when Nixon ended the diplomatic boycott of China.)

Never in American history have the difficulties of framing, and sticking to, a coherent foreign policy been more severe than since World War II. It was then that the heaviest burdens of world leadership fell on what must surely be the most complex, many-layered, loose-jointed democracy the world has ever seen. Sometimes it has seemed that we must either tighten up our system of making foreign policy—confine it more to a governing elite, insulated against the heedless pulling and hauling of petty politics—or give up the pretense of being the world's leader. But we have done neither; yet, in spite of many a dire prediction, the world has not yet fallen victim either to communism or to nuclear war, or to any of the other fatal ills that are said to await it.

The successes, such as they are, can be no ground for complacency. United States foreign policy could not have done as well as it has since we arrived at superpower status had it not been for the extraordinary exertions of countless able people who made the complex and cranky American political and bureaucratic system work in a world of new challenges for which it was never designed. The challenges that will face us in the decades to come will be no less novel and difficult. Lincoln's words of 120 years ago still ring with meaning: "The occasion is piled high with difficulty, and we must rise with the occasion."

The second part of this book discusses some four decades of U.S. involvement with different countries, regions, and problems of the world. There is much in the story of that period to support a hopeful, though far from complacent, view of the future. Even with American power far less overwhelming than it was in 1945, and with the Washington foreign policy process in its customary semidisorder, the system may still work well enough in decades ahead to keep the nation and its friends independent and secure and to hold the most dangerous conflicts within limits—and, with luck, even to move them toward solution. But that is a hope, not a prediction. If there is to be a fair chance of turning it into fact, untiring study and effort will be demanded of countless able and wise Americans, not all of whose names will appear in history books.

Making Policy in a Crisis:
The Cuban Missile Case

On October 14, 1962, a U.S. reconnaissance plane obtained photographic proof that Soviet military deliveries to Cuba included—contrary to repeated Soviet denials—medium-range nuclear missiles capable of reaching the United States. President Kennedy, convinced that if the missiles stayed, the world power balance would be widely viewed as having shifted toward Moscow, was determined to get them removed.

The crisis that followed came dangerously close to a shooting war between the superpowers. But by October 28 a combination of nonstop diplomacy and U.S. naval blockade (or "quarantine") around Cuba induced Moscow to back down and remove the missiles without a shot being fired. Instrumental in the result were two U.S. assurances, both subject to removal of the missiles: that the United States would not invade Cuba, and that U.S. nuclear missiles in Turkey, near the Soviet border, would be withdrawn (they were outmoded and due for removal in any case).

Both assurances had been demanded by Moscow as its price for removing the missiles; Washington, however, insisted they reflected unilateral U.S. policy and were not part of a deal.

Looking back after 20 years, six of Kennedy's top advisers during that famous crisis joined in September 1982 in a brief assessment of the lessons to be learned from it. Their comments shed light on several key aspects of the foreign policy process: the necessity for top-level policy control, the role of intelligence, the interplay of diplomacy and military power, the importance of usable conventional rather than nuclear weapons, and the complications of foreign alliances and domestic politics.

The authors, and the offices they then held, are: Dean Rusk, Secretary of State; Robert S. McNamara, Secretary of Defense; George W. Ball, Under Secretary of State; Roswell L. Gilpatrick, Deputy Secretary of

Defense; Theodore C. Sorenson, special counsel to the President; and McGeorge Bundy, special assistant to the President for national security affairs.

In the years since the Cuban missile crisis, many commentators have examined the affair and offered a wide variety of conclusions. It seems fitting now that some of us who worked particularly closely with President Kennedy during that crisis should offer a few comments, with the advantages both of participation and of hindsight.

FIRST: The crisis could and should have been avoided. If we had done an earlier, stronger and clearer job of explaining our position on Soviet nuclear weapons in the Western Hemisphere, or if the Soviet government had more carefully assessed the evidence that did exist on this point, it is likely that the missiles would never have been sent to Cuba. *The importance of accurate mutual assessment of interests between the two superpowers is evident and continuous.*

SECOND: Reliable intelligence permitting an effective choice of response was obtained only just in time. It was primarily a mistake by policy-makers, not by professionals, that made such intelligence unavailable sooner. But it was also a timely recognition of the need for thorough overflight, not without its hazards, that produced the decisive photographs. The usefulness and scope of inspection from above, also employed in monitoring the Soviet missile withdrawal, should never be underestimated. *When the import-* *ance of accurate information for a crucial policy decision is high enough, risks not otherwise acceptable in collecting intelligence can become profoundly prudent.*

THIRD: The President wisely took his time in choosing a course of action. A quick decision would certainly have been less carefully designed and could well have produced a much higher risk of catastrophe. The fact that the crisis did not become public in its first week obviously made it easier for President Kennedy to consider his options with a maximum of care and a minimum of outside pressure. Not every future crisis will be so quiet in its first phase, but *Americans should always respect the need for a period of confidential and careful deliberation in dealing with a major international crisis.*

FOURTH: The decisive military element in the resolution of the crisis was our clearly available and applicable superiority in conventional weapons within the area of the crisis. U.S. naval forces, quickly deployable for the blockade of offensive weapons that was sensibly termed a quarantine, and the availability of U.S. ground and air forces sufficient to execute an invasion if necessary, made the difference. American nuclear superiority was not in our view a critical factor, for the fundamental and controlling reason that nuclear war, already in

79

1962, would have been an unexampled catastrophe for both sides; the balance of terror so eloquently described by Winston Churchill seven years earlier was in full operation. No one of us ever reviewed the nuclear balance for comfort in those hard weeks. *The Cuban missile crisis illustrates not the significance but the insignificance of nuclear superiority in the face of survivable thermonuclear retaliatory forces. It also shows the crucial role of rapidly available conventional strength.*

FIFTH: The political and military pressure created by the quarantine was matched by a diplomatic effort that ignored no relevant means of communication with both our friends and our adversary. Communication to and from our allies in Europe was intense, and their support sturdy. The Organization of American States gave the moral and legal authority of its regional backing to the quarantine, making it plain that Soviet nuclear weapons were profoundly unwelcome in the Americas. In the U.N., Ambassador Adlai Stevenson drove home with angry eloquence and unanswerable photographic evidence the facts of the Soviet deployment and deception.

Still more important, communication was established and maintained, once our basic course was set, with the government of the Soviet Union. If the crisis itself showed the cost of mutual incomprehension, its resolution showed the value of serious and sustained com-

munication, and in particular of direct exchanges between the two heads of government.

When great states come anywhere near the brink in the nuclear age, there is no room for games of blindman's buff. Nor can friends be led by silence. They must know what we are doing and why. *Effective communication is never more important than when there is a military confrontation.*

SIXTH: This diplomatic effort and indeed our whole course of action were greatly reinforced by the fact that our position was squarely based on irrefutable evidence that the Soviet government was doing exactly what it had repeatedly denied that it would do. The support of our allies and the readiness of the Soviet government to draw back were heavily affected by the public demonstration of a Soviet course of conduct that simply could not be defended. In this demonstration no evidence less explicit and authoritative than that of photography would have been sufficient, and it was one of President Kennedy's best decisions that the ordinary requirements of secrecy in such matters should be brushed aside in the interest of persuasive exposition. *There are times when a display of hard evidence is more valuable than protection of intelligence techniques.*

SEVENTH: In the successful resolution of the crisis, restraint was as important as strength. In particular, we avoided any early initiation of battle by American forces, and indeed we took no action of any kind that would have forced an instant and possibly ill-considered response. Moreover, we limited our demands to the restoration of the *status quo ante*, that is, the removal of any Soviet nuclear capability from Cuba. There was no demand for "total victory" or "unconditional surrender." These choices gave the Soviet government both time and opportunity to respond with equal restraint. *It is wrong, in relations between the superpowers, for either side to leave the other with no way out but war or humiliation.*

EIGHTH: On two points of particular interest to the Soviet government, we made sure that it had the benefit of knowing the independently reached positions of President Kennedy. One assurance was public and the other private.

Publicly we made it clear that the U.S. would not invade Cuba if the Soviet missiles were withdrawn. The President never shared the view that the missile crisis should be "used" to pick a fight to the finish with Castro; he correctly insisted that the real issue in the crisis was with the Soviet government, and that the one vital bone of contention was the secret and deceit-covered movement of Soviet missiles into Cuba. He recognized that an invasion by U.S. forces would be bitter and bloody, and that it would leave festering wounds in the body politic of the Western Hemisphere. The no-invasion assurance was not a conces-

sion, but a statement of our own clear preference—once the missiles were withdrawn.

The second and private assurance—communicated on the President's instructions by Robert Kennedy to Soviet Ambassador Anatoli Dobrynin on the evening of Oct. 27—was that the President had determined that once the crisis was resolved, the American missiles then in Turkey would be removed. (The essence of this secret assurance was revealed by Robert Kennedy in his 1969 book *Thirteen Days*, and a more detailed account, drawn from many sources but not from discussion with any of us, was published by Arthur M. Schlesinger Jr. in *Robert Kennedy and His Times* in 1978. In these circumstances, we think it is now proper for those of us privy to that decision to discuss the matter.) This could not be a "deal"—our missiles in Turkey for theirs in Cuba—as the Soviet government had just proposed. The matter involved the concerns of our allies, and we could not put ourselves in the position of appearing to trade their protection for our own. But in fact President Kennedy had long since reached the conclusion that the outmoded and vulnerable missiles in Turkey should be withdrawn. In the spring of 1961 Secretary Rusk had begun the necessary discussions with high Turkish officials. These officials asked for delay, at least until Polaris submarines could be deployed in the Mediterranean. While the matter was not pressed to a conclusion in the following year and a half, the missile crisis itself reinforced the President's convictions. It was entirely right that the Soviet government should understand this reality.

This second assurance was kept secret because the few who knew about it at the time were in unanimous agreement that any other course would have had explosive and destructive effects on the security of the U.S. and its allies. If made public in the context of the Soviet proposal to make a "deal," the unilateral decision reached by the President would have been misread as an unwilling concession granted in fear at the expense of an ally. It seemed better to tell the Soviets the real position in private, and in a way that would prevent any such misunderstanding. Robert Kennedy made it plain to Ambassador Dobrynin that any attempt to treat the President's unilateral assurance as part of a deal would simply make that assurance inoperative.

Although for separate reasons neither the public nor the private assurance ever became a formal commitment of the U.S. Government, the validity of both was demonstrated by our later actions; there was no invasion of Cuba, and the vulnerable missiles in Turkey (and Italy) were withdrawn, with allied concurrence, to be replaced by invulnerable Polaris submarines. Both results were in our own clear interest, and both assurances were helpful in making it easier for the Soviet government to decide to withdraw its missiles.

In part this was secret diplomacy, including a secret assurance. Any failure to make good on that assurance would obviously have had damaging effects on Soviet-American relations. But it is of critical importance here that the President gave no assurance that went beyond his own presidential powers; in particular he made no commitment that required congressional approval or even support. The decision that the missiles in Turkey should be removed was one that the President had full and unquestioned authority to make and execute.

When it will help your own country for your adversary to know your settled intentions, you should find effective ways of making sure that he does, and a secret assurance is justified when a) you can keep your word, and b) no other course can avoid grave damage to your country's legitimate interests.

NINTH: The gravest risk in this crisis was not that either head of government desired to initiate a major escalation but that events would produce actions, reactions or miscalculations carrying the conflict beyond the control of one or the other or both. In retrospect we are inclined to think that both men would have taken every possible step to prevent such a result, but at the time no one near the top of either government could have that certainty about the other side. *In any crisis involving the superpowers, firm control by the heads of both govern-*

ments is essential to the avoidance of an unpredictably escalating conflict.

TENTH: The successful resolution of the Cuban missile crisis was fundamentally the achievement of two men, John F. Kennedy and Nikita S. Khrushchev. We know that in this anniversary year John Kennedy would wish us to emphasize the contribution of Khrushchev; the fact that an earlier and less prudent decision by the Soviet leader made the crisis inevitable does not detract from the statesmanship of his change of course. We may be forgiven, however, if we give the last and highest word of honor to our own President, whose cautious determination, steady composure, deep-seated compassion and, above all, continuously attentive control of our options and actions brilliantly served his country and all mankind.

Reprinted from TIME Magazine (September 27, 1982).

Part II
The Regions

The world we have to deal with politically is out of reach, out of sight, out of mind. It has to be explored, reported, and imagined. Man is no Aristotelian god contemplating all existence at once . . . . Yet this same creature . . . is learning to see with his mind vast portions of the world that he could never see, touch, smell, hear, or remember. Gradually he makes for himself a trustworthy picture inside his head of the world beyond his reach.

Walter Lippmann
Public Opinion (1922)

4

The Superpowers and Europe

The two nuclear-armed superpowers, the United States and the Soviet Union, are the heavyweights of world politics, in a class that no other state even approaches. Both have the power not only to govern and defend their own very large territories; they have extended their strategic predominance far beyond their own borders and their competing influence into every region of the world.

For the United States, the problem of relations with the Soviet Union has held a top priority ever since World War II. And rightly so—for the combination of deeply opposed purposes and extremes of nuclear destructive power makes this the most dangerous and perplexing international relationship on earth. As the tone of U.S. Soviet relations has ranged back and forth from bitterly hostile to almost peaceful, various labels have been invented to describe it: cold war, competitive coexistence, détente, protracted conflict. But through all the fluctuations the basic reality has remained: a mixture of some cooperation with much conflict, but always, thus far, carefully short of direct combat between the two.

In the course of this long conflict, each superpower has become the center of a wide-ranging network of alliances and alignments aimed against the other.

Europe in the Middle

Both superpowers have strong reasons for being preoccupied with Europe. It contains by far the greatest concentration of economic power and technology outside the superpowers themselves. To the Russians, with one foot geographically and culturally in Europe and the other outside it, the rest of Europe has been for centuries a fascinating but disturbing next-door neighbor, admired for its brilliant achievements but feared as a source of ideological contamination and as a historic springboard for aggression against Russia.* To Americans it is the main ancestral home, the source and sharer of their culture, and, taken as a region, their greatest trading partner. Either superpower would view with the utmost alarm any substantial gain in the other's power and influence in Europe.

It was from the mutual struggle to prevent such gains that the two alliances arose. For about three decades, armed forces under the seven-nation Warsaw Pact, headed by the Soviet Union, have faced armed forces of the North Atlantic Treaty Organization (NATO), headed by the United States and now comprising 16 nations, along a front line whose most sensitive sector runs through the middle of divided Germany. There has not been so much as a military skirmish between the two forces in all that time. If large-scale shooting ever did start in such a formidably armed and strategically vital spot, the chances of stopping it short of a global nuclear holocaust would be highly uncertain.

What brought America and Russia to their preeminence in Europe—and the world—was the shattering impact of the two world wars (1914–1918 and 1939–1945). The main political consequences, as matters stood in 1945, were these:

- Germany, so recently the terror of Europe, was crushed and divided between the occupying armies of the Soviet Union in the east (except for West Berlin, where the Western allies were in charge) and the United States and its British and French allies in the west.
- Britain and France, once the world's mightiest powers, were so weakened

---

*These fears long antedate the Soviet Union. Napoleon's invasion of Russia in 1812 exposed the weakness of the autocratic czarist state and introduced Western democratic ideas. A generation later Western Europe, with its growing class of uprooted and aggrieved factory workers, became the seedbed of the socialist doctrines of Karl Marx. By the twentieth century Marx's European socialist heirs had split into quarreling factions, some insisting on democracy and free debate, others—including those called Bolsheviks and, later, Communists—insisting on a centralized one-party dictatorship. The former element came to dominate Western socialism; the latter, led by the Russian exile V.I. Lenin, prevailed in Russia's October 1917 revolution and organized the Third (Communist) International. Thus Lenin and his successors in the Kremlin, although claiming to be the only true heirs of one Western idea, socialism, became bitter foes of another—multiparty democracy.

by the effort of defeating Germany that neither they nor all of Western Europe together could fill the power vacuum left by Germany's fall.

- The Soviet Union, successor to the czarist Russian Empire which had collapsed during World War I, was now a rapidly industrializing great power with a revolutionary Communist ideology and a battle-tested army dominating Eastern Europe including eastern Germany. Having suffered an estimated 20 million military and civilian deaths, and great physical devastation, in fighting Germany's aggression, the Soviets gave top priority to keeping postwar Germany divided and weak.
- The United States, which had fought decisively in both world wars and had emerged from the second one with unrivaled economic power and sole possession of the new atomic bomb, was now the only power strong enough to balance the Soviet Union.

From that day to this, these two huge states—one wholly and the other partly outside of Europe—have been the rival power centers on which the political destiny of Europe largely depends.

The Map of Europe Redrawn

Power relations, and many political boundaries as well, were drastically revised in Central and Eastern Europe in the three years immediately after World War II. The revision was all in favor of the Soviet Union. Much of it was accomplished over the indignant objections of the United States— which, however, made no move to challenge the results militarily.

From Poland southward to Bulgaria, within the belt of Eastern European countries from which it had driven Hitler's armies, Josef Stalin's government used its military and political supremacy to bring about the triumph of Communist-dominated governments subservient to Moscow and the suppression of political opposition.*

In occupied Germany, the Soviets passed up opportunities to share with the Western victors in joint administration of the whole country, preferring to keep an exclusive grip on their own occupation zone in the east. (Related to their desire to tighten that grip were their repeated attempts to end the Western presence in Berlin, which had become a magnet for disaffected East Germans.) In addition, during and after the war

---

*Significantly, Soviet predominance did not last in Yugoslavia, which had fought Germany with little help from Soviet forces. There, the Communist chief, Marshal Tito, shook off Soviet domination in 1948. It was the first break in Soviet control over the international Communist movement.

the Soviet Union extended its own borders westward by diplomatic pressure and armed force to include various lands, most of them formerly ruled by the czars: parts of Finland, the three Baltic republics of Latvia, Lithuania, and Estonia, part of what had been German East Prussia, a large eastern portion of Poland (which was compensated with large chunks of eastern Germany), and smaller pieces of Czechoslovakia and Rumania.

There is controversy to this day as to what interest led the Russians to act in this way. Was it a naked power grab by a world-conquering Communist empire? Or was it a defensive move to insulate Russia against still another aggression by Germany or even by the nuclear-armed United States, whose prewar hostility to the Soviet revolution was well known?

Whatever Moscow's real motives, its actions were perceived by its erstwhile allies in the West as aggressive and menacing. What most Western politicians, especially in the United States, saw, or believed they saw, was the world headquarters of an antidemocratic, anticapitalist, totalitarian system called communism, possessing great military power, thrusting its control deep into the heart of strategic Europe. Still proclaiming its revolutionary message with the fervor of a religious movement, it backed a Communist-led civil war in Greece, controlled large and obedient Communist parties in France and Italy, and harassed and threatened the Western position in West Berlin. To Western eyes, it seemed to want to extend its power everywhere, and especially in Europe, as far as it could.

From this perception arose the U.S. policy known as *containment*. As its original proponent, the American diplomat and Sovietologist George F. Kennan, explained it, the policy was essentially defensive. Its main thrust was to oppose further Communist encroachment beyond the lines already reached, while trying to avoid head-on collisions and hoping that Western firmness would eventually wear down Soviet belligerence.

Some early variations on the containment theme sounded a more aggressive note. By 1950 secret U.S. policy papers, later published, were picturing the Kremlin in stark terms as determined on nothing less than world domination. They proposed that the United States, by both open and covert means, should exploit Soviet weak spots and work for "retraction," not just containment, of Soviet power in Europe and elsewhere. In 1953 President Eisenhower's Secretary of State, John Foster Dulles, dramatized the same theme, calling for a "rollback" of Soviet power. But the proposed means—mainly propaganda to stir up discontented nationality groups within the Soviet sphere—proved ineffective.

Thus, as time went on, events forced Washington into painful choices. Should the United States decisively support East European revolts against Soviet oppression? Or should it pursue the path of stable coexistence with Soviet power along the geographic lines that emerged after 1945? Each time the issue has arisen, Washington has swallowed hard and taken the latter course.

Two Alliances, Two Germanys

The pursuit of containment in Europe involved the United States in European affairs more deeply than ever before. The involvement took two main forms: massive U.S. financial aid under the Marshall Plan (1948–51) to assist the economic recovery of non-Communist Europe, and aid to the region's military defense.

The economic recovery effort was a spectacular success, paving the way for the creation of the Common Market. Among other things, it gave Western Europe's governments the strength and confidence to talk back to Washington. (And, as time went by, some West European Communist parties began to go "Eurocommunist" and talk back to Moscow.) Strategically, its main result was to strengthen Western Europe for the military burdens it was about to assume.

The foundation of the military effort was the North Atlantic Treaty of 1949—the first peacetime alliance outside the Western Hemisphere in the nation's history. The treaty, still in force, now joins 16 countries, all European except the United States and Canada, in a pledge that they will treat an armed attack on any of them in Europe or North America as an attack on all. As the alliance expanded to include Greece and Turkey (1952) and West Germany (1955), some of Europe's oldest rivalries were sunk—forever, the optimists hoped—in this anti-Soviet partnership.

In 1950—a year of acute cold-war anxiety brought on by the Soviet atomic bomb and events in Asia—the North Atlantic Treaty Organization (NATO) was established in Europe and a multinational military force was assembled under an American general, Dwight D. Eisenhower, already famous as the Allied commander in Europe during World War II. As a key contingent in the force, six U.S. Army divisions were stationed in West Germany, backed by supporting air and naval forces. United States forces at essentially the same level remain in the NATO lineup to this day, and the supreme NATO commander is still an American general.

Parallel with these military developments was a step-by-step evolution in the political status of that historic European storm center, Germany.

With Soviet-Western talks on Germany's future hopelessly deadlocked, a "two-Germany" solution became inevitable. The Western occupation zones became the Federal Republic of Germany (FRG), more familiarly known as West Germany. The Soviet zone became the Communist-ruled German Democratic Republic (GDR), known as East Germany. In 1955, after years of reluctance, especially in France, the NATO powers decided to admit West Germany to NATO. The aim was twofold: to increase their troop strength on the central front, and to solidify West Germany's commitment to the West. German troops soon became NATO's largest national contingent. In the same year Moscow, as if in retaliation, formalized its military domination of the East by creating the Warsaw Pact, including East Germany, under Soviet command. Thus Germany's two parts were firmly tied into their respective alliances.

Still, tension remained high, and Germany was its focus. There was the chronic problem of Western access to West Berlin. There was the endless tide of East Germans "voting with their feet" by migrating to the richer and freer West—some 3 million passed through Berlin alone from 1949 to 1961—until eventually the flow was almost stopped by the Communists' construction of the Berlin Wall and other barriers patrolled by armed guards. Above all, there was the refusal of West German politicians, sensitive to patriotic opinion, to give up on the eventual reunification of their country. Out of respect for these feelings, and despite intense Soviet pressure, no NATO government for many years would give formal recognition to the GDR.

By the late 1960s, however, West German political pressure for reunification had begun to moderate, enabling the government to develop a more conciliatory *Ostpolitik* (East policy). This trend coincided with the superpowers' developing détente, which in 1971, at long last, led to an agreement with Moscow guaranteeing Western rights in West Berlin. By 1973 the two Germanys had normalized their relations, and the GDR had been recognized by all Western governments. Trade between West Germany and the Soviet bloc began to flourish, and West Germans long detained in the East were allowed to return.

Finally in 1975, at a conference in Helsinki, Finland, the heads of 35 nations in Europe and North America, including all members of the two alliances, signed a "final act" declaring that the existing borders of states in Europe are "inviolable" and may not be changed by force. Politically, although not a legally binding treaty, the document was a substitute for the general European peace treaty that had never been written after World War II. It legitimized the border changes the war had produced—most importantly, the frontiers of the two Germanys. In return, Moscow consented to include a series of pledges to uphold human rights—particularly the free flow of information, ideas, and people between East and West. Its subsequent violation of these pledges has diminished its moral authority, but not its physical domination, in Eastern Europe.

West Germans still cling to the idea of peaceful reunification somehow, someday; to them, East and West Germany are not two nations but "two states within one nation." But *Ostpolitik* and the Helsinki declaration went a long way toward ending nightmares of a reunified, newly aggressive Germany, which had long haunted not only the Soviet Union but Germany's former enemies in the West.

Détente Begins

On issues other than Germany, the cold war had begun to show signs of détente by the mid-1950s. In March 1953 Stalin died, and his successors appeared to moderate the Stalinist public posture of relentless hostility toward the capitalist world. That summer the Korean War ended. In 1955 a peace treaty with Austria at last ended the ten-year military occupation of that country by Soviet and Western forces and established its neutrality in the East-West conflict. In the same year the leaders of the United States, Britain, France, and the Soviet Union held the first East-West summit meeting since 1945, settling nothing but stirring new hopes of peace. Life in the Soviet Union and Eastern Europe became a little less harsh; the new leader, Nikita S. Khrushchev, stressed the necessity of peace in the age of nuclear weapons; and Moscow began to present a more smiling countenance to the world.

In the quarter century since then, détente has become a recurrent theme in the East-West conflict. Like two teams in a tug-of-war, both sides slacken their hold now and then as if they feared the rope might break. Then something alarming happens and the rope tightens again. But a limit to the tension is set by the nuclear might and nuclear vulnerability of both sides. This ambiguous relationship seems fated to go on as long as the two superpowers confront each other—so strong that they dare not make war, so deeply opposed that they cannot make peace.

Restraint Between Giants: The Balance of Terror

Examples of the caution and restraint on both sides are numerous. In 1948–1949, when the West broke a Soviet land blockade of West Berlin by an 11-month airlift, the Russians could easily have shot down the Western planes, but they did not. In 1956, when Soviet tanks crushed a popular uprising in Hungary, Western protests were loud and anguished and some diplomatic and economic sanctions were applied, but not one Western shot was fired. The same was true of the Western response to the repression of democratic reforms in Czechoslovakia (1968) and to the Soviet-inspired crushing of Solidarity in Poland (1981–1982). In 1962, the frightening crisis over Soviet nuclear missiles in Cuba ended with removal of the missiles, a U.S. pledge not to invade Cuba, and no shooting. In 1968, when Leonid I. Brezhnev of the Soviet Union explained his country's military intervention in Czechoslovakia by the so-called "Brezhnev doctrine"—that as leader of the "socialist camp" it has a right to intervene in any "fraternal" country where it judges that its version of socialism is threatened—the United States roundly condemned the doctrine but did nothing to challenge it by force. Nor have the Soviets made a directly menacing military move against any NATO member.

Moreover, even in the worst cold-war periods, communication between the two governments' embassies and foreign ministries has been uninterrupted. Every American President from Truman through Carter has held at least one face-to-face meeting with a top Soviet leader. There is even a White House-Kremlin telegraphic "hot line," installed in 1963 after the Cuban missile episode, for direct top-level communication in moments of crisis.

There are various reasons for this mutual caution, including the fact that both sides have, thus far, been led by a generation with indelible memories of World War II. But a more basic reason is the enormous weight of the military power centered on Europe. For decades each alliance has maintained close to a million armed men in Europe, thousands of tanks, antitank weapons, bombers and figher planes; and, still more daunting, thousands of short-range and medium-range nuclear weapons. And that is not all. The superpower "anchor man" on each side is armed with thousands of *strategic* nuclear weapons of intercontinental range. If the order to fire were ever given, both sides—in North America and Europe and in the Soviet Union—could be destroyed as functioning societies, with casualties in the hundreds of millions, in a matter of hours. The phrase "balance of terror" is no exaggeration.

These strategic weapons have been part of the European military equation from the outset of the Atlantic Alliance in 1949. The Russians, although they achieved their first nuclear explosion in that very year, still had no deliverable nuclear weapon. The NATO governments reasoned that their electorates would not be willing, over the long pull, to maintain peacetime armies strong enough to balance those of the dictatorial Soviet Union. So, the argument went, the only sure way to deter a Soviet attack on NATO was by the threat of "massive retaliation" against the Soviet homeland with nuclear-armed bombers or, later, ballistic missiles. In the 1960s, when the Soviets acquired a comparable ability to devastate Western Europe, and soon afterward the United States, this threat lost much of its credibility as a shield for Europe. The Americans then deployed *battlefield* nuclear weapons (mainly artillery warheads) in Europe—only to be countered soon afterward by similar weapons on the other side. Meanwhile Britain and France, having developed smaller nuclear arsenals of their own, were deploying them on land and sea in the NATO area.

The mutual deterrence created by these terrifying arsenals is about all that can be said in their favor. On the negative side is the fact that advancing weapons technology and mutual distrust have combined to cause an unceasing nuclear arms race, a source of chronic public anxiety and a threat to the one vital interest that both superpowers obviously have in common: survival.

The Road to SALT

Inevitably in this situation, the idea of détente—of limits to the cold war— has found its main expression in attempts to stop the arms race—especially the nuclear arms race—by negotiation. The diplomatic sparring over the nuclear issue goes back to 1946, when the Soviet Union, then working to develop its own A-bomb, reacted coldly to a U.S. proposal—the so-called Baruch Plan—to put all nuclear weapons and other "dangerous" nuclear activities under a powerful international monopoly.*

The first break did not come until 1963, when the nuclear race was already in high gear. Both sides then agreed to ban test explosions of nuclear weapons in the oceans or the atmosphere—a practice that had produced alarming worldwide radioactive fallout. In 1968 the super-powers, along with Britain, sponsored the Treaty on Nonproliferation of Nuclear Weapons (NPT), designed to prevent the spread of nuclear weapons to still more countries (Britain, France, and China had already joined the "nuclear club").

---

*For further discussion of this episide, see page 206.

The NPT included a pledge by the superpowers to negotiate for mutual reduction and eventual abolition of their own nuclear arsenals, but the pledge was no guarantee of success. Up to then, East-West exchanges on this issue had been little more than a propaganda contest while the arms race itself accelerated—with the Soviets during the 1960s steadily narrowing the American lead, especially in intercontinental ballistic missiles (ICBMs). Underground nuclear tests on both sides, permitted under the 1963 pact, proved fully adequate to keep the competition in warhead design going full blast.

By the late 1960s—if not, indeed, considerably earlier—a situation of *mutual deterrence* existed, in which neither side could launch a nuclear *first strike* without grave risk of being destroyed in retaliation. Moscow could then negotiate from what was generally perceived as a position of equality, and the first *Strategic Arms Limitations Talks* (SALT) began in 1969.

The result, signed in 1972, was a pair of agreements known as SALT I. On each side, the number of strategic missile launchers (ICBM silos on land and "tubes" on submarines) was frozen at its then existing level for five years. An accompanying treaty placed a permanent, and very low, limit on the antiballistic missile defenses each side could maintain against the other—the hope being that in this way each side's vulnerability to retaliation would continue to deter both.* Actual nuclear arms reductions were to be sought in a later negotiation.

However, SALT I did not stop or stabilize the nuclear race. For one thing, bombers—in which the Americans had a wide lead—were not covered. More important, any military significance the agreed ceiling on missile launchers might have had was quickly bypassed by technology. The United States, technologically more advanced, had already perfected the MIRV, a multiwarhead missile in which each warhead could be aimed at a different target. The Russians soon followed suit—and on a larger scale, since their more powerful rockets could carry more megatonnage on each missile. And the accuracy of their ICBM guidance systems, originally far behind those of the United States, rapidly improved.

After SALT I, other U.S. inventions reached the advanced development stage. Perhaps the most important of these was a pilotless, long-range, low-flying subsonic aircraft known as the cruise missile. It is hard to find and shoot down, highly accurate, able to carry a nuclear

---

*In SALT I as in other cases, high technology came to the aid of arms control by providing means to verify compliance—including satellite photography—without the on-site inspections that Moscow had long resisted.

warhead, and small enough for one big bomber to launch as many as 30 while flying outside enemy territory.

Part of the American idea behind such innovations had been to use the mere prospect of them as bargaining chips, not actually producing or deploying them at all if the Soviets would make enough concessions in return. But no such deal concerning the MIRV was struck in the SALT I agreement, and the negotiators for a follow-up SALT II treaty had to try to halt the race at a point much further along the road. The treaty, signed in 1979, ran into a storm of controversy in the United States. Not only did the new agreement fail to embody the sharp cuts in strategic forces (especially Soviet "heavy" ICBMs) which President Carter had proposed as his opening bid; it was complex and hard to explain, and its advocates could not clear it of charges that it would give strategic superiority to the Soviets. Damaged by these charges, and by a general souring of détente over other issues, the treaty could not muster enough support in the Senate and was left in legislative limbo by President Carter after the Soviet invasion of Afghanistan. However, as late as 1982 both super-powers, by tacit consent, were abiding by its terms while starting a new round of negotiations.

The outlook for success in the new talks that opened in Geneva in June 1982 was unclear. The opening positions of the two sides were far apart. Meanwhile both continued the race to build new weapons systems whose power and accuracy, some critics feared, might further undermine confidence in the stability of mutual deterrence. A popular antinuclear movement arose, closely controlled in the Soviet bloc but spontaneous and vigorous in the West—evidently a response to the NATO govern- ments' alarm at the Soviet nuclear buildup and their announced determination to match it.

The political dilemma facing the United States was familiar: whether to alienate the "peace" vote by pursuing the nuclear arms race still further, or to work out a treaty, inevitably a compromise, whose terms could once again be denounced by hard-liners as handing strategic superiority to the other side.*

The European Dimension

Still further complicating the nuclear weapons problem is the role of these weapons in the military balance in Europe. During the 1970s, side by side

---

*This problem is discussed further in Chapter 8.

with the strategic arms race, a steady buildup of the Soviets' mid-range nuclear weapons in Europe set off a new round in the nuclear weapons competition in that crucially important region.

What worried the NATO governments most was a fast-growing force of new, powerful, and accurate Soviet SS-20 missiles and nuclear-capable "Backfire" bombers in Eastern Europe, of sufficient range to reach and demolish any city in Western Europe. A large Warsaw Pact advantage in some types of ground forces, especially tanks, was another concern. By the late 1970s the NATO governments had agreed that the perceived imbalance on the Soviet side would have to be redressed—if possible by negotiation, but if necessary by a Western counterbuildup in NATO strength. Part of the buildup would consist of modernizing NATO's conventional (nonnuclear) forces in order to increase the chance of stopping a Soviet attack without recourse to nuclear weapons. But increased nuclear defenses were also decided on, and it was these that drew the most attention.

Some of the new nuclear weapons involved in the Western plans were in the tactical or battlefield category. Most controversial among these is the so-called neutron or *enhanced radiation* weapon, viewed by military experts as more usable against a massive Soviet ground attack than earlier, more indiscriminately destructive weapons in this class. Opponents argue that "first use" of *any* nuclear weapon, no matter what the type, against a non-nuclear attack could rapidly escalate to a global holocaust. The subject of off-again-on-again waffling by the Carter Administration, the neutron weapon got a new lease on life from the Reagan Administration but has yet to be deployed.

Even more devastating are the intermediate-range (1,500 to 3,000 miles) nuclear delivery systems on both sides, including ballistic missiles like the Soviet SS-20 or France's submarine-launched M-20, as well as some types of cruise missiles and manned bombers. These could lay waste whole cities anywhere in Western Europe and in much of the western Soviet Union. In 1979 NATO, to match the SS-20s especially, announced that 572 new-model U.S. ballistic and cruise missiles of intermediate range would be deployed in Western Europe by the mid-1980s. But the antinuclear backlash to this announcement in Western Europe was so strong as to raise doubt whether the deployments would be politically possible. It was in response to this problem that the Reagan Administration, hoping to soften its warlike image in European eyes, started in November 1981 a long-heralded negotiation with the Soviet Union aimed at setting agreed limits on the European theater nuclear arsenals of both sides. Meanwhile still another set of East-West arms control talks, begun in 1973, dragged along in Vienna between NATO and Warsaw Pact delegations, aimed at reducing—and, the NATO side hoped, equalizing— the two alliances' massive conventional forces in Europe. Early agreement on either of these subjects seemed unlikely.

The Political Balance: How Stable?

As the 1980s began both NATO and the Warsaw Pact were having problems of disunity and faltering leadership that could ultimately affect the balance of power.

For the Soviets, the trouble centered in Poland, whose location between Russia and Germany gives it great strategic importance. The Polish people, crushed more than once in times past in a Russian-German strategic nutcracker, are fiercely nationalistic and devoutly Catholic and have long presented a difficult problem for Soviet-sponsored Communist rule.

During the 1970s, taking advantage of the spirit of détente, Poland's government had borrowed heavily from Western banks, hoping to modernize its limping economy. The effort failed, weighed down by the worldwide recession as well as bureaucracy and corruption in the ruling Communist party. In 1980 a new round of food price increases caused widespread trouble—not for the first time; but this time the result was different. Industrial workers created a new union movement and called it Solidarity. Strikes swept the nation; Solidarity gained millions of members. A desperate government, its authority gravely undermined, made unprecedented concessions including the right to independent unions, freedom from censorship, and the right to strike—things unheard of in an orthodox Communist state. But in December 1981, under rising threats of Soviet military intervention, a new hard-line Communist leadership under General Wojciech Jaruzelski cracked down. Solidarity was suppressed, its leader Lech Walesa was interned, and the main concessions were revoked. A sullen Polish nation, poorer than ever, remained a weak link at a most strategic point in the Warsaw Pact lineup.

Aside from the Polish crisis, as the Brezhnev era ended there were severe problems in the Soviet Union itself. Its economy, in addition to being weighed down by a vast military establishment, was long past its years of rapid growth, bureaucracy-ridden, and a technological parasite of the West. The low productivity of its agricultural system—still saddled with the inefficient collective farm system which Stalin had ruthlessly imposed on it in the 1920s—had turned massive food imports into an annual habit. Its most original minds were silenced or exiled. Its 270 million people— among whom the underprivileged non-Russian "nationalities" now made up the majority—were frustrated by long denial of the better life they had been promised. Even the ethnic Russians, although intensely patriotic, had long since ceased to believe in the official ideology of progress toward a Soviet utopia, let alone that of a world Communist triumph. More and more, the strength that this great Soviet power projected into the world seemed to be neither ideological nor economic, but chiefly military.

NATO, being an alliance of argumentative democracies, is much more accustomed to public disunity than the Warsaw Pact organization. Through the decades there have been resounding clashes of U.S. and European interests involving—among other things—the sharing of NATO costs; competition for NATO defense contracts; threats from Washington to reduce U.S. troop strength in Europe; conflicting strategic and commercial interests in trade with the Soviet bloc; trade battles involving steel and farm products; high U.S. interest rates, seen in European countries as prolonging their recession; European dissent from U.S. policy in the Middle East, whose oil remains critically important to Western Europe; Europeans' worry lest their interest be sacrificed in secret deals between the superpowers; and, on the other hand, a recurrent European nightmare—revived by every public debate over nuclear weapons in Europe—in which a helpless Europe is reduced to ashes in a "limited" war between the superpowers. And there have been still other frictions involving one or two European powers: French sensitivity about what Paris considers overbearing U.S. behavior; British complaints of Irish-American money being smuggled to Catholic terrorists in Northern Ireland, and of Washington's neutral stand at the outset of the Falklands war; seemingly endless disputes between Greece and Turkey, mainly over Cyprus; and Spain's still-unfulfilled claim to the British colony of Gibraltar. On top of all this, antidemocratic forces, ethnic quarrels, and other internal disorders have continued to threaten civil peace in Turkey and in the newest alliance member, Spain.

Does this long litany of troubles mean that NATO, and perhaps even the system of rival alliances on which the world power balance is centered, might come apart? Might the system be succeeded by some sort of neutral Europe, a "third force" between Moscow and Washington? Such speculations are almost as old as NATO itself, but their early realization seems highly unlikely. For more than three decades the system has weathered many a harsh crisis. Yet it is undeniable that it contains elements of potential instability:

- There is chronic worry—among experts as well as the general public—that the mutual deterrence of the superpowers is less stable than had been thought, and that a nuclear cataclysm could happen through accident or mutual miscalculation.
- There is fear in some quarters that the European partners in NATO, tired of military burdens and eager for Soviet trade, might gradually "Finlandize" themselves, avoiding offense to Moscow and serving as reliable high-technology suppliers to the failed Soviet economy.
- Others even fear that, if economic disaster or some other cause should seriously weaken the alliance system on one or both sides, a reunited Germany might once again appear and dominate the continent.
- The competition among Soviet political leaders after the death of Leonid Brezhnev in 1982 could, some observers fear, produce a more aggressive and dangerous Soviet foreign policy.
- For the West, one especially painful price for maintaining the system has been self-restraint in the face of the heavy-handed suppression of human and national rights in Hungary, Czechoslovakia, and Poland. If that restraint should fail in some similar case in the future, both the system and the peace could be shattered.
- Finally, the Europe-centered balance does not extend reliably into the third world. Like the Balkan wars of 1912–1913, third-world conflicts could some day lead to global war. Aware of this, the superpowers signed in Moscow in 1972 a mutual pledge to "exercise restraint" worldwide, and thus avoid "a dangerous exacerbation in their relations." Each, in its own interests, has indeed shown some restraint in the third world; but, as will be seen in Chapter 6, their competition remains vigorous—and could become more so.

The list is enough to remind us that no human institution, however stable, is eternal or free of risks. But no better system seems to be in prospect. And on the credit side can be set two very large facts. There has been no war in Europe, and no nuclear war anywhere, since 1945.

5

Northeast Asia and the Superpowers

Northeast Asia, so different from the West in history, race, and culture, has become a region of high strategic importance to both superpowers—second only to Europe and the Atlantic Ocean. Their interest in the region centers partly on each other—Soviet and American territorial waters actually meet at the Bering Strait—but mainly on two great nations, China and Japan, which have asserted their power in Asia repeatedly in times past. Both superpowers have had both China and Japan as enemies at one time or another in the present century; at other times both have engaged in complex stratagems, alliances, and political maneuvers involving China and Japan as well as their lesser neighbor, Korea.

In recent years the United States has been far more successful in this contest than the Soviet Union. Japan is firmly in the American camp. China, although Communist, has quarreled bitterly with its former Soviet ally and now has constructive relations—but no alliance, formal or otherwise—with the United States. Korea has been divided into two states since World War II, the south allied with the United States and the north balancing between its Soviet and Chinese neighbors. How U.S. relations with the region are likely to develop in future years can best be guessed by looking at some of the recent history of these countries and their interactions.

China

China has more than one-fifth of the world's people, great resources, and an extraordinarily rich and proud civilization. When the imperial and

103

industrial power of the West was entering a phase of explosive growth some two centuries ago, China was left behind and became a prey to economic exploitation by the Western powers. It has gone through more than a century of wars and revolutionary convulsions in its struggle to throw off the humiliation of Western and Japanese domination, to modernize, and to reassert its former power in Asia.

During World War II China was torn by a three-way contest between Japanese invading armies and two rival Chinese authorities: the U.S.- backed Kuomintang (Nationalist) government under Chiang Kai-shek and the Communists under Mao Zedong. After Japan's defeat in 1945 the Communists won in a four-year civil war; Chiang withdrew his remaining forces to China's island province of Taiwan; and the red flag of the People's Republic of China was raised over the capital city of Beijing (Peking). The Communist government quickly gained control over virtually all mainland China*—the first Chinese government to do so since the eighteenth century. It set out to transform China's backward society by persuasion and force, replacing private farms with big peasant communes. And in 1950 it signed an alliance with the world headquarters of communism, the Soviet Union.

These events were a great shock in the United States, coming as they did during the depths of the cold war with Moscow. After several months' hesitation, in June 1950, following the invasion of South Korea, President Truman placed the U.S. Seventh Fleet between Chiang's bastion on Taiwan and the Communist forces on the mainland. Thereafter Washington steadfastly maintained relations with its admired wartime ally, Chiang, treating him as the head of the only lawful government of China and exerting worldwide pressure for the votes needed to keep his delegates in China's seat at the United Nations. The United States signed a defense treaty with Chiang in 1954, although opposing his dream of reinvading the mainland. Thanks to its own business enterprise and to a model land reform program adopted under American guidance a generation ago, Taiwan's economy today is one of the most prosperous in Asia.

For over two decades "Red China" was ostracized by U.S. diplomacy and kept off limits to American visitors. Repeatedly, America's hostile feelings were reinforced by Beijing's actions: its raucous anti-American

---

*The exceptions are two coastal cities—Britain's thriving colony of Hong Kong and Portugal's smaller colony of Macao. Hong Kong's status serves a complex of Chinese as well as British interests, chiefly commercial; but Britain's lease on most of the territory expires in 1997 and its future—and Macao's too—is in doubt.

propaganda, its massive participation in the Korean War (see below), its threats to "liberate" Taiwan by force, and its aid to Communist North Vietnam during the Vietnam War.

The main strategic fact behind U.S. hostility, however, was China's alliance with the Soviet Union. This seemed to confirm the then prevailing American view of a monolithic, aggressive Sino-Soviet Communist bloc directed from Moscow. But soon old antipathies between China and the Soviet Union began to surface. They quarreled angrily over ideology, with China accusing Moscow of softening toward the enemy, the United States. They became competitors for influence in the third world. There was a military buildup on both sides of the long border. Finally in 1960 Moscow abruptly ended its large aid program in China. By the early 1960s the alliance was close to being a dead letter. In 1964, as if to underline its new independence, China conducted its first nuclear weapon test.

In these new circumstances, it began to appear that a thaw in the frozen relations between China and the United States would serve the interests of both. But before the potential could be realized, a decade of convulsive events had to pass. China's violently antiforeign Cultural Revolution, begun in 1966, and America's commitment to the war in Vietnam seemed insuperable obstacles. In 1971, with both obstacles removed or much diminished, President Nixon launched his "opening to China," climaxed by his trip to Beijing in 1972. There an agreement was signed to "normalize" U.S.-Chinese relations. Both governments soon opened diplomatic liaison offices—embassies in function, though not in name—in each other's capitals. Trade, scientific, and cultural contacts began. The 23-year estrangement of China and America was over. Meanwhile in late 1971, after the U.S. policy shift was made known, the UN General Assembly at last voted to seat the People's Republic of China and—over last-ditch U.S. opposition—to expel the Taiwan government.

Both sides knew the relationship could not go much further unless they could compromise, or at least maneuver around, the emotional issue of Taiwan. Washington still had full diplomatic relations with Chiang's government, while Beijing insisted on its right to reimpose control over that undisputedly Chinese province. Finally in 1979 President Carter cut this Gordian knot, transferring official U.S. recognition from Taiwan to Beijing and terminating the U.S.-Taiwan defense pact. Semiofficial U.S.-Taiwan relations continue, and U.S. trade with prosperous Taiwan still far exceeds that with the People's Republic. Beijing seems well aware that the new friendship would be ruined if it tried to take Taiwan by force, and it seems to have no early intention of making the attempt—in which, besides, some authorities say it might fail militarily. Instead, it has pursued its aims with a carrot instead of a stick. In 1981 it publicly invited the Kuomintang leaders to reunite Taiwan with the mainland and accept high posts in the central government, while continuing to rule Taiwan with wide autonomy. The Kuomintang scornfully refused, but Beijing later publicly renewed the offer. Meanwhile it strenuously protested the continued sale of U.S. military aircraft to Taiwan.

China's relations with the United States and other industrial powers have continued to develop. To strengthen its antiquated military defenses against the Soviet Union, it has begun buying modern weapons in Europe and some nonlethal military items in the United States. But its main priority is technological and economic modernization, for—despite its nuclear weapons—China's development is still only skin-deep and its economy as a whole remains very poor and backward. (With over a billion Chinese to feed, China is a major food importer.) It is in this sense that the U.S. connection is especially important.

The connection is not an alliance, and Beijing still plays an independent diplomatic hand. Its habitual attacks on "hegemony" by the superpowers in various parts of the world are often cast in terms that can refer to the United States as well as to the Soviet Union. It has opposed all arms control agreements with Moscow and favored a NATO arms buildup to draw off Soviet strength from the Chinese front. In case this strategy should fail, or its American connection go sour over Taiwan or some other problem, Beijing has never closed the door on a possible thaw in its cold war with Moscow. NATO would presumably view such a thaw with dismay, since some 46 Soviet army divisions and a large Soviet nuclear missile force are tied down along the 5,000-mile border that separates China from the Soviet Union and its big landlocked satellite, the Mongolian People's Republic.

The Soviet Union in Asia

When China and the United States renewed contact, it became apparent that a new triangular relationship had arisen between China and the two superpowers. Each of the three, pursuing its own interests, worries lest it become "odd man out," the other two cooperating at its expense. Each may try to play the other two off against each other, or to gain the cooperation of one against the third. But the potential for all such maneuvers is limited by the parties' conflicting interests. Hence the triangle is never quite stable, and may even undergo sudden shifts.

The U.S.-Chinese thaw of 1972 was one such shift—perhaps not the last. It was said then that America had "played its China card," but it would be just as true to say China played its American card. Moscow reacted with indignant charges against China for collusion with the capitalist enemy—an echo of Stalin's charges of "capitalist encirclement" in the decades before World War II.

The Soviet antipathy toward China has many roots. It stems partly from racial prejudice among the people of European Russia who dominate Soviet life. It also reflects resentment against anybody who dares to compete with Moscow for influence in the world Communist movement. Finally, geography is a factor, for Russia has been a competitor in the power struggles of Asia since the great conquests of the czars centuries ago. Its port of Vladivostok on the Sea of Japan is much nearer to Tokyo and Beijing than to Moscow, and eastern Siberia is a source of many resources important to the Soviet economy.

Soviet relations with modern China, despite their common revolutionary experience, are a story of wary cooperation repeatedly derailed by clashing interests. In the 1920s, Soviet agents coached, and tried to dominate, the Kuomintang revolution in south China. They even induced the new Chinese Communist party under Mao Zedong to merge with the Kuomintang. The merger ended in bloody fighting, and Mao rebuilt his battered Communist forces without Soviet help. All through the 1930s and during World War II, the Soviets sought to divert Japanese aggression away from Siberia and toward China—then, with Japan defeated, moved to regain czarist Russia's old sphere of influence in Manchuria. These unhelpful Soviet moves during China's time of troubles were not forgotten by Mao's regime in its hour of victory in 1949. Late in 1982 a new attempt at "normalizing" Sino-Soviet relations was under way. But if the 1950 alliance is ever revived, some bitter feelings will have to be overcome on both sides.

As will be seen below, Soviet policy toward Japan and Korea has also had its difficulties.

Japan

In 1945 the United States, having borne the brunt of the war in the Pacific, and having brought Japan to its knees with the first—and thus far the only—nuclear bombings in all history, became—over Soviet protests—the sole occupying power in defeated Japan. Thereupon Japan, stripped of half a century's vast colonial conquests and reduced to its home islands,

drastically revised its national self-image and its view of Japanese interests.
It began a double transformation: from military dictatorship to democracy,
and from great power to strategic ward of the United States. It adopted a
new constitution renouncing war and armed forces. (Japan, nevertheless,
has a small, U.S.-equipped military establishment, tactfully named the
"Self-Defense Forces." It costs about 1 percent of the nation's GNP,
compared to 5.5 percent in the United States and 2 percent in neutral
Switzerland.) The United States established military bases in Japan and, by
a mutual defense treaty signed in 1951, extended its nuclear umbrella to
shield a then virtually unarmed Japan against hostile pressure. And the
Japanese proceeded to rebuild their crowded island nation into the world's
third most productive economy, while achieving the lowest rate of
population growth in Asia.

Japan has developed increasingly cooperative relations with China,
but its relations with the Soviet Union remain cool. Although it eventually
signed peace treaties with all its other World War II enemies, it has refused
to sign one with the Soviets until they return several small northern islands
they seized in 1945 as the war was ending. When Japan signed its peace
treaty with China in 1978, Moscow signaled its displeasure by sending
10,000 soldiers to garrison the disputed islands.

Poor in energy and mineral resources, Japan depends heavily on
imports, especially of Middle East oil. It pays for these by its huge volume
of manufactured exports and by highly profitable direct investments
abroad. Its climb to world economic power has been helped by intensive
technological research and development, a close partnership between
government and business, and a homogeneous, hardworking, and highly
disciplined population. Wages are far above prewar levels but still modest
by U.S. standards, and tax-supported social benefits are low.

Japan's high economic posture and its low military posture have both
become sticky issues in relations with its most important friend, the United
States. Since 1980 Washington has been pressing, thus far with small
success, for a sharp increase in Japanese military strength. Whether—or
when—Japan will again be a great military power in its own right, and for
what purposes its power might then be used, are weighty questions for the
world's statesmen to ponder.

Korea

"When the elephants fight, the grass gets trampled," says an African
proverb. In Northeast Asia in the past century, Korea, the only country in

the region that is not a great power, has served as the grass time and again—dominated, fought over, and trampled by all four of the nearby elephants.

For centuries a "hermit kingdom" under Chinese protection, Korea was opened to world trade by Japan in 1876. In 1905 the Japanese, having eliminated both Chinese and Russian influence from Korea, imposed a harsh colonial rule, built industries and railroads, and ran Korea until their defeat in 1945. Then Korea's new troubles began. By Soviet-American agreement, Japan surrendered in North Korea to an invading Soviet force; in the South, to the invading Americans. The arbitrary dividing line was the 38th parallel at the peninsula's narrow waist. Then, much as in the German story, the opposing powers failed to agree on how to reunite the country; the 38th parallel demarcation line became a border; and two mutually hostile Korean states arose, one under Soviet, and the other under American, protection.

Soon afterward the United States took two steps that many critics, with the benefit of hindsight, have called unwise. In June 1949, having built a mediocre South Korean Army, and having concluded that Korea was not important enough to American interests to fight for, it withdrew U.S. combat troops from South Korea soon after Soviet troops were withdrawn from the North. Then early in 1950, a public address by the Secretary of State, in full harmony with the U.S. military doctrine of the time, defined the U.S. "line of defense" in Asia as including Japan and the Philippines—but with no mention of Korea. This omission might well have been taken by Moscow and its North Korean clients as a signal that the Americans didn't much care what happened to South Korea.

In any case, in June 1950 a highly trained Soviet-equipped North Korean Army launched a massive surprise invasion of the South. Immediately the United States showed that it did care after all. Suddenly the attack on South Korea was seen in Washington as the first great test since 1945 of whether law-abiding nations would fight together to defeat naked aggression against any of them. More pragmatically, it was also seen as a threat to the U.S. position in Japan. American combat troops were flown from Japan to Korea. Washington assembled a 16-nation army (mostly American and South Korean) under the UN flag, and staged a spectacular counteroffensive which by autumn was racing deep into North Korea.

But one more surprise was to come. As the American-led UN command approached the Chinese border, a million-man Chinese army poured across and drove the UN forces back in near-panic. Overruling—

and finally dismissing in a celebrated public brawl—the brilliant but headstrong American commander, General Douglas MacArthur, President Truman and his Pentagon advisers refused to extend the war by bombing China lest too much strength be diverted from Europe, the main theater in the world contest. Limited to the Korean peninsula, the war remained stalemated until an armistice was signed in 1953—leaving a devastated Korea still divided along a line not far from the old 38th parallel. The United States and South Korea promptly signed a mutual defense treaty to deter further aggression from the North.

To this day, 38,000 U.S. military personnel, plus nuclear-armed aircraft, plus a large U.S.-equipped South Korean army, stand guard against a heavily armed North Korea. In 1972 the two Korean governments finally started talking about unification, but ten years of intermittent talks have led nowhere. Shooting incidents along the border are frequent and hostility remains high.

South Korea is a fast-industrializing nation under a tough military dictatorship whose corruption and repression of dissent have often embarrassed Washington. Its security still ranks as a key interest of the United States and of Japan as well. (In 1977 the Carter Administration began a gradual withdrawal of the U.S. ground combat units, but the plan got a nervous reception, especially in Japan, and was stopped.)

North Korea is also rapidly industrializing under the iron dictatorship of Soviet-trained Kim Il Sung. Kim has done a careful balancing act in the Chinese-Soviet feud, both sides of which aid him and compete for his support. How Korean unification will ever be achieved in this tangled situation is not clear.

Asian Complexities in the World Balance

From this brief account it can be seen that the Northeast Asian end of the superpower balance—second in strategic importance only to Europe—contains complications not present in Europe, primarily because of China. Since 1949 China has leaned first to the Soviet side, then to the Western side. Geographically it is half a world away from America, and politically and culturally its distance from *both* superpowers is perhaps even greater. Pursuing its own interests, China could shift again—either toward Moscow or, more likely, to maneuver independently between the two superpowers. Which way China moves will matter increasingly if it succeeds in overcoming its enormous economic and military inferiority and approaches superpower status in its own right.

Japan's position is less problematical now, but events could change the picture. The growth of individualism and consumer-mindedness in the younger generation of Japanese seems likely to affect the nation's economy and politics profoundly, although in unforeseeable ways. A world economic depression would be disastrous for such an export-dependent nation and could put a strain on its commitment to peace and democracy. And the postwar Japanese aversion to militarism, and even to nuclear weapons, might not outlive the World War II generation now in office, particularly if security in the region should again be upset.

The United States, in its long-range efforts to stabilize the world power balance and achieve world order, will have to take account of such destabilizing possibilities in Northeast Asia, even though that end of the alliance system looks solid enough today.

6

Instability in the Third World

Although the lion's share of the world's political and military power is concentrated in the great alliance systems, most of the people live elsewhere. They are citizens of close to 100 countries in South and Southeast Asia, the Middle East, Africa, and the Pacific and Indian oceans. All but a handful of these countries tend to identify with what is loosely called the third world, as distinguished from the two antagonistic worlds centered on the superpowers.* Each has its own character, interests and political outlook, in some cases more or less compatible with those of the United States, or of the Soviet Union; in many cases with neither. Although the superpower contest strongly affects them, it is by no means as central to their world outlook as it is to ours. Washington, preoccupied with the world's main power centers, has often been accused of neglecting third-world problems that could damage its interests—only to be jolted later on by crises whose origins Americans knew little or nothing about.

The countries of the third world are so extremely diverse, and some are changing so fast, that few broad statements can be made about them without the word "but":

---

*China often calls itself a third-world country, and resembles that category in being underdeveloped, anticolonial, and not truly aligned with either superpower. But its huge size, growing nuclear weapons stockpile, and deep involvement in the superpower contest put it in a class by itself. Australia, New Zealand, Israel, and white-ruled South Africa are geographically located in third-world regions but do not identify with the third world politically or psychologically. Among European countries, on the other hand, neutral Yugoslavia plays a leading role, and Malta and Cyprus lesser ones, in third-world politics. For the unique position of Latin America, see Chapter 7.

- They are generally poor—especially those in South Asia and most of Africa—and at an early stage of economic and technological development; but some are swimming in oil wealth, and parts of Brazil and India have been developing rapidly, as have some small states such as Singapore and the Ivory Coast.
- Most have small populations—under 5 million—but Indonesia has over 150 million; Bangladesh 90 million; Pakistan and Nigeria over 80 million each; and India, the most populous, has close to 700 million—one-seventh of the world's people in one country.
- The great majority were colonies or protectorates of Western countries until World War II; but a few, like Thailand and Ethiopia, have been independent almost continuously for many centuries.
- Most of the ex-colonies won independence by peaceful agreement; but India and Pakistan won partly by campaigns of passive resistance; and several, notably Algeria, Indonesia, Vietnam, and Zimbabwe, won only after years of armed rebellion.
- Predominantly nonwhite, many contain a wide diversity of language and ethnic groups within the borders of a single state.
- None weighs very much in the scales of world power; but several, such as India, Vietnam, Nigeria, Iran, and Saudi Arabia, have exerted strong influence within their own regions.
- In the superpower contest nearly all call themselves "nonaligned," but the reality is infinitely varied: some stand aloof, many deal opportunistically with both superpowers, some switch from one camp to the other, and some are linked more or less solidly with one side.

Nonalignment and the Big Powers

The political and economic problems of the emerging third-world nations have been staggering. Words like "less developed" or "developing" are commonly applied to their economies, but the same words could apply to their political situation as well. They have had to wage a many-sided struggle against poverty and internal instability. Many national leaders have political strength in one section of the country but little national authority. Rival factions, tribes, and religious and language groups jockey for power and often fight each other, sometimes across national borders. And in one area, southern Africa, harsh struggles still continue against the white man's rule.

To serve their two most urgent interests—economic and technical development and security from attack by political rivals—virtually all third-world governments have sought outside economic and military aid. Some, notably in French-speaking West Africa, looked to their former colonial rulers, as did many members of the Commonwealth of Nations, which Britain widened to include all its newly independent ex-colonies. Others turned to the United States and other industrial democracies, or to UN agencies, or a combination of these. Some Marxist leaders, as well as non-Marxists struggling through their "wars of national liberation," received aid from the Soviet Union or China or both.

But whichever way they turned, most third-world leaders, intent on strengthening their independence and bargaining power, kept a certain distance between themselves and the superpower conflict. Partly with this in mind, they formed broad regional groups, such as the Arab League and the Organization of African Unity. Still broader was the movement called *nonalignment,* promoted in the 1950s mainly by India and Indonesia and later by Algeria and Yugoslavia.

The Conference of Nonaligned Countries, whose heads of government meet annually, now has 96 members. Its future is a question mark. Officially, its complaints and demands are aimed impartially at both superpowers, but in reality its main targets have been the United States and its NATO allies (in political shorthand, "the West"). It has stretched the meaning of nonalignment to include countries as solidly allied to the Soviet Union as Fidel Castro's Cuba, recently a major influence in the conference. Seldom critical of the Soviet Union, the conference was badly split in 1980 by the Soviet invasion of Afghanistan, one of its members.

That nonalignment could acquire such an unbalanced meaning suggests that the Soviet Union must enjoy some immunities in the third world that are denied to the West. And indeed it does—but that is not the whole story. The interests, assets, and liabilities of the two superpowers and their allies in dealing with the third world are very different, and the advantages are not all on one side. A summary of the situation might read something like this:

Interests:

In *economic* terms, the Western powers need third-world oil, minerals, and tropical products such as coffee and tea. They also seek third-world markets and investment opportunities, which, indeed, are essential to their future prosperity. The Soviet Union has little trade and less investment in the third world, and what there is is usually for political reasons.

In *political and diplomatic* affairs, partly because of their greater economic stakes, the Western powers' interests are many, and generally favor the status quo: friendly relations with the countries they once ruled;

stability and peaceful change, minimizing opportunities for revolutionary violence or for Soviet inroads. Soviet interests, as befits the less influential side, are more single-minded: to gain leverage at the expense of the West, often backing violent "liberation" movements against Western colonial rule. (However, in some cases—the Congo [now Zaire] in 1960, Angola in 1975, and Afghanistan since 1980—where pro-Soviet elements seemed about to win out or had actually done so, the roles have been reversed, with the United States supporting armed factions opposed to them.)

Strategic interests of the West include heavy dependence on third-world oil (likely to diminish over the years) and strategic minerals. Also important are military and naval facilities, satellite tracking stations, and so forth, to support Western interests both locally and in global strategy. The Soviet Union resembles the West in its need for military facilities, but is still self-sufficient in oil and nearly so in minerals.

Ideologically, each side has shown some interest in exporting to the third world its political principles and its ideas of economic and social justice, and human rights; but for neither side has this been the top priority.

Against these often clashing interests must be set the common interest of both superpowers in avoiding a direct military encounter between them anywhere in the world. No ground rules exist for observing their 1972 pledge to "exercise restraint," but the vital need for some prudent restraint seems to be obvious to both sides.

Assets and liabilities:

The advantages of the Soviet Union are mainly in two fields: military and psychological. Its *military* capacities in several third-world areas—Indochina, Afghanistan, and parts of Africa—steadily increased during the 1970s with expansion of its navy and its long-range air cargo fleet, its use of Cuban troops as surrogate forces in Africa, and its greatly increased flow of weapons to favored governments and insurgent groups. Meanwhile the United States, distracted by its troubles in Indochina, let its armed forces decline until near the end of the 1970s, when a new military buildup—accelerated by the Reagan Administration—included a substantial effort to develop conventional forces usable in the third world.

Moscow's *psychological* advantages, such as they are, have historical roots. Most important, and somewhat ironic, is the fact that the Soviet Union, unlike the United States and several of its allies, has no former colonies. Its own empire, stretching across Eurasia, remains intact, an integral part of the Soviet Union, and is voiceless in world affairs. The fact that its non-Russian—and largely nonwhite—ethnic groups are looked down on by the dominant European Russians is known to some people in the third world but not as an important issue. The same can be said of the Soviet Communist party's bare toleration—indeed, active discouragement—of scores of millions of Muslim, Christian, and Jewish believers within their realm.

By contrast, Western colonial rule is a vivid, and not always pleasant, memory to most leaders and educated citizens in the third world, and Marxist ideology has been attacking it without mercy for more than a century. In the version spread by the Communist International (Comintern) in the days of Lenin and Stalin, that ideology found a ready following among many Asian and African intellectuals who were still living under colonial rule. Its influence has since been reinforced by Soviet aid and propaganda support to insurgents in anticolonial wars from Vietnam to southern Africa.

The United States, on the other hand, seized the Philippines from Spain in 1898 and ruled there until 1946, and still retains some small colonies in the Pacific and the Caribbean. More important, it is allied to the great European colonial powers of the past and has tended to back them, or at least not oppose them, in all their colonial wars since World War II. The military actions of the United States itself in Vietnam, the Caribbean, and elsewhere have been pictured by Moscow as colonialist. And U.S. reluctance to take strong measures against South Africa has been exploited by Soviet propaganda in black Africa as evidence that the United States is a racist nation.

Weighing against these Soviet advantages is another set of facts favoring the United States. The Soviet invasion of Afghanistan in 1979 was a shock to many third-world countries, especially those where Islam predominates. U.S. economic, technical, and humanitarian aid to the third world—directly and through international agencies—although widely criticized as inadequate, far exceeds that of the Soviet Union. Still more important to third-world economies are their exports to, and capital investments from, the Western world; the Soviet Union is no match for the West in that respect. Soviet aid has been focused on strongly anti-Western governments and has been mainly military rather than economic. In a few cases, such as Egypt and Guinea, Soviet aid has involved such interference that the recipients sent the Russians home.

Finally, many third-world citizens are well aware that the United States gained its own independence in an anticolonial revolution; and that, with all its faults, it is a free country with a basic respect for individual rights—and the Soviet Union is not. And the immensely greater success of the U.S. economy is known throughout the world.

America in the Third World: Globalism and Regionalism

For a few years after World War II, U.S. attention was so concentrated on Europe and Northeast Asia that there was not much attention to spare for the old colonial empires from which European power was already rapidly pulling out or being pushed out. Generally, Washington was content to let Britain, France, the Netherlands, Belgium, and Portugal extricate themselves, salvaging whatever influence they could.

Beginning in the early 1950s, however, bad news from several third-world areas caused U.S. policy to take a more active turn. A nationalist faction in oil-rich Iran came to power, nationalized the British-owned oil company, and waged a two-year war of nerves against the West before being overthrown. In Egypt the monarchy was toppled in 1952, and soon President Gamal Abdel Nasser, a fiery Arab nationalist, turned to the Soviet Union for support and pushed his demands on the West to the crisis point. In Indochina, France's colonial war ended in disaster. Even Latin America seemed less safely in the American camp when Guatemala in 1954 elected a left-wing president who promptly opened relations with Moscow.

In all these events, what mainly troubled Washington, preoccupied as it was with cold-war conflicts in Europe and a shooting war in Korea, was the opportunity they opened for extensions of Soviet power. Just as communism had been contained on the Eurasian mainland, the United States was determined to contain it elsewhere. The approach of President Eisenhower's Secretary of State, John Foster Dulles, was much the same in the third world as in Europe: find reliable friends in strategically situated countries; make mutual defense treaties with them; back them with military and economic aid and, where appropriate, covert operations. Local tactics would vary, but the overriding aim would be to prevent or defeat Communist penetration.

The security treaties Dulles negotiated in Southeast Asia and the Middle East are now obsolete, and his enthusiasm for this approach has been much derided as "pactomania." However, the point of view that gave rise to the treaties is still very much alive, although more pragmatic in execution. Indeed, as Soviet capabilities to exert power and influence in the third world have increased, this view has taken on added importance.

Today it is commonly called the *globalist view*. It emphasizes firm ties with proven anti-Communist friends, tends to emphasize military power, and is impatient with fence-sitters who flirt with both sides. It takes an interest in local issues primarily as these are seen to bear directly on the East-West competition.

Opposed to this is what is sometimes called the *regionalist view*. It concentrates on the specific problems and grievances of each country or region: poverty, underdevelopment, denial of national or racial rights, local wars, and arms races. As the regionalist sees it, the best way to thwart Communist and other extremist forces and advance the prestige and interests of the United States is to work with all groups—even those that also accept Communist support—that seem able to solve the problems on which extremism thrives. These problems, the argument goes, are important in their own right and would merit U.S. attention even if communism didn't exist.

As will be apparent in the sections that follow, U.S. policy in the third world has necessarily combined the globalist and regionalist approaches, with one or the other predominating at different times and places—and with widely varying success. Much the same could be said of Soviet policy, despite Moscow's less complicated interests in this part of the world.

SOUTHEAST ASIA: THE INDOCHINA WAR AND AFTER

Southeast of China lie the smaller lands of Indochina and the Malay Peninsula and the island chains of Indonesia and the Philippines. Their total population is about 375 million, or 8.5 percent of the world's people.

Before World War II, this whole region was under Western colonial rule except for the ancient kingdom of Thailand. In 1946 the United States, keeping a prewar promise, set the Philippines free after less than half a century under the American flag. Elsewhere, Japan's wartime conquests had struck a stunning blow to the power and prestige of the European rulers. Their postwar return was opposed everywhere by native independence movements. Communist parties, some backed by the Soviets, others by the Chinese, did their best to dominate the independence fight where they could; but in Indonesia, Burma, Malaysia and Singapore, independence was achieved under non-Communist leadership. Recently the foreign policies of the countries just named have ranged from neutrality in self-isolated Burma to military alliance with the United States in the Philippines. Indonesia leaned toward China for a time, but a new military regime seized power in 1965, crushed the Communist party, and has looked to the West ever since.

Far different is the story of **Indochina**, consisting of the three states of Vietnam, Laos, and Cambodia (Kampuchea). All three are now dominated by Vietnamese Communists backed by the Soviet Union. The events that led to this result was a great tragedy for Indochina—and the prelude to new tragedies not yet finished. For the United States they were a disaster that still reverberates in American life, politics, and foreign policy.

The states of Indochina were conquered and colonized by France in the nineteenth century. In 1940, after Hitler's invasion of France, they were seized by Japan. After Japan's defeat, the returning French found themselves facing a nationalist uprising in Vietnam, the largest of the three countries. Increasingly, the nationalist movement was taken over by a Communist faction under Ho Chi Minh. Beginning in 1950, the United States, fearing that the Communist triumph in China might create a "falling domino" effect in nearby areas, gave military aid to the French, while Ho's forces received aid from both China and the Soviet Union.

The struggle to maintain French dominance—either directly or through unconvincingly "independent" client states—proved unwinnable, and in 1954 France gave up. A conference in Geneva, with all the combatants and big powers present, announced the independence of Cambodia and Laos and accepted the temporary division of Vietnam into two parts. North Vietnam was ruled by Ho's Communists. The United States replaced France as South Vietnam's big-power sponsor and set out to build a strong anti-Communist nation out of a bewildering array of cultures, religions, and competing political factions.

The Geneva accords called for elections throughout Vietnam within two years to choose a single government for the whole country; meanwhile neither side was to attack or subvert the other. But the accords were fatally flawed, for the United States refused to accept them unequivocally, while its South Vietnamese client rejected them outright—especially the call for national elections, which all sides seemed to agree the Communists would win. So the elections were never held, while North Vietnam increasingly ignored the Geneva ban on subversion, smuggling aid and reinforcements to Communist insurgents in the south.

Thus Vietnam's destiny was decided not by elections but by a steadily intensifying military-political struggle that devastated large parts of

Vietnam and did not end until 1975. Although fought mainly in South Vietnam—whose survival as a non-Communist state was Washington's basic war aim—the war spilled over extensively into Laos and Cambodia and included periods of heavy U.S. bombing of North Vietnam.

The Americans failed much as France had failed before. A succession of South Vietnamese governments, stigmatized as American puppets, never managed to gain solid political authority in the villages or to capture the nationalist cause from the Communists, who fought a relentless village-based guerrilla war. The latter received a steady flow of military aid (but no combat troops) from the Soviet Union and China, which were already competitors for influence in the area. South Vietnam's U.S.-trained army proved largely ineffective. Massive U.S. "carpet bombing" and chemical defoliation of South Vietnam's forests failed to root out the guerrillas. Heavy bombing of North Vietnam failed to stop the southward flow of troops and supplies. U.S. combat strength in Vietnam mushroomed from under 2,000 in early 1962 to over half a million in 1968. Victory kept on receding until more and more Americans, viewing scenes of the agonizing struggle on their TV screens, turned against the war.

The climax came in February 1968. The Communists' fierce, month-long "Tet" offensive against cities and towns throughout South Vietnam, repulsed with heavy losses on both sides, dramatically discredited U.S. claims that the enemy was weakening. In March a despairing President Lyndon B. Johnson turned down his field commander's request for another 205,000 soldiers, decided to seek a negotiated peace, and announced his withdrawal from political life.

Johnson's successor, Richard M. Nixon, elected partly on the war's unpopularity, pursued two contrary objectives: to get the American troops out and yet somehow preserve a non-Communist South Vietnam. The first objective was attained; the second, despite years of U.S. negotiation with North Vietnam, was not. In April 1975 South Vietnam's army, fighting alone, collapsed, and Vietnam soon became one Communist state. Almost simultaneously in Cambodia, whose neutrality had been grossly violated by both sides in the war, insurgents led by a Cambodian Communist named Pol Pot seized power from a pro-American military regime.

Regional Aftermath of the Vietnam War

Indochina's agony was not over yet. Life under the new Vietnamese regime was harsh enough; in Pol Pot's Cambodia it was brutal in the extreme.

Cambodia's 6 million people were reduced to a primitive existence in which at least 1 million (some estimates go much higher) died despite massive international food relief. Meanwhile, the Pol Pot regime, backed by China, launched a series of attacks along the border with its traditional enemy, Vietnam. Vietnam severed its wartime Chinese connection and turned to the Soviet Union. In November 1978 Vietnam signed a 25-year friendship treaty with Moscow. It then invaded Cambodia, drove Pol Pot's forces into the western mountains, and set up a pro-Vietnamese government. Even a brief counterinvasion of Vietnam by China failed to discourage the Vietnamese. Meanwhile they were completing their takeover of neighboring Laos, making themselves masters of Indochina.

Thus an ancient Indochinese feud became a proxy war between the two giants of world communism. The Soviet Union seemed the big winner. Without firing a shot, it had a toehold on China's southern flank and air and naval facilities in Vietnam—a potential threat to Japan's vital sea-lanes to the Middle East and Europe.

The United States, still licking its wounds, played little part in these events. Having staked enormous national resources for more than a decade on what its leaders believed to be a vital interest in Indochina, and lost, the nation quickly redefined its interests in the region at a far more modest level. Its main effort was a refugee program that brought some 600,000 Indochinese—Vietnamese "boat people" and Cambodian and Laotian refugees—to this country between 1975 and 1982. Politically, Washington made the distasteful decision to join China and the UN majority in accepting the remnant Pol Pot regime, rather than the one sponsored by Vietnam, as the lawful government of Cambodia. Nothing came of brief U.S. peace talks in 1978 with Vietnam, which by then appeared to be solidly in the Soviet camp; it still has no trade or diplomatic relations with the United States. Modest U.S. military aid went to Thailand, which felt threatened by Vietnam's westward lunge; but no more dominoes fell. Otherwise, the United States reverted to its traditional "offshore" strategy in Asia, based on long-standing defense treaties with Australia, New Zealand, the Philippines, and Japan and on U.S. facilities in the islands of Micronesia.

Meanwhile Indochina's non-Communist neighbors set about reducing their dependence on Washington while seeking to insure themselves against any further Soviet or Chinese encroachment in the region. For this purpose they upgraded the Association of Southeast Asian Nations (ASEAN), founded in 1967 by Indonesia, Malaysia, the Philippines, Singapore, and Thailand. At first an economic grouping, it now took on an added political dimension, aiming at what a Malaysian official called "a judicious policy of equidistance" between the great powers. ASEAN's main links, however, are still with the West and Japan. Thus far the threat its members fear has not materialized. By late 1982 its effort to persuade Vietnam to withdraw from Cambodia had not succeeded. Whether impoverished Vietnam's desire for U.S. aid and investment will bring a change in its foreign policy remains to be seen.

AUSTRALASIA AND THE SOUTHERN OCEAN

In the vast stretch of salt water comprising the South Pacific and South Indian oceans, the big power is Australia. The 15 million people of that country, on a continent-sized island nearly as big as the "lower 48" states of the United States, together with their smaller neighbor New Zealand (3 million) account for three-quarters of the population and 97 percent of the economic product of the two dozen political units into which the thousands of islands scattered through the southern ocean are divided.

Australia and New Zealand do not belong politically to the third world, but their presence in it is a fact of geography. They are as many miles from the Western world, to which they belong in every other respect, as it is possible to be without leaving the planet.

Australia was settled beginning in the eighteenth century by British emigrants who quickly overwhelmed the small aborigine population. New Zealand's settlement followed a similar pattern a few decades later. Today both countries are bound to the Atlantic world by many links. They are original members of the British Commonwealth and of the Organization for Economic Cooperation and Development (OECD), a predominantly Western group of industrial democracies. Most of their trade is with OECD members. In strategic terms they are firmly aligned with the United States through a mutual security treaty, the ANZUS Pact, dating from 1951. Both countries fought on the Allied side in the two world wars, and both sent contingents to serve under the American command in the Korean and Vietnam wars.

Australia, although most of its great expanse is arid, boasts a highly skilled population, major agricultural exports, substantial industry and fast-developing natural resources. It has a considerable potential for increased influence in Asia and the Indian Ocean in times to come.

In all the rest of this region there are about 15 independent states, all recently emerged from colonial status, ranging in size from Papua New

Guinea (3 million people) to Tuvalu (7,400). There are also a handful of small island groups still under French, British, or American rule. All these islands were taken over by Western powers, mostly at the height of the colonial era a century or more ago. The motives were various: natural resources, Christian missionary enterprise, prestige, and naval coaling stations.

As noted in Chapter 2, the United States was not immune to such considerations. The American flag still flies over Wake, Midway, Guam, and American Samoa, all acquired in that era. In addition, after fierce battles during World War II, the United States took over from Japan some 2,100 small islands in that vast stretch of the tropical western Pacific now known as Micronesia or the Trust Territory of the Pacific Islands (TTPI). In administering the TTPI, the United States must report annually to the United Nations, but in practice it has had a largely free hand. It has been criticized for showing more attention to strategic concerns in the region (including nuclear weapons tests in the 1950s) than to the interests of some 126,000 islanders, but the island's political status evolved considerably in the late 1970s.

Most of the U.S. Pacific dependencies are considered strategically important as links in the chain of American air and naval power off the Asian mainland. As the TTPI moves toward autonomy in the 1980s—the plan is to divide it along cultural lines into four self-governing dependencies—the United States expects to retain its strategic facilities there.

SOUTH ASIA: INDIA AND ITS NEIGHBORS

From the high Himalayas south to the Indian Ocean lies one of the world's oldest civilizations, the product of thousands of years of invasion and interaction among peoples of different races, languages, and religions. (Over 800 languages are spoken in India alone, and 16 of them have official standing in the Indian government.) Between the dominant religion, Hinduism, and the second in importance, Islam, there is perpetual conflict. The population of the whole region is approaching 1 billion people. Over two-thirds of them are in **India**, whose modest industrial base is swamped by a vast, impoverished, tradition-bound rural majority. Thus far U.S. relations with India have been troublesome, but have seldom claimed a high priority in Washington. Crises in the region, however, have raised the priority from time to time, and may do so again.

Until World War II, the Indian subcontinent was one vast colonial complex, "British India"—the greatest single part of the worldwide British Empire. But nonviolent agitation for Indian self-government, and later for independence, led by the revered Mohandas K. Gandhi, had been steadily mounting since shortly after World War I and was further stimulated by Britain's troubles during World War II. In 1947, amid great violence and bloodshed between Hindus and Muslims, India gained independence as two republics, India and **Pakistan**. The latter, created for India's large Muslim minority, emerged as two widely separated "wings," culturally and linguistically quite different, on India's northwestern and eastern flanks. But India kept a number of heavily Muslim areas, including most of the rich and disputed northwestern province of Kashmir.

Tension remained high, exploding into renewed war in 1965 when Pakistan attempted to drive India out of Kashmir. The attempt failed, but worse trouble was in store for Pakistan. In 1971 the Bengalis of Pakistan's impoverished east wing revolted against the rule of the less populous but politically dominant west. In the struggle some 10 million Bengalis fled into India; India invaded West Pakistan; and the latter, overpowered again, agreed to the secession of the east wing. Today it is the overcrowded, desperately poor, politically fragile republic of **Bangladesh**.

Not long after independence, both Pakistan and India were led by their mutual hostility to seek support from opposing superpowers. In 1954 Pakistan moved into the American orbit by becoming a member of the Southeast Asia Treaty Organization (SEATO), receiving U.S. military aid in return. In 1971 it played a key role in the secret preparations for the U.S. "opening" to China. India turned increasingly to the Soviet Union for arms and diplomatic support, and in 1971—despite its long-standing leadership in the nonaligned movement—signed an Indian-Soviet friendship pact. Although SEATO no longer exists and India's link to Moscow is well short of a full alliance, the tilt of these quarreling neighbors toward their respective superpower patrons still persists.

India, however, was not content to rest its security on the Soviet connection. Despite its clear superiority over Pakistan, in 1974 it made and exploded its own nuclear device, technically equivalent to a nuclear weapon.

What led India to take this fateful step has never been fully explained, but the country India fears most is probably not Pakistan but China. By taking over Tibet in 1950, China acquired a long mountain border with India and its small Himalayan neighbors, Nepal and Bhutan. In 1959 Chinese repression caused the Dalai Lama, leader of Tibetan Buddhism, to flee to India. In 1962 Chinese armies attacked India at three disputed points along the border. One of the seized areas, Ladakh in northeastern Kashmir, is still in Chinese hands. Then in 1964 China became a nuclear power. It cultivated cordial relations with Pakistan; and in 1972 it began a new relationship with the United States. Some of these moves were doubtless aimed against the Soviets, but India saw them from its own perspective.

Unfortunately, whatever India's motives, two results of its nuclear explosion did not serve its interests. One was a new cloud of uncertainty over continued supply of U.S. nuclear fuel for India's important nuclear energy program. The other, much more ominous, was a determined effort by Pakistan to achieve a nuclear-weapon capability balancing India's.

The Indian threat is only one reason why Pakistan feels insecure. Although nearly all Muslim, it is a patchwork of languages and tribal groups, some of them overlapping into neighboring Iran and Afghanistan, and all of them resentful of the Punjabi officer class, which dominates the military government. On top of all this, in December 1979 Pakistan's insecurity was further heightened when the Soviet Union invaded Afghanistan.

Russia's Afghan War

Peopled by many warring Muslim tribes, Afghanistan in the early twentieth century came under the protection of Britain, which regarded it as a buffer state to keep the Russians out of India. When Britain withdrew from the region after World War II, a succession of Afghan governments adopted a neutral stance, accepting aid from both the Soviet Union next door and the distant United States. But during the 1970s U.S. aid and influence in Afghanistan dwindled while the Soviet presence grew. Finally Prime Minister Mohammed Daud became alarmed at the hordes of Soviet advisers in his country and set out to reduce their influence. In 1978 Daud was assassinated by Marxist revolutionaries, who thereupon made Afghanistan a close ally of Moscow.

Where the revolutionaries seem to have blundered was in attempting a headlong Marxist revolution among the country's largely illiterate, devoutly Muslim tribes. The result was nationwide rebellion and chaos. The Soviets, unwilling to see a new Marxist client state on their very doorstep go down the drain—and undoubtedly realizing that U.S. military intervention, especially in the midst of the Iranian hostage crisis, was very unlikely—moved into Afghanistan with their own army, installed a handpicked Afghan Communist as the new leader, and set out to suppress the tribal rebellion.

It was the first time Soviet armed forces had ever fought in the third world. Aside from Western economic and diplomatic reprisals, the invasion cost Moscow its first UN vote of condemnation in many years, an unprecedented rebuke from the 34-nation Islamic Conference, and a loss of prestige among the "nonaligned." Three years later the Afghan war still ground along indecisively. Some 2.5 million Afghans, well over one-tenth of the country's population, fled into Pakistan, which became a base for their guerrilla struggle against the Russians.

Thus Pakistan became a plausible target for possible Soviet attack— and a candidate for large-scale U.S. military aid. By late 1981, despite a congressional ban on aid to countries that refuse to forswear nuclear weapons, a $3.2 billion, six-year U.S. program to strengthen Pakistan's armed forces was agreed to, to be financed partly by Pakistan's oil-rich, anti-Communist, and devoutly Muslim friend, Saudi Arabia.

In times past, India might have been expected to react by moving closer to Moscow. This time, Prime Minister Indira Gandhi's political need to show progress in India's stagnant economy—plus, it appeared, her annoyance with the Russians over Afgahanistan—led her to take a different course. She reopened the stalled talks with China over the border dispute, meanwhile turning to Western Europe rather than the Soviet Union for new fighter planes to balance Pakistan's expected purchase. In 1982 she visited the United States—her first American visit in over a decade—mainly in search of economic aid and private capital, and was expected, in return, to ease India's tight curbs on foreign investment. The outlook seemed to brighten for an improvement in India's long-strained relations with China, the United States, and possibly even Pakistan itself.

Such a regional détente is much needed, for recent tensions have not only raised fears of war—possibly even nuclear war in South Asia but have also distracted attention from the enormous domestic ills that afflict all the countries of that region. Their success or failure—above all India's—in coping with poverty, excessively rapid population growth, and political disorder will be an important factor in shaping the world of the next century.

THE MIDDLE EAST—ZONE OF TURBULENCE

Of all regions of the world, the Middle East in recent years has appeared to pose the greatest danger of war between the superpowers. The danger has at least three sources:

- *Geography.* The region is a unique strategic crossroads—a land bridge connecting three continents and a maritime gateway between two oceans. And its northern edge borders on the Soviet Union, which is wary of any American activity near its frontiers.
- *Resources.* The oil of the Persian (or Arabian) Gulf is—and will remain for years, although probably to a diminishing degree—a vital source of energy for the industrial democracies.
- *Nationalism, religion, and development.* The religion of Islam—both the Sunni branch that predominates in the Arab states and the Shiite branch whose main center is Iran—has combined with intense nationalism to arouse passionate conflicts within the region and resentment against the former colonial rulers of the West. These tensions have been further sharpened by the pressures of rapid development and "Westernization."

Politically, the main focus of anti-Western feeling in the Arab states is the Jewish state of Israel, along with its chief sponsor and protector, the United States. Israel's nationalism, in turn, is just as passionate, and as deeply involved with religion, as that of the Arabs. Ever since its founding in 1948, Israel has been in a state of war or armed truce with its Arab neighbors—all four of them, in fact, until 1979 when it signed a peace treaty with Egypt. It still occupies lands long regarded by Arabs as rightfully theirs. Despite its small size and population, its people's technological skill and high morale, plus massive aid from the United States, have made it by far the strongest military power in the region.

Religion plays a greater *political* role in the Middle East today than in any other region of the world. From Iraq, Saudi Arabia, and Egypt all the way across North Africa to Morocco, 21 states—plus one aspirant to statehood, the Palestine Liberation Organization—belong to the Arab League. They share one dominant religion, Islam (although there are important Christian minorities in Lebanon and Egypt) and one language, Arabic. These are the twin legacies of Islam's Arabian prophet, Muhammad, whose followers conquered and converted all those countries in an irresistible tide of "holy war" some 13 centuries ago. The Islamic faith, minus the Arabic language, spread still farther—into Iran and Turkey, the far reaches of Asia, and much of Black Africa.

In the Arabic-speaking countries, language and religion together have formed the basis for a somewhat amorphous brand of nationalism—that of the *Arab nation*. Politically, the Arab nation is little more than an unrealized dream and a loose association, embodied in the Arab League but split by bitter rivalries—Algeria vs. Morocco, Syria vs. Iraq, Libya vs. Egypt, among others. But all Arab League members tend—with varying degrees of fervor—to close ranks against Israel, deeply resented as a Western intruder.

The NATO allies and Japan have a greater stake in the region than the Soviet Union, which produces (thus far) more than enough oil and gas for its own needs and has no commitment either to preserve Israel or destroy it. Defensively, however, Moscow is sure to be sensitive to any increased U.S. influence in an area so close to its own territory. Moreover, some studies suggest that rising Soviet energy needs will one day make it a competitor for Middle East oil. Its advance into Afghanistan has even renewed speculation that the Kremlin may still cherish Russia's old imperial dream of dominating the Middle East. Whether it does or not, it has built substantial military facilities in the region and has seized many opportunities to support anti-Western, especially anti-American, forces— but always short of actions that could risk a direct superpower clash.

Western Rule—And the Rule of Oil

Western dominance in the Middle East reached its height during the late nineteenth and early twentieth centuries as the old Ottoman (Turkish) Empire crumbled and finally collapsed in World War I. Britain and France then became the chief powers of the region and remained so until after World War II, when their protectorates and colonies, from the Persian Gulf through Syria all the way to Morocco, became independent one after another.

Even after independence, Western interest in the Middle East remained high. Control of the strategic Suez Canal was one reason; the proximity of an unfriendly Soviet Union was another. A third reason, of growing military and economic importance, was oil. Britain had begun to produce oil in Iran in the early 1900s, and later in Iraq and the smaller sheikdoms of the Gulf. In the 1930s American companies began oil production in Saudi Arabia, whose reserves later proved to be the greatest in the non-Communist world. Algeria and Libya also became important oil producers.

The West had a brief scare in Iran in 1951 when the xenophobic government of Mohammed Mossadeq nationalized the British-owned oil company. But in 1953 Mossadeq was overthrown in a U.S.-engineered coup, and Iran's big oil production, though still nationalized, continued to flow at bargain prices. It was during the 1950s, in fact, that Middle East crude oil, produced and controlled by Western companies and sold for as little as $2 a barrel, became a vital necessity for economic growth in Japan and most of Western Europe. By the early 1960s the United States was beginning to show a similar, though lesser, dependence as its large domestic oil and gas production fell behind booming demand.

Unluckily for the West, this oil dependence came at a time of rising self-assertion by the oil-exporting countries. By the early 1970s the most important of them—mostly in the Middle East and Arab North Africa, but also including Indonesia, Nigeria, and Venezuela—were cooperating in an export cartel called the Organization of Petroleum Exporting Countries (OPEC) to multiply their oil income. Successive waves of OPEC price rises in seven years (1973–80) more than quintupled the real, inflation-discounted price of oil and helped drive the West—as well as the oil-importing developing countries—into a deepening economic swamp called stagflation. And the big oil states, especially Saudi Arabia, began to be counted among the major financial powers of the world.

The results for the West were not only economic but strategic. An alarm signal was flashed during the Arab-Israeli War of 1973: an Arab embargo on the sale of oil to Israel's friend, the United States. The Arab states had shown that they could use economic sanctions as a foreign policy instrument. The embargo, though short-lived, raised the specter of the oil faucet being turned off altogether if anti-Western forces should ever dominate the Gulf. Since Britain's military withdrawal from the Gulf in 1971, the United States had taken on responsibility for the security of that area. The approach adopted became known as the *twin pillars* policy: close U.S. relations with the Gulf's two oil giants, Saudi Arabia and Iran. The policy worked for seven years, then went up in flames in Iran's revolution.

The revolution in Iran was a shock to the West. In the 1970s Iran's autocratic Shah Mohammed Reza Pahlavi had worked urgently to modernize his backward nation of 35 million people and build its military power while the oil lasted. United States capital and technology, and the most modern weapons (except nuclear), were sold to Iran in abundance. The shah, of course, had his opponents: conservative Shiite Muslim clergy; millions of uprooted, devoutly religious peasants crowding Iran's cities; Western-trained intellectuals and students; Kurdish, Arab, and other non-

Iranian minorities; the small Soviet-controlled Tudeh (Communist) party; and influential Iranians opposed to the rising corruption surrounding the royal court. But all this, it then appeared, was kept under control by the shah's presumably loyal armed forces, the momentum of his development program, and his hated but efficient secret police.

The reality was otherwise. Beginning in early 1978 anti-shah and anti-U.S. protests from these diverse sources coalesced and built into a hurricane of revolutionary violence. Within a year the shah was deposed, and the rule of Islamic zealots began under Ayatollah Ruhollah Khomeini. Iran's huge oil exports stopped, then resumed at a trickle; world oil prices jumped again. Iran's relations with the United States, dubbed by Khomeini the "great Satan," fell to zero. A sea of new troubles engulfed the revolution: endless factional feuds; assassination and repression; the 444-day crisis over the American embassy hostages; and the border war with invading Iraq. Soon the Soviet Union, although held at arm's length by the Khomeini regime, was making efforts to gain some influence over the confused Iranian political scene.

All this had its effect on America's other "pillar," Saudi Arabia, and its neighboring Gulf sheikdoms. They were alarmed at American impotence in Iran and felt threatened both by Islamic radicals stirred up by the Iranian revolution and by Soviet-backed Arab radical states. Seeking a quick way to reassure them—and to warn Moscow—President Carter declared in January 1980 that "an attempt by any outside force to gain control of the Persian Gulf region will be regarded as an assault on the vital interests of the United States of America. Such an assault will be repelled by any means necessary, including military force." To put teeth in this pronouncement, Washington worked to arrange for U.S. air and naval facilities in nearby countries—Kenya, Somalia and Oman—to supplement those it had already acquired on Britain's Indian Ocean island of Diego Garcia. Plans were laid for creation of a highly mobile U.S. "rapid deployment force," chiefly with the Gulf in mind.

But nagging questions remained. How much security could the Saudi kingdom, financial and spiritual heartland of the Arab world, derive from protection by the United States, the principal backer of the Arabs' chief enemy, Israel? And what about that other big Persian Gulf oil producer, Iraq—mired in its rash war with Iran; unsure of further military aid from its Soviet patron, yet loath to turn to any friend of Israel? Clearly, a U.S. policy for the Gulf must reach beyond the Gulf itself to deal with that most pervasive and intractable of all Middle East problems, the Arab-Israeli conflict.

Israel and the Arabs

About a century ago—a time of rising nationalism, and also of anti-Semitism, in Europe—persecuted Russian Jews began to emigrate to Palestine, hoping to create a nation of their own in that ancient homeland of the Jewish people. The world Zionist movement soon adopted the same cause on an international scale. Palestine's small population, which was then ruled by the crumbling Turkish Empire, was mainly Muslim Arab, and shared the nationalist feelings that had begun to sweep the Arab world.

No great issue arose over the matter until World War I. In 1917 Britain, in the famous Balfour Declaration, promised the Zionists to support creation of a "Jewish national home" in Palestine after its liberation from Turkish rule. Britain's Arab nationalist allies were indignant, having expected that the whole region would be theirs. Nevertheless, after the war Jewish emigration to Palestine, which by then was ruled by Britain under a League of Nations mandate, continued and increased. During the Hitler era, hundreds of thousands of European Jews arrived, most of them fleeing Nazi persecution and, finally, the horror of the Nazi Holocaust. As Jewish numbers in Palestine increased, so did Arab-Jewish violence.

In 1947 Britain, burdened with postwar troubles at home and abroad and determined to leave unruly Palestine, brought the issue to the United Nations. The UN General Assembly, over strong Arab opposition but with vigorous support from the White House, endorsed a plan to partition Palestine into an Arab state and a Jewish state. The Zionists agreed but the Arab governments refused. Britain, at the end of its patience, pulled out. On May 14, 1948 the state of Israel raised its flag in Tel Aviv. On President Truman's orders it was recognized within minutes by the United States, where Zionism enjoyed dedicated support from the Jewish community and broad sympathy among citizens of all faiths. Recognition by the Soviet Union and other major powers quickly followed.

Simultaneously, the first Arab-Israeli War began. The Israelis soon gained the upper hand. A UN armistice, signed in 1949 by Israel and its four neighbors—Egypt, Jordan, Syria, and Lebanon—left Israel in possession of half again as much land as it would have had under the UN plan, including the western half of Jerusalem, which soon became the Israeli capital. In 1950 those parts of Palestine near the West Bank of the river Jordan not won by Israel—including East Jerusalem, site of shrines sacred to Jews, Muslims, and Christians—were declared annexed by the kingdom of Jordan, while Egypt held onto a 135-square-mile district on the Mediterranean known as the Gaza Strip.

The armistice was not peace. Over 600,000 Palestinian Arabs crowded UN refugee camps near the armistice lines in Jordan, the Gaza Strip, Lebanon, and Syria—"temporary" camps, still in existence today—or started life anew in other countries. A like number of Jews, expelled from Arab countries, settled in Israel. The Arab governments refused to recognize Israel and demanded that it be abolished and that the Palestinian refugees be allowed to return to their homes.

The Arab demands seemed empty words at first, but as Western-oriented monarchies were overthrown by Arab nationalists in Egypt (1952), Iraq (1958), and Libya (1969), words were increasingly matched by action. Soon both Jordan and the revolutionary government in Egypt were backing Palestinian commando raids against civilians in Israel. Egypt's leader, Gamal Abdel Nasser, having tried vainly to buy arms in the United States (which was then refusing arms to both sides), began to buy arms from the Soviet bloc. Meanwhile he was supporting Algerian nationalists in their fight for independence from France. In July 1956 he seized the Suez Canal, until then controlled by Britain. That October, Britain, France and Israel responded with a secretly planned invasion of Egypt—only to withdraw under Soviet threats and American pressure. For the Europeans, it was the last hurrah of imperial power in the Middle East. For Israel, it was a sharp reminder that the United States also had Arab relationships to protect.

To help prevent further trouble, a small multinational peacekeeping force, under the UN flag, was stationed behind Egypt's border with Israel. The arrangement held for over ten years, during which Nasser emerged as the leading Arab champion and foe of Israel. In May 1967, as border incidents mounted between Israel and Egypt's ally Syria, Nasser forced the removal of the UN peace force, blockaded Israel's exit to the Red Sea through the Gulf of Aqaba, and marched his Soviet-equipped army up to Israel's border. His bold stroke proved to be a colossal blunder. In June Israel replied with a lightning offensive, which broke the blockade and smashed Egypt's and Syria's forces—as well as Jordan's, which had rashly joined the fight. In six triumphant days Israel not only overran the remainder of the old Palestine territory, ousting Jordan from the West Bank and Egypt from Gaza; it also seized Syria's menacing Golan Heights and, the biggest prize of all, Egypt's Sinai Peninsula.

Closest to Israeli hearts was the conquest of the old eastern section of

Jerusalem, the site of the ruins of the original temple of Solomon, Judaism's holiest shrine. Although the same area also includes shrines sacred to devout Muslims and Christians, and is thus a highly emotional bone of contention in Middle East politics, Israel brushed aside objections from Washington and elsewhere and formally annexed it.

Israel, exultant and militarily supreme, at first offered to withdraw from most of the conquered lands (but not East Jerusalem) in exchange for full peace. The Arab states—still unable to face the permanence of Israel—did not reply; so Israel stayed. And the Americans, pro-Israel in popular feeling and preoccupied with Vietnam, were in no mood this time to press it to withdraw. Yet Washington also had Arab attitudes to consider. The upshot was the famous UN Security Council Resolution 242 of November 1967—a unanimous, but purposely ambiguous, call upon the warring parties to make peace with "secure and recognized borders," and on Israel to withdraw "from territories" (all? most? some?) occupied in the June war. Repeated attempts to start negotiations on that basis got nowhere. Meanwhile Israeli civilian settlements appeared in growing numbers in all the occupied territories, including the West Bank, from which a new wave of Palestinians had fled as war refugees.

Once again the Palestinians turned to hit-and-run terrorism. Small guerrilla squads launched frequent raids on Jewish communities in the West Bank, Gaza, and Israel proper. Behind the raids was a political purpose. Already in 1964 several exiled Palestinian groups, backed by Arab governments, had joined in what was to become the Palestine Liberation Organization (PLO). Its declared aim was to replace Israel with a state in which all Palestinian Arabs would have the right to live. Ever since, the PLO and rival factions within it have received money, weapons, training, and diplomatic support from various Arab governments and from the Soviet bloc.

In the early years the PLO had little impact. It suffered a heavy blow in 1970–1971 when King Hussein of Jordan, in bitter conflict with the PLO over who should ultimately rule the West Bank, drove 10,000 Palestinians out of his country in bloody fighting. Most PLO groups thereafter operated from Lebanon. In 1974, however, the PLO's star rose. The Arab states, heartened by the outcome of the 1973 war (see below) and flushed with OPEC's oil victory, declared the PLO to be "the sole legitimate representative of the Palestinian people," poured new money into it, and endorsed its demand for a Palestinian state. The UN General Assembly—over strong U.S. objections—adopted the Arab position; gave the PLO leader, Yasir Arafat, a triumphal reception; and authorized the

PLO to post a permanent observer at UN headquarters in New York. As time passed the PLO also gained a measure of support in Western Europe and Japan.

Israel had denounced the PLO from the outset as a terrorist organization bent on Israel's destruction. Beginning in 1972 it kept guerrilla attacks in check by periodic raids on PLO bases in Lebanon, and later by an informal alliance with armed Lebanese Christians. In 1976, with civil war raging among Lebanese and Palestinian factions, Syria sent its armed forces into Lebanon both to maintain its own influence there and to counterbalance Israel's. Multinational Arab and UN peacekeeping units also helped to muffle the conflict. Lebanon itself almost ceased to exist as an independent state.

Egypt's Separate Peace

Meanwhile, almost unnoticed, events were moving toward the first great split in the solid Arab front against Israel. The crack had begun to open after the death of Egypt's Nasser in 1970. His successor, Anwar el-Sadat, took little interest in replacing Nasser as leader of the Arab world. He put his emphasis instead on modernizing Egypt's backward economy and avenging its humiliation in the 1967 war. He rebuilt the armed forces with renewed Soviet aid, then ousted his Soviet military advisers. On October 6, 1973, the high holy day of Yom Kippur in the Jewish religious calendar, he led a surprise Egyptian-Syrian attack on Israel in the occupied Sinai and the Golan Heights.

Militarily, the Yom Kippur War came close to being another Arab disaster, for a crushing Israeli counteroffensive regained all the lost ground and more. But Sadat's bold stroke had inflicted punishing losses on Israel and marked him as the man who had redeemed Arab honor. Moreover, Sadat could now turn for aid to the United States, which had duly noted his ouster of the Russians. United States aid and Arab oil money began to patch up Egypt's ragged economy. And in 1974–1975, Egypt and Syria gained through the diplomacy of U.S. Secretary of State Henry A. Kissinger what they had failed to gain in battle: permanent Israeli withdrawals from parts of the Sinai and of the Golan Heights. Israel, in compensation, received increased U.S. military aid, the protection of new UN peace-keeping units, and an important diplomatic assurance: that Washington would not recognize or negotiate with the PLO until the latter recognized Israel's right to exist.

Sadat now felt strong enough to move the Middle East toward the peace that both he and the Americans urgently desired. The most obvious method would have been to reconvene a piece of diplomatic machinery called the Geneva Conference, which included the warring parties as well as the United States and the Soviet Union—the latter's consent having long been viewed in Washington as important, possibly even essential, to any general settlement of the conflict. A small edition of such a conference, with delegations from the two superpowers, Egypt, Israel, and Jordan—the first official diplomatic meeting ever held between Israel and the Arabs—had met fruitlessly for one day after the 1973 war; but the obstacles to further such meetings in Israeli, Arab, and PLO politics proved insuperable.

So, in November 1977, Sadat dropped his bombshell. He flew to Jerusalem and made a ringing appeal for peace to the Knesset, Israel's parliament. The Arabs' anti-Israel front was shattered; Sadat was denounced as a traitor to the Arab cause; and Egypt was denied further aid from Saudi Arabia. In 1979 it was suspended from membership in the Arab League.

Undaunted, Sadat joined with Israeli Prime Minister Menachem Begin in negotiating two agreements, mediated by President Carter at Camp David in September 1978. The first agreement led in March 1979 to a full Israeli-Egyptian peace treaty, including an Israeli pledge to complete evacuation of a demilitarized Sinai Peninsula by April 1982. The second agreement, in answer to Sadat's Arab critics, called for steps toward a solution of the Palestinian problem. A Palestinian authority with "full autonomy" would take over temporarily from the Israeli military government in the West Bank and Gaza; five years later the final status of the territories—the toughest issue—would be decided. Details were to be settled in talks among Israel, Egypt, Jordan, and elected Palestinian representatives.

The "autonomy talks" were crippled at birth, for neither Jordan nor the West Bank Palestinian leaders would touch a project so far from the Arab position. The talks began just between Israel and Egypt, with U.S. officials sitting in. By 1980 they were stalemated, the two sides poles apart on whether "autonomy" meant local administrative authority only (Israel's view) or something broad enough to pave the way toward statehood or confederation with Jordan (Egypt's view). Meanwhile Israeli settlements in the West Bank and Gaza continued to increase. Worried European and Japanese officials started their own contacts with the PLO and prodded Washington, without success, to do the same.

The Dangerous Struggle Continues

With the region's most poisonous issue still unsettled, the Israeli-Egyptian peace was uneasy, and the tensions it raised on both sides were evident.

On Egypt's side, Sadat's "act of betrayal" was the main count brought against him by the Islamic fundamentalists who assassinated him in October 1981. Sadat's successor, Hosni Mubarak, immediately reaffirmed the peace treaty with Israel. He was rewarded the following April when Israel completed on schedule its promised evacuation of the Sinai despite anguished outcries from the uprooted Israeli settlers and their sympathizers in Israel proper. With that major goal attained, Mubarak proceeded to mend his fences in the Arab world and to apply pressure on all concerned—Israel, the United States, and the Palestinians—for a solution that many had viewed as inevitable ever since 1967: a Palestinian state—or else a Palestinian-Jordanian federation of some kind—living in peace with Israel, the latter withdrawn to something approximating its 1967 borders.

Mubarak's counsels made little headway. On the Arab side, even pro-American Saudi Arabia remained tantalizingly vague about peace with Israel on any terms—seemingly fearing violent reactions from diehard anti-Zionists in its midst. Yasir Arafat, the often mild-sounding head of the PLO, seemed held back in similar fashion by quarreling PLO factions and hard-line Arab governments, especially that of Syria.

On the Israeli side the picture was no brighter. Already in 1981 the Begin government had flexed its muscles by bombing a nuclear reactor in Iraq and by virtually annexing its occupation zone in the Golan Heights, historically part of Syria—acts that seemed to say that any Arab authority less friendly than Egypt will get no quarter from Jerusalem.

After the evacuation of the Sinai, Israel's mood, as if in compensation, seemed to grow still tougher. Its heaviest blow fell on Lebanon, still the PLO's main stronghold. In June 1982 a full-scale Israeli invasion of Lebanon was launched. Israel's declared aim as the campaign began was to clear the PLO from a 25-mile belt of southern Lebanon, so that PLO guns could no longer shell northern Israel. But as the invasion progressed, so did Israeli demands. Having surrounded Beirut, Lebanon's battered capital and host to the main PLO headquarters, Israel demanded that the PLO leave Beirut altogether or be destroyed; and that Syria's large forces leave Lebanon. Thereupon the Reagan Administration sent a veteran negotiator, Philip. C. Habib, to work out terms for the various withdrawals and, it was hoped, help to restore Lebanon's shattered sovereignty. In late August a U.S.-French-Italian peacekeeping force stood guard as PLO contingents moved out of Beirut to Syria, Jordan, Tunisia, and other Arab countries. But by year's end the Israeli and Syrian forces—and some remaining PLO fighters under Syria's wing—were still in Lebanon; and so were the peacekeepers.

What had Israel achieved by its Lebanese venture? Its armed forces had certainly demonstrated once again their overwhelming superiority to those of Syria, the only Arab country that had dared to fight them. And, for a time at least, the PLO had been moved out of range of Israel's borders. But against these successes there were some serious minus quantities in the account. To start with, there was anxiety lest Lebanon should turn out to be Israel's Vietnam—impossible to pacify and nearly impossible to leave. This impression grew when the new president of Lebanon, although elected virtually under Israeli guns, shied away from Israel's demand for a peace treaty or a security pact.

No less ominous was a rising criticism of Israel's tough posture, both in Israel and in the United States. The change seemed to be triggered by a revulsion against the violence of the Israeli assault. Civilian deaths and injuries from Israeli shells and bombs were numerous and prominently covered by the news media. Most damaging of all was a vengeful massacre of hundreds of Palestinian civilians, including women and children, by Lebanese Christian forces acting with what looked like Israeli acquiescence. Fairly or not, Israel's reputation as a humane democracy had suffered a sharp blow. In Washington there was new doubt about the ready support for Israel, whatever its policies, that had prevailed for many years in American politics.

Finally, aside from the question of excessive violence, many Americans and Israelis challenged the strategic wisdom of the Lebanese assault. Its uncertain outcome seemed to demonstrate once again that force alone cannot solve the Palestinian problem any more than a pillow can be crushed by punching it with a fist. Now as before, the Palestinians are at the core of the Arab-Israeli conflict. They are a people with a strong sense of nationhood—created most of all by their grievance against Israel. Scattered through the Arab world, they are widely resented as intruders and feared as revolutionaries. Indeed, the Arab governments' pressure for a Palestinian state reflects not only solidarity with their Palestinian brethren, but also a desire to be rid of this restless and threatening presence.

But where could the Palestinians go? On that central question, the opposing sides in the wake of the Lebanese invasion seemed as far apart as ever. The Arab side, at best, was evasive; the Israelis, blunt and unyielding. The Begin government, going further than any of its predecessors, had consistently held that Israel's 1967 conquests, especially the West Bank (in biblical terminology, Judea and Samaria), were Israel's by divine right, would never be surrendered in whole or in part, and were open to Jewish settlement as Israel might decide. Begin accordingly put the narrowest possible construction on the Camp David accord he had signed on Palestinian autonomy. He insisted that the autonomy he had promised was not a prelude to statehood, or to territorial concessions, but only, in Begin's own phrase, a "quasi-" or "pseudo-" government, its authority limited to people, not land. Seen in this light, Israel's refusal to talk to the PLO seemed less a stand against terrorism than a refusal to discuss what even the most reasonable PLO factions wanted: a state of their own in some substantial part of the land in which all the Palestinian people had once lived.

In this situation the United States, its national interest deeply involved with both sides, saw a chance to act. For years Washington had followed a cautious policy, concentrating on "damage control" at moments of crisis, and exerting little strong pressure for a comprehensive peace among all the parties to the conflict. But U.S. policy had never excluded the idea of a Palestinian state carved out of the occupied territories, living in peace next door to a permanently recognized Israel; indeed, this was a conceivable outcome of the negotiating process set in motion by the 1979 accords at Camp David. As long as the Arabs remained evasive about such an outcome, the United States could be evasive too—and thus escape, or postpone, what would probably prove a wrenching political battle with Israel and its American backers. This stalling, however, always carried a risk of so alienating Arab feeling as to jeopardize the security of the whole Middle East.

It may have been such thoughts, in the wake of the Lebanese crisis, that caused American hesitancy to turn to boldness. In late August 1982 President Reagan, working with his new Secretary of State, George Shultz, made the first purely American proposals for a comprehensive Arab-Israeli peace in many years. To both Israel and the Arabs he proposed a set of principles, all bearing on the core issue of territory:

● an immediate freeze on Israeli settlements in the occupied territories;
● inclusion of "land," not just "people," in the definition of Palestinian autonomy;

- a final peace settlement based on "an exchange of territory for peace," with the territory given up by Israel to be proportionate to the extent of peace offered in return;
- and, for the West Bank and Gaza, no independent Palestinian state but, instead, Palestinian self-government in association with Jordan.

For the Arabs, including the Palestinians, his message was: "Accept the reality of Israel" and negotiate directly with it.

The Reagan initiative was quickly rejected by the Begin government but welcomed by Israeli opposition leaders. On the Arab side it was seen as a forward step by the two figures most concerned, Arafat of the PLO and King Hussein of Jordan. Whether it could dislodge hard-liners on both sides from decades of rigid hostility was not immediately apparent. Significantly, however, the Soviet Union, still an important backer of Syria and other comparatively inflexible Arab governments, sounded a new note. Even while predicting failure for the Reagan plan, Moscow scolded the "rejectionist" Arabs for their rigidity and called on the PLO to accept Israel. With both superpowers thus competing for the support of Arab moderates, it even seemed possible that, after nearly four decades, the feud between Israelis and Arabs might begin to give way to the common interest in peace.

Any such progress, in turn, would greatly ease U.S. relations with the Arab states of the Persian Gulf. But it would by no means automatically solve them, for the politics of the Gulf present U.S. policy-makers with difficult questions that have little to do with Israel. What to do about Iran's revolutionary regime, still strong enough to beat back Iraq's invasion, and still hostile and virtually inaccessible not only to the United States but to most of its Arab neighbors? How to help build Saudi military power without running the risk that that power might one day be used against Israel or even, as in Iran, against pro-American rulers? And how to "project" U.S. military power in such a remote and politically sensitive area, where U.S. military facilities are as vulnerable as the governments that grant them?

Theoretically, a big part of the answer to such questions might be found if Washington and Moscow could agree on what their 1972 joint declaration about exercising "restraint" in dangerous situations actually means in that most dangerous of all regions, the Middle East. Can the United States be assured that the Russians will not use Afghanistan as a jumping-off point for an invasion of the Gulf, will not manipulate Iranian politics against the West, and will not connive in any plots to "strangle" the West by shutting off the Gulf's oil? Can Moscow be assured that the United States will not some day use a pro-Western, post-Khomeini government in Iran, or an insurgent movement in Afghanistan, as a pressure point against the Soviet Union? Can both sides somehow moderate their competition for influence in the various states of the region? If so, the danger of superpower conflict in the Middle East could be much reduced, and the outlook for stability improved.

There are still no answers to questions of this kind. Both within the region and in the policies of the two superpowers, the materials for future conflict in the Middle East are plentiful.

AFRICA—FROM THE MEDITERRANEAN TO THE CAPE

Africa, its huge bulk stretching about 5,000 miles from north to south, divides politically and geographically into three fairly distinct zones. Five Arab countries share its Mediterranean northern coast. In and to the south of the Sahara Desert, a barrier as forbidding as any ocean, are the 45 mainland and island states of Black Africa. Dominating the temperate south is that bastion of white minority rule, South Africa, embroiled in racial conflict but—with its advanced skills, thriving industry, and enormous gold production—by far the strongest economic and military power in the continent.

North Africa

For thousands of years the peoples of Mediterranean North Africa have developed within the orbits of the powerful civilizations of Europe and the Middle East. In successive eras, part or all of the region has been ruled by ancient Greece, Rome, the Arab caliphs, Ottoman Turkey and, beginning in the nineteenth century, the colonial powers of Europe. Despite Europe's recent dominance, Islam remains the prevailing religion and Arabic the common language. (Algeria, Tunisia, and Morocco are collectively called the *Maghreb*—the Arabic word for West.) As the colonial system dissolved after World War II, all the states of the area—Egypt, Libya, Tunisia, Algeria, and Morocco—joined the Arab League and became involved in varying degrees in the conflicts of the Middle East. But all are also active members of Africa's regional body, the Organization of African Unity (OAU).

In international politics, the interests and policies of these five states vary widely. Only Tunisia, the smallest of the group, keeps a low international profile. Policies toward Israel range from Egypt's peace treaty and Morocco's moderate stance to the "rejectionism" of Algeria and Libya, the last named being the most militantly anti-Zionist of the five.

In African affairs, Egypt's attention has centered on quarrels with Libya and cooperation with its big southern neighbor Sudan, which it once ruled.

Libya, a big oil producer, was an Italian colony until World War II. Its devoutly Muslim dictator, Colonel Muammar el-Qaddafi, has pursued an adventurous course, investing heavily in Soviet arms. He has used both armed force and subversion against relatively pro-Western governments in nearby African countries including Egypt, Sudan, Uganda, Chad, Somalia, and recently Algeria. His relations with Washington have been embittered by these actions as well as by his hard line against Israel and his alleged use of hit men to murder Libyan dissidents abroad.

France's former colony of Algeria is the only one of the five that fought a war for independence, which it gained in 1962. For many years its leaders combined Algeria's oil and gas wealth with a radical world view to make their country a standard-bearer in the anti-Western politics of the third world. In its own corner of Africa, Algeria has sponsored an insurgent movement, the Polisario Front, fighting for the independence of the former Spanish colony of Western Sahara, now ruled by Morocco. Morocco's conservative King Hassan has received U.S. arms and limited U.S. support for his country's claim to the disputed area. However, U.S. relations with Algeria have improved somewhat since a change of government in 1979. Algeria is host to substantial U.S. private investments, and in 1980–1981 its government was a key intermediary in the negotiated return of the U.S. hostages in Iran.

United States interests in North Africa generally take a low priority except where Middle East politics or Mediterranean military questions are involved. Economically, the region continues to look mainly toward Europe, the main market for its oil and agricultural products and the employer of much of its rapidly growing population.

Black Africa

The huge area now known as Black Africa did not begin to find its own voice in world affairs until barely a quarter of a century ago. Until then, for many centuries two great streams of influence had flowed into the region: one from the Arab world, the other from Europe.

Arab trade and Arab conquests long ago made Islam a major religion, in some cases the dominant one, in all the Black African countries along the southern rim of the Sahara, and in East Africa as far south as Tanzania. Even in Nigeria, the region's chief power today, the Hausa people of the north, who are Muslims, claim to be more numerous than the coastal Christians. This religious tie, fortified by Arab oil money, gives the Arab states substantial influence in Black Africa today.

Europe's impact on the region was first felt before 1500, when Portuguese explorers set up trading stations along the tropical African coasts. For centuries, what mainly drew Europeans to Africa, to the shame of later ages, was the transatlantic slave trade. Only after slavery in the Western Hemisphere was abolished, however, did Europe's domination of Africa reach its height. For over half a century beginning around 1880, European flags flew over all of Black Africa except Ethiopia and Liberia. For the Europeans, Africa meant raw materials, national prestige, and pride in what white rulers and Christian missionaries saw as their "civilizing mission." For millions of Africans, it was a disruption of ancient ways and an apprenticeship—sometimes cruel, sometimes benevolent—in the ways of the modern West.

In Black Africa as elsewhere, decolonization began soon after World War II. In the single year 1960 independence came to 16 African countries. Today, faithfully following the arbitrary colonial frontiers, Africa is divided into more states than any other continent. The regional body, the Organization of African Unity, has 50 members.

The giant of Black Africa is Nigeria, with one-fifth of the region's population and great oil reserves. It exports more oil to the United States than any country except Saudi Arabia. It has the region's largest cadre of trained administrators and professionals. It also has large problems, among them economic policies that penalize saving, encourage corruption, and, critics say, squander much of the oil wealth on which national development depends. Also, like most countries embracing many language and ethnic groups, Nigeria has had severe problems of maintaining unity. Secession by the Ibo people in the oil-rich coastal state once called Biafra was prevented only by an exhausting civil war (1967–1970). Since then Nigeria appears to have restored unity under a new federal constitution; but the structure remains vulnerable.

Still, Nigeria is a leading voice in African affairs, opposed both to

South Africa and to the widening influence in the region of radical Arab Libya.

Black Africa needs all the leadership it can muster, for its problems are great. Here we focus on three major interests which concern the whole region and raise policy questions for the United States.

1. National development. For reasons of both national power and human betterment, Black African governments are determined to develop their economies and strengthen their political systems. Their production per capita is below that of any other major region except the Indian subcontinent. For export earnings, most depend heavily on one or two mineral or agricultural commodities the world prices of which rise and fall unpredictably. Most countries are woefully lacking in roads, communications, schools, health services, technological research institutes—all the infrastructure essential to economic growth. Agriculture has lagged badly and dependence on imported food has increased. Rising demand for something better than the grinding poverty of rural life has brought hordes of untrained people to the already swollen cities where even menial jobs are scarce. Very rapid population growth rates—Kenya's, an extreme case, is estimated at 4 percent a year, which means a doubling of population in 18 years—has further aggravated problems of illiteracy, malnutrition, and endemic disease. In times of drought the people of some countries, especially in the Sahel region just south of the Sahara, have suffered acute hunger and even famine in recent years.

All these difficulties are compounded by shortages of experienced managers, planners, and technicians, and by political conflict within nations that are constantly troubled by tribal and linguistic rivalries. A few countries have suffered periods of misrule by corrupt and brutal tyrants. Others have found able and durable leaders. But for all, despite substantial flows of foreign aid, political and economic development has a long way to go. For the poorest countries of the region, some experts foresee long periods of great hardship before life gets better.

2. Peace. African nations have attempted to reduce the risk of war by nonalignment (in principle, though not always in practice) in the superpower rivalry and by respecting the borders inherited from the colonial era. Yet wars still happen. Among their main causes have been the spillover of tribal conflicts across national borders and entanglement with the disputes of the Middle East—which, in turn, tend to draw in the superpowers.

Internal ethnic or tribal conflict has afflicted many African states. Many such conflicts, like the Biafra war in Nigeria, have been contained within national borders; but others have created massive international refugee problems—Africa has long been high on the agenda of the UN High Commissioner for Refugees—and consequent friction with neighboring countries. Ethiopia's ethnic struggles have caused an estimated 2 million Muslims to flee into Somalia and the Sudan. And in the desert republic of Chad, once a French colony, power struggles between tribes have led to repeated armed intervention by France, then by Libya; support of dissident Chadian factions by Sudan; and then an attempt by Nigeria and the OAU to uphold Chad's independence with an all-African peace force. In Zaire in 1978, when armed bands exiled from the mineral-rich province of Shaba staged a bloody invasion of their homeland from across the border in Angola, French and Belgian paratroopers were sent in to help Zaire's incompetent army repel the invaders. In 1979, Uganda's notorious Idi Amin Dada was replaced by the tribal foe he himself had ousted, Milton Obote, following an invasion by the army of Tanzania where Obote had been exiled.

Most worrisome—and most tempting—to global political strategists are the conflicts in the east, where Africa overlaps with the Arab world. Libya's intrusion into Chad is part of that picture. But at least five countries in the area are involved, and their interactions with each other and with the superpowers provide a textbook example of the strange reversals that can happen in third-world politics.

In the 1960s, the United States had two conservative friends in northeast Africa: the Arab king of Libya and the Coptic Christian emperor of Ethiopia. Both received American arms and welcomed American military installations. In the same area at the same time, the Soviet Union enjoyed similar cooperation with three clients, all Arab dictatorships: Egypt, Sudan, and Somalia. Both Sudan and Ethiopia had domestic insurgencies to cope with, but otherwise the region seemed quiet.

By 1981 the situation was transformed. America's two royal friends had long since been deposed. A self-styled Marxist regime in Ethiopia and Colonel Qaddafi's radical Arab regime in Libya were both now backed by the Soviet Union. Together, they were doing their best to undermine one of Ethiopia's main enemies, Somalia, which had recently failed in a rash attempt to "liberate" Ethiopia's ethnically Somali province of Ogaden. Somalia too had switched sides and had become a military client of the United States, despite Washington's disapproval of its Ogaden venture. Soviet military advisers and Cuban troops, having helped Ethiopia in the Ogaden campaign, were now helping it fight the Eritrean rebels in the north. Libya's Qaddafi was trying to get Ethiopia to repay his help against

Somalia by helping him to subvert the government of Sudan, which (along with Qaddafi's arch-foe, Egypt) was now leaning toward the United States. Despite these power plays, Ethiopia and Sudan, two dirt-poor countries with enough trouble on their hands already, seemed in no mood to fight each other. Just what this strategic square dance was likely to mean for the superpower balance in the Middle East was far from clear. But for the peoples of the area it clearly meant more war and more misery.

3. Ending white minority rule. The one interest that has long united all of Black Africa is hostility to the "white redoubt" in southern Africa.

By 1965, the only major pockets of white rule left on the African continent were in the south: Portugal's big colonies of Angola and Mozambique, Britain's rebellious crown colony of Southern Rhodesia, South-West Africa (also called Namibia) under South African rule, and South Africa itself. Since 1960 the black majorities in all these countries had been swept by independence fever from the north, and violence against white rule had begun to increase, aided by the Soviet bloc and by China.

The first big change came in 1974 when Portuguese generals, in despair after 13 years of hopeless colonial war, overthrew the dictatorship in Lisbon. Within a year the new government had granted independence to virtually all Portuguese colonies throughout the world, including Angola and Mozambique. In both countries, insurgent factions backed by the Soviet Union came to power.

Pressure then rose against the self-proclaimed republic of Rhodesia—the future Zimbabwe—where in 1965 the ruling whites under Ian Smith had broken with Britain, the legal sovereign, and issued a "unilateral declaration of independence" rather than yield power to the black majority as London had insisted. In the 1970s guerrilla armies with African, Soviet, and Chinese backing stepped up terrorist attacks inside Rhodesia from bases in neighboring Mozambique and Zambia. In 1978, under pressure from all sides to end the escalating war, Smith attempted a compromise "internal settlement" giving unarmed black groups inside Rhodesia a share of power, but excluding the armed Patriotic Front. The war ground on for another year until all factions, under British pressure, agreed on a constitution making Zimbabwe independent under majority rule but guaranteeing certain rights to the white minority. Robert Mugabe, head of the stronger guerrilla organization, became president. Although calling himself a Marxist-Leninist, Mugabe in his first year in office turned conspicuously toward the West for aid and investment. But his government has been tormented by ex-soldiers of the minority Matabele tribe, who have mounted a terrorist campaign against Mugabe and against the nation's dwindling number of highly productive white farmers. Between this problem and the control of landlocked Zimbabwe's best export routes by an unfriendly South Africa, the young nation faces a difficult future.

The Shrunken "White Redoubt": Namibia and South Africa

The temperate, resource-rich southern bulge of Africa was first settled by white men—seafarers from the Netherlands—over three centuries ago. Their white Afrikaner descendants, plus a lesser number of whites mainly of British descent, make up the 4.5-million minority whose highly industrialized democracy rules over a voteless 23.2 million nonwhites in the powerful but deeply troubled Republic of South Africa. South Africa, in turn, still exercises colonial rule over a dependent neighboring country which it still calls South-West Africa but other countries now call Namibia.

In the 1980s, with Zimbabwe independent, it was South Africa more than ever that felt the world community's pressure against white minority rule—a practice of the colonial era, long since abandoned everywhere else. The immediate focus, however, was Namibia, the one remaining buffer between Black Africa and South Africa proper.

Bigger than Texas, Namibia has vast mineral wealth and a sparse population, about a million. It was handed to South Africa in 1920 as a League of Nations mandate. In 1966 the UN General Assembly, with U.S. support, voted that South Africa, by imposing its apartheid system on Namibia, had forfeited its right to rule there and must leave. Soon a nationalist group called the South-West African People's Organization (SWAPO) demanded independence and started terrorist attacks.

For years South Africa defied the UN, fought SWAPO's guerrillas, and continued to rule. But after neighboring Angola gained independence, the new Soviet-backed government there began to let SWAPO use Angolan bases. South Africa responded with periodic raids into Angola, apparently aimed not only at SWAPO but also at helping insurgent Angolans overthrow the government. U.S. covert action briefly aimed at the same result until stopped in 1975 by act of Congress. Meanwhile Angola accepted the aid of a 20,000-man Cuban expeditionary force to help defend it from its domestic and foreign foes. South African raids continued; so did the Cuban presence. Washington refused to open diplomatic relations with Angola unless the Cubans left.

Despite its overwhelming military power, South Africa has had diplomatic reasons for wanting to solve the Namibian issue by negotiation—mainly its desire to repair its relations with the West and with its Black African neighbors. Negotiations took place on two parallel tracks. On one track, in an echo of the Rhodesian story, South Africa worked out an "internal settlement" with the ruling whites and a group of black tribal units—excluding SWAPO, the strongest black organization—on terms that would still leave the whites in a dominant position. But implementation was stymied by SWAPO partisans and, at the other extreme, by hard-line whites opposed to any concessions at all.

On the other track, South Africa has negotiated with a group of five Western governments, led by the United States, with a mandate from the UN Security Council. They have sought agreed ground rules for UN-supervised elections—in which SWAPO would participate—to choose a government of an independent Namibia. But neither SWAPO nor South Africa seems willing to risk an election it might lose. In 1982 the Reagan Administration was hoping to break the impasse by obtaining constitutional guarantees for the white minority's rights even if SWAPO, as expected, wins a fair election. And U.S. talks with Angola, begun during the Carter years, were resumed in hopes of getting the Cubans removed as part of a Namibian package deal. But on all sides, hard-liners were digging in against any compromise.

Meanwhile, international pressure has continued against the main target of Black Africa's wrath, South Africa itself. For over three decades, governments chosen by South Africa's all-white electorate have adopted one device after another to perpetuate the system known to the world as *apartheid*, under which whites rule over the four-fifths of the population that is nonwhite and, by white South African standards, poor. Only whites may hold public office. The races are kept separate in residence, marriage, education, and, with few exceptions, jobs. Ten small, scattered, poverty-stricken tribal "homelands" have been created by South African law; three have been recognized by South Africa, but not by the outside world, as "independent," and the rest are being prepared for that status. Every black South African, according to his tribal ancestry, is assigned as a citizen of a homeland and, when the government so pleases, as one of its permanent residents. Most blacks live in South Africa proper, where the jobs are, but their rights there are closely restricted. Black political activity is a criminal offense. Minor exceptions to these and other rules, following the violent

Soweto riots of 1976, have been limited by the government's fear of a white Afrikaner backlash.

Opposition to apartheid is both domestic and international. Within South Africa, leaders of banned black political organizations, such as the African National Congress (ANC) and the younger "black consciousness" movement, are either in jail or operating underground. But they receive aid and sympathy from a minority of dissident whites, and financial and other aid from the Soviet bloc as well as from the OAU. The ANC has recently conducted a few small hit-and-run attacks on targets inside South Africa, using nearby Black African countries as operating bases. In one of these, Mozambique, South Africa is reported to have retaliated by covertly backing an armed antigovernment faction, much as it has done in Angola.

International pressure against apartheid began decades ago. A continuous war of words is carried on against it at the UN. There is a UN embargo on arms transfers to South Africa. Various diplomatic and symbolic pressures have also been applied. United States participation in these pressures was visibly increased during the Carter Administration, but never to a point that could endanger the considerable U.S. business stake in South Africa, which accounts for about 1.25 percent of U.S. foreign trade.

There has long been sharp controversy within this country over policy toward South Africa. Advocates of strong American pressure against apartheid—including an increasingly influential black community—argue that apartheid is not only morally wrong but politically doomed; and that by opposing it so ineffectively the United States arouses deep resentment from the nonwhite third world and especially from Black Africa, where the U.S. stake in trade, investment and strategic minerals is at least as great as in South Africa itself. South Africa's rulers, this view maintains, unless faced with economic and other pressures that only the United States can exert, will not abandon apartheid until forced to so by race war—an outcome from which only communism or other extremist forces can benefit.

The other view, to which President Reagan and many members of his Administration have adhered (although somewhat less rigidly since taking office), argues that South Africa's and Namibia's mineral resources and geographic position are strategically important to this country; that the alternative to white rule with order and prosperity is all too likely to be black dictatorship with chaos, communism, or both; and that, in any case, outside pressure only raises Afrikaner hackles. Instead, it is argued, existing internal forces—especially the white economy's increasing need for black skilled workers—should be given a chance to bring about needed reforms.

Most Americans seem to agree that the U.S. interest requires a peaceful South Africa in which the rights of all, white and nonwhite alike, are fulfilled. But how to move toward that goal, and what priority the effort deserves in U.S. policy—these remain highly controversial questions that will continue to claim the nation's attention until the problem is solved.

7

The Western Hemisphere

In many respects countries of the Western Hemisphere, except the United States and Canada, resemble the third world. They are classed as developing countries; politics in many of them is unsettled; a few have become arenas of superpower competition; and some have even affiliated themselves with the world conference of the nonaligned. Yet in other ways the Latin American and Caribbean countries clearly do not follow the third-world pattern. They have roughly a century and a half of independence. In most, the dominant classes are largely European in ancestry and culture. And geography and history have destined them to have a close—if often quarrelsome—relationship with one superpower, the United States.

That relationship has been changing. All through the first half of this century, the supremacy of the United States in its own hemisphere was so self-evident as to seem beyond challenge. What shook the nation out of this complacent view was the successful defiance of U.S. power by Fidel Castro, who took over Cuba in 1959 and aligned his country with the Soviet Union. This was an early and spectacular sign that the postwar ability of the United States to shape events had begun to decline even among its hemispheric neighbors.

As elsewhere, the difficulties are both economic and political. Rapid development in a few Latin American countries has given them more international clout. And the drive for development has raised popular expectations and sharpened political conflict in most of Latin America as well as in eleven small-to-tiny Caribbean states* recently declared independent. In some areas, explosive population increase has swamped the supply of food and jobs and swelled the tide of migrants entering the United States, legally or otherwise.

Meanwhile America's neighbor, Canada, has been wrestling with chronic problems of national identity, complicated by economic difficulties, that have a complex effect on its relations with the United States.

CANADA'S IDENTITY PROBLEMS

Canada—the United States' NATO ally, main trading partner, and close cousin in national culture—has always had difficulty in resisting the gravitational attraction of its giant neighbor to the south. It was a stronghold of British loyalists during the American War of Independence, but many Canadians soon caught independence fever themselves. By the 1830s Canadian insurgents against British rule were recruiting illegal help from across the American border. The step-by-step loosening of Britain's grip on Canada—the latest step was taken in 1982—owned much in its early stages to British anxiety lest a resentful Canada slip into the American orbit.

Even today, Canada's problems of maintaining its national identity still persist. In fact, Canada entered the 1980s wrestling with three interlocking identity problems. Domestically, it is torn by the pull of ten highly autonomous provinces, especially French-speaking Quebec. This problem was entangled until 1982 with that of its lingering constitutional link with Britain. And from the south, Canadians still feel the powerful economic and cultural pull of the United States.

The Quebec problem is the oldest. After 1763, when England finally defeated France for control of Canada, Quebec was allowed to keep its French language and culture—virtually a nation within a nation. Even now French-Canadians—about a quarter of the country's population, located mainly in Quebec Province—lag far behind most of Canada economically, and a wide psychological gulf divides most of them from the English-speaking majority. Emotions have run high since the mid-1970s when the

---

*In 1982, ten Caribbean islands or island groups were still under French, British, or Netherlands rule, and two—Puerto Rico and the U.S. Virgin Islands—under American rule. All are self-governing in varying degrees. Puerto Rico has about 3.5 million people; the rest add up to 1.4 million.

fiery René Lévesque, elected premier of Quebec, moved to impose the French language on the province's powerful English-speaking minority and started maneuvering Quebec toward total independence.

As the 1980s began the Quebec issue collided with the constitutional one. Canada was still living under the federal constitution of 1867—an act of the British Parliament, which alone had legal power to amend it. London had long been willing to end this state of affairs as soon as Canadians could agree on a constitution of their own; but Ottawa and the provinces deadlocked over the division of powers between central and provincial governments. In 1981 Premier Pierre Elliott Trudeau won approval of a new draft constitution from all provinces except Quebec, where the Lévesque government's insistence on French-language education was again the sticking point. Despite Quebec's objections the draft was duly submitted to and approved by the British Parliament, and in April 1982 Queen Elizabeth—still Canada's monarch by Canadian choice—traveled to Ottawa to declare it in effect.

Whether this achievement will cement a new Canadian unity-in-diversity remains to be seen. Not only Quebec but other provinces too exert a constant centrifugal pull against the federal power. This is notably true of Alberta, which has quarreled frequently with Ottawa about the division of power over the oil industry and its large revenues.

If Canada does hold together, as most observers fully expect, one reason will be Canada's determination to resist U.S. domination. Most of Canada's 24 million people live within 100 miles of the U.S. border. The American influence is so pervasive that English-speaking Canadians and Americans are often hard to tell apart in speech and dress. About half of Canada's largest businesses are U.S.-controlled, and in the key oil and gas industry Canadian ownership of total production was up to only 35 percent in 1981 despite a government-backed program of takeovers. Repatriation of profits by American companies accounts for a major chunk of Canada's balance-of-payments deficit. American TV shows and magazines outsell their domestic competitors in the Canadian mass market. No wonder Canadians feel they have to remind the United States that their country is independent.

The strains are a long way from the crisis level. Early U.S. hopes of annexing Canada faded over a century ago. The common border is famous as the longest unfortified international border in the world. The two countries' common interests are not only economic but strategic: Canada has given this country important support in ballistic missile defense, in NATO, and in international conflicts from Korea to the Middle East. And

Canada's exceptional services to UN peacekeeping and peacemaking have served a basic world interest in which the United States shares.

In bilateral relations, Washington has sensibly steered clear of the Quebec issue. The issues that do arise—such as Ottawa's curbs on U.S. investment in Canadian oil, or friction over U.S. fishing rights in Canadian waters, or pollution from U.S. smokestacks falling as acid rain in Canada— are all matters that diplomacy can solve, or at least keep under control, so long as both sides are mindful of their common interests and of each other's needs.

ANGLOS AND LATINOS: CULTURES IN COLLISION

Far deeper are the tensions and conflicting interests that have long troubled U.S. relations with Latin America; for along its southern frontier this country is a close neighbor to nations whose histories are profoundly different from its own, and which now number about half again as many people as there are in the United States itself. These tensions cannot safely be neglected, for great common interests are also at stake: hemispheric security, human rights, and, most conspicuously, economic well-being. Latin America ranks just after Canada and the European Common Market in trade with the United States—Brazil, Mexico, and Venezuela accounting for the lion's share of the total.

In many respects—size, population, climate, resources, ethnic composition, and culture—the Latin American republics are extremely varied. But most of them (Mexico in recent times has been a conspicuous exception) share one basic political problem: inability to agree on a constitutional means of deciding who has the legitimate right to rule. Political instability is the result.

This problem is a legacy of Latin America's colonial past. For over 300 years the region was ruled by the absolutist kings of Spain and Portugal through their local viceroys. Representative government was unheard of. Between 1810 and 1824, after the two monarchies were overthrown during the Napoleonic wars, the Latin American provinces declared themselves independent. They then attempted to superimpose republican constitutions on rigidly stratified societies—people of European ancestry at the top, those of mixed race (mestizos) in the middle, Indians or African slaves or their descendants at the bottom. There was little sense of nationhood and still less experience with self-government. The most important political loyalties were personal ties, usually to leading families or exceptional individuals on the local or regional scene. Ever since, most Latin American republics have been chronically embroiled in struggles over the right to rule, with periods of democracy alternating with periods of dictatorship. Often, when political party struggles were mainly among local factions, the armed forces have emerged as the only group with a strong enough national sense to hold the country together, usually by dictatorial means.

But even military governments could not prevent frequent intervals of violence as factions competed for political and economic power. In recent decades the violence and disorder have tended to widen as landless farm workers and others at the bottom of the socioeconomic ladder, once inactive politically, began to enter the political arena in countries as diverse as Brazil, Colombia, and the small republics of Central America, and to press their demands for a larger share of the goods of life.

Yet, despite all the instability and arbitrary rule, Latin Americans throughout the hemisphere—some in office, some in opposition, some in exile—have upheld the rights and dignity of the individual and the ideal of lawful, constitutional republicanism. At times this has seemed little more than a verbal ideal, perhaps mere lip service; but many Latin American politicians have striven mightily, often at risk of life and limb, to translate it into political reality.

In Chapter 2 we recalled how the United States, from its very beginnings, exerted an influence on Latin America—first as an anticolonial inspiration; then under the Monroe Doctrine as a self-appointed protector; then as an aggressively expansionist power at the expense of Mexico and later in the Caribbean; and finally, in the early twentieth century, as builder and master of the Panama Canal and the dominant presence throughout the Caribbean. Again and again in that last phase, the United States intervened with troops in Caribbean and Central American countries to restore order, protect American lives and investments, and keep the Europeans out.

After 1945: Latin Challenge, U.S. Response

Although the United States had formally renounced its policy of intervention years before World War II, when the war ended in 1945 it seemed to be more supreme in the hemisphere than ever. To be sure, the Treaty of Rio de Janeiro, a mutual defense pact between the United States and all the Latin American republics signed in 1947, made the hemispheric system formally multilateral, an association of equals. The same is true of the Organization of American States—an outgrowth of the old Pan-American Union—formed in 1948 to implement the defense treaty and promote economic and social cooperation. These were Washington's concessions to Latin American pride, and perhaps something more—steps toward a less lopsided, more truly reciprocal, inter-American community.

But there was never much doubt when meetings were held at OAS headquarters in Washington which member had the decisive voice. Nor was there any doubt that the outside threat which had primarily brought the Rio Pact into being came from the Soviet Union, the global rival of the United States. Defense of the hemisphere against Soviet penetration became, in effect, the new Monroe Doctrine—embraced not only by the United States but by numerous Latin American governments that looked to this country for protection against domestic as well as foreign challenges. Significantly, until the Cuban revolution of 1959 only two out of the twenty Latin American republics, Mexico and Argentina, maintained diplomatic relations with Moscow.

It soon turned out that the age of U.S. military intervention—what Theodore Roosevelt had called the "big stick"—was not over after all. In 1954 a leftist government in Guatemala, which had expropriated plantations of the U.S.-owned United Fruit Company, was overthrown by an invading right-wing army organized by the CIA. In 1958 in Venezuela, by contrast, a U.S.-backed anti-Communist democratic coalition restored free elections and multiparty government after years of right-wing dictatorship—and Venezuela's major reserves of oil, produced by the U.S.-owned Creole Petroleum Company, continued to flow unmolested to heat and illuminate the U.S. East Coast. The message seemed to be: Washington prefers freely elected governments so long as they side with it in the world struggle and are not excessively hostile to U.S. economic interests.

In 1959 the anti-Communist effort suffered a spectacular reverse. The scene was Cuba, where a fragile democracy had been crushed in the 1930s by the dictator Fulgencio Batista, and whose shaky economy depended mainly on a sugar industry dominated by U.S. firms. The charismatic Fidel Castro, after three years of guerrilla war, overthrew Batista and became "maximum leader." He shot or banished his political rivals, imposed a one-party Communist dictatorship, confiscated U.S. properties, vilified the United States, turned to the Soviet Union, and set out to spread his revolution in Latin America. Washington answered with an embargo on trade and diplomatic relations—later joined by all Latin America except

Mexico—and then with a CIA-organized invasion by Cuban exiles. Their landing in the Bay of Pigs in April 1961 was a fiasco. Castro redoubled his hostility, received Soviet military aid, permitted the building of Soviet military and naval facilities, and in 1962 briefly became host to the Soviet nuclear missiles that led to the most dangerous crisis in the history of U.S.-Soviet relations.*

U.S. interventions elsewhere still continued, and some were effective. In the 1960s U.S. covert action helped unseat leftist governments in Brazil and Guyana. In 1965 President Johnson sent Marines to the Dominican Republic to help opponents of the leftist Juan Bosch prevent him from assuming the presidency to which he had been elected. (In that case the eventual political outcome was more democratic than those of other interventions elsewhere: in 1978, for the first time in Dominican history, an opposition party took office after winning an election.) And in Chile in 1973, when the freely elected government of Salvador Allende, a Marxist, ran into furious domestic opposition and was overthrown by a right-wing military junta, the CIA and U.S. business firms—whose Chilean properties Allende had expropriated—had a hand in the proceedings.

Such tough actions, however, were not the only U.S. answer to Castro. Beginning in 1960, and still more in 1961 under President Kennedy's Alliance for Progress policy, Washington framed economic development programs to relieve the poverty and injustices on which extremism feeds. And later, in 1977, President Carter used the lever of U.S. aid to promote another idealistic goal in Latin America, the protection of human rights. Neither aim was pursued long enough or vigorously enough to make a fair test of its practicality. But one lesson was clear: no government likes to be told in public by a foreign power—least of all by a superpower—what to do about its domestic problems. This was shown, for example, by the indignant reactions in Argentina, Brazil, and Uruguay, all of which were then going through a cycle of left-wing terrorism and governmental repression, when Carter sought to apply pressure on them in behalf of human rights. Suspension of small, symbolic U.S. military aid programs was a self-defeating gesture, giving all three governments a cost-free opportunity to thumb their noses at Washington by canceling the programs for good.

*See pages 78–83.

Washington's New Hemispheric Agenda

As in earlier times, the parts of the hemisphere of highest importance to the interests of the United States in recent years have been those near its southern border: the Caribbean, Central America, and Mexico. But trouble spots in South America need constant watching too, for the economic and strategic importance of that continent is already considerable and likely to increase.

An acute tension point in the Caribbean area until very recently was the **Panama Canal** issue. Beginning in 1964, anti-U.S. riots in Panama led to 13 years of on-and-off negotiations to replace the one-sided treaty of 1903. In 1978 the Senate, after bitter debate, narrowly approved two new treaties, one to turn over the canal and Canal Zone to Panama by stages, ending in the year 2000; the other giving the United States a permanent responsibility for the canal's security and neutrality. There could still be friction in future years over implementation of the treaties. The Senate, in consenting to them, attached a reservation asserting the right to send U.S. forces into Panama proper if necessary to defend the canal—a provision that was deeply resented in Panama and would surely raise a hemispheric storm if ever acted on. Politically, fulfillment of both treaties' terms— including relinquishment of U.S. military facilities in the Canal Zone— could hinge on success or failure between now and 1999 in dealing with anti-U.S. political movements nearby, especially in Central America.

Relations with **Cuba** had begun to ease by the 1970s. Washington had failed to unseat Castro; he had failed to manage his economy or export his revolution; the situation was a standoff. In 1974 talks began on possible renewal of U.S.-Cuban diplomatic relations—only to be broken off in 1975 when Cuban forces turned up in Angola.

Cuba remains a thorn in America's side both in Africa and in Central America. In the Caribbean, however, Castro's influence has been fading. His championship of independence for the U.S. Commonwealth of Puerto Rico has aroused more interest at the UN than in Puerto Rico itself. His most important Caribbean friend, the socialist Michael Manley, who was prime minister of the island republic of Jamaica, lost that office in a 1980 election after years of economic mismanagement. The victor, Edward Seaga, a strong free-enterprise man, sent Manley's Cuban advisers home. Heartened by this news, the Reagan Administration sought the cooperation of Mexico and Venezuela in planning for a new "Caribbean basin" economic development program—a project still largely in the talk stage in 1982 as the other partners disputed Washington's emphasis on private investment as the main theme. Whatever the means, some improvement in the region is a clear U.S. interest. The Caribbean's crowded, poverty-wracked islands—notably Haiti, the poorest and worst-governed of them all—are an important source of illegal immigration to this country and a breeding ground for political trouble.

Central America's Agony

In Central America in the 1970s, military regimes controlled mainly by big landowners came increasingly under attack. First to succumb was the 46-year Somoza dynasty in Nicaragua, toppled by a left-wing coalition in 1979 after 18 months of civil war. Months later in El Salvador, after years of sputtering warfare between the military and leftist guerrillas, a coalition of civilians and colonels deposed the dictatorship and, with U.S. backing, started a sweeping land reform program. But most of the political center, although still in office, quickly lost power as the old murderous pattern of left versus right reasserted itself, and the tide of indiscriminate killings rose again. The official land reform languished, sabotaged by both extremes, which saw it as an obstacle to their competing bids for exclusive power. Fighting was still under way in El Salvador in 1982 and was spilling over into neighboring Honduras. Washington accused Cuba and Nicaragua of giving military aid to the insurgents, and responded by giving U.S. military aid to the established governments. It also began to support Nicaraguan exiles in their efforts to subvert the Nicaraguan government.

In late 1981 the Salvadoran government was being urged by Mexico, Venezuela, and France—and, later, Spain—to negotiate with its foes for a political compromise; but the Reagan Administration took a tougher stand. It pinned its hopes on a March 1982 national election for a provisional government, in which insurgents who laid down their arms would be entitled to vote. Although the insurgent armies boycotted the election and did their best to sabotage it, the turnout was large. To the consternation of the moderates, the biggest gainers were the parties of the extreme right, said to be financed by Salvadoran exiles in Florida. Killings by right-wing death squads resumed, with U.S.-supported politicians of the moderate center among the victims; the half-implemented land reform program was cut back further; and the war continued. The U.S. Congress, having called for periodic presidential reports on El Salvador's human rights performance as a condition of further aid, reacted skeptically to

President Reagan's certification that the Salvadorans were improving in this respect.

Meanwhile there was spreading conflict nearby. The Salvadoran guerrillas, crossing northeast into neighboring Honduras, found themselves fighting alongside Honduran insurgents against the U.S.-backed Honduran army. On its Nicaraguan frontier, Honduras was working with the U.S. Army and with Indian refugees from Nicaragua in what looked like a low-level border war. Nicaragua's own revolution, originally a coalition affair, had moved steadily into Cuba's orbit. And in Guatemala, a big power by Central American standards, hope faded for an early or moderate solution to an increasingly brutal guerrilla war, already two years old and spilling over into southern Mexico. There, too, the adversaries were landowners backed by the army on one side, and on the other side a coalition of Communist and non-Communist groups mainly representing the landless poor. Many of the unassimilated Indians who make up the majority in Guatemala, and who had customarily had nothing to do with the white man's politics, had joined the guerrillas. Only Costa Rica, famed as Central America's citadel of democracy, still hoped to steer clear of the region's turmoil; but its own situation, strained by economic crisis and pressure from warring neighbors, also looked precarious.

Why all this turbulence in these Central American countries once derided as the sleepy home of "banana republics"? Gross inequality is part of the answer: plantation wealth in the hands of a few families, with the majority remaining in poverty. Not all the violence against this inequality is new. In Nicaragua the revolutionaries of 1979 took their name, Sandinista, from a murdered revolutionary of the 1920s; insurgents in El Salvador were crushed in 1932 with tens of thousands killed; and Guatemala's aborted left-wing movement of 1954 is not forgotten. But the trouble came to a head in the late 1970s chiefly because of the corrupt excesses of the U.S.-backed Nicaraguan dictator, the young Anastasio Somoza, who appropriated a large part of the country's wealth to himself and suppressed all opposition. The spark was provided in 1979 when an outburst of bitter criticism of Somoza in the Nicaraguan press, whose freedom had been briefly restored under Carter Administration pressure, was answered by the murder of a leading opposition editor.

Soon the Sandinistas' example was being followed in neighboring countries, eagerly assisted in all cases by Castro's Cuba. Again and again, Washington's intermittent attempts to steer the politics of Nicaragua and its strife-torn neighbors toward a middle, tolerant, democratic course were blown away in the whirlwind of battle between the two extremes; and the United States found itself reluctantly siding with the extreme right.

Mexico: Big Problems Next Door

Perhaps weightiest of all for U.S. interests, although still entirely nonviolent, is the problem of relations with **Mexico**. As the 1980s began, Mexico had a strong and stable government but a formidable set of economic problems: persistent rural poverty, an alarmingly rapid growth in population, very high unemployment, bulging cities, rising food import bills—and an annual emigration to the United States, mostly illegal, estimated as high as one million. The great weapon against all these difficulties, Mexico hopes, is its enormous new oil wealth, against which it has borrowed heavily from foreign banks. It seems determined to use oil exports not only to finance its neglected agricultural and rural development but to influence U.S. policy on migration, trade, and investment. But its acute financial crisis in 1982, when sagging world oil prices left Mexico with a mountain of unpaid foreign debts, gave new proof of how vulnerable any economy is that relies heavily on exports of one commodity.

For Mexico, emigration across the Rio Grande is an economic safety valve. For the United States it is an economic and political threat, especially in a time of recession and high unemployment. Thus far the main U.S. answer, none too effective, has combined tougher deportation efforts and border controls with proposals to increase the number of legally admissible migrants and to legalize the status of many "illegals" already on U.S. soil. Mexico argues that a better method would be U.S. cooperation to help Mexico grow more of its own food, sell more products in U.S. markets, and improve the quality of its rural life, thus reducing the incentive to emigrate. It remains to be seen how Washington will respond—and, for that matter, whether any Mexican government is politically capable of effective aid to its sadly neglected and fast-growing rural population.

South America: Trouble Beyond Our Reach?

In April 1982, like a bolt from the blue, Argentina invaded and seized the disputed Falkland Islands (it calls them the Malvinas), a small group with less than 2,000 British inhabitants some 400 miles off Argentina's South Atlantic coast. The islands had been held by Britain for a century and a half, and claimed by Argentina for at least as long. Negotiations on the dispute had been under way for years and were seemingly progressing when the blow fell. In Argentine politics, the invasion was apparently a desperate move by a shaky military junta to rally a discontented people at a time of economic distress.

By mid-June the fighting was over, Britain had regained the islands at painful military cost, and a new group of Argentine generals had thrown out the government that ordered the attack. Most observers thought the war had been completely unnecessary—one which Argentina had no good reason to start, but which Britain had failed to anticipate and had done little to prevent diplomatically or prepare for militarily.

Diplomatically, the war created nothing but problems for the United States. At first, perhaps partly because Argentina was helping in the antiguerrilla wars of Central America, the Reagan Administration had played the role of mediator—thereby infuriating the British who expected more of their NATO ally. When mediation failed and the war turned in Britain's favor, so did the United States—thereby not only infuriating the Argentines but evoking angry rhetoric from much of the rest of Latin America, especially Guatemala and Venezuela, which have territorial bones to pick with former British colonies.

Small though it may be in the eye of history, the Falklands conflict was one more reminder that South America, a continent only tenuously within reach of U.S. influence, contains much potential for political trouble. Colombia is a fragile democracy, long threatened by a chronic insurgency of the poor. Ecuador and Peru, rich in oil and minerals but still poor in living standards, strive to maintain democratic government despite economic stress and only feeble authority over their large Indian populations in the high Andes. Mountainous, mineral-rich Bolivia, most of whose people are also Indian, has had on the average more than two changes of government per year since World War II. Chile, largely a mining state but partly industrialized, still stifles politically under the right-wing dictatorship that overthrew the chaotic Allende government in 1973. Landlocked, agricultural Paraguay is a tight one-man dictatorship. Recently Uruguay, once a shining example of democracy in South America, has been wracked with guerrilla warfare and ruled by a military junta.

But the continent's greatest uncertainties come from the rising power of Brazil and Argentina, the two most populous and powerful countries in South America. Their histories tell of brilliant cultural and scientific achievements and of struggles to establish stable democracy—but also of political turmoil, civil wars, terrorism, and repression. Although the early 1980s found them overextended financially and heavily in debt to foreign banks, they have important economic and technological capacity and still greater potential. Both, however, are still politically unstable and ruled by military governments—though they keep trying to return to democracy and regular multiparty elections. Adding to Washington's worries is the fact that both have made important progress in nuclear technology and have never unequivocally promised not to acquire nuclear weapons.

Argentina and Brazil are both loners in Latin American politics. Brazil is the sole hemispheric heir to Portuguese culture. Argentina, once Spain's southernmost colony, is proudly European in ancestry and culture and disdainful of neighboring countries with a strong Indian or African heritage—preferring, in fact, not even to be called "Latin American." The two have a long history of wars and bitter disputes and are generally regarded as regional rivals—a fact that adds an edge to their nuclear aspirations. Highly resistant to pressure from the United States, these two states seem destined to play an increasing role in the power equations of the hemisphere. How to reconcile that role with U.S. interests, and with the common interest in hemispheric peace, is sure to be a nagging question on Washington's foreign policy agenda for many years to come.

Part III
The Issues

Hence we see very plainly that warlike pursuits, although generally deemed honorable, are not the supreme end of all things, but only means. And the good lawgiver should inquire how states and races of men and communities may participate in a good life, and in the happiness that is attainable by them.

Aristotle
Politics, Book VII

8
Global Issues I: War, Peace, and Human Rights

As the preceding chapters demonstrate, many of the problems that arise for U.S. foreign policy in different parts of the world bear a family resemblance. This chapter and the next will look a little further into five broad groups of issues of this kind. The five headings are: (1) peace and security; (2) human rights; (3) economic and social needs; (4) the planetary environment and human population; and (5) world order.

It will become clear as we proceed that these large issues are global in more than a geographic sense. In all cases there is a *global interest* in solving them in a generally acceptable way. The terms of any particular solution, of course, are likely to arouse controversy. But even where controversy is sharpest, all nations share an interest in finding solutions that will at least be more tolerable than continued conflict. That common interest is often forgotten in the heat of the struggle but it does not cease to exist.

The five categories used here must not be taken too literally, for reality cannot be tucked neatly into boxes. Issues in one category can be linked in many ways to those in another. Some linkages are in the nature of the case—as between population growth, economic growth, and environmental problems. Others arise simply from the tendency of governments to bargain: "I'll do this political favor for you if you'll do that economic favor for me." This latter kind of linkage can sometimes break a stubborn deadlock; at other times it can turn a simple dispute into a complex and durable one.

PEACE AND SECURITY

Finding ways to maintain national interests without war; limiting wars when they happen; avoiding or at least controlling arms races—such peace-and-security issues probably have long been at the top of the foreign policy agenda, but two modern circumstances have focused increased attention on them. First, the news media have made ordinary citizens more vividly aware of the once remote horrors of the battlefield. Second, there has been a quantum jump in the destructiveness of weapons. Nuclear powers especially, although they often exchange hot words and sometimes get into conventional wars against lesser powers, are exceedingly cautious about direct confrontation with each other.

This is notably true of the strategic contest between the two superpowers, whose power balance in Europe has proved remarkably stable ever since World War II. It was mainly Soviet power—first the fear of it in the West, then the reality of it in the East—that brought the two alliances into being; but the resulting balance of power is maintained by mutual nuclear deterrence and mutual fear. To the West, the Soviet Union is still the dominant power of the Eurasian continent, a largely closed system, self-isolated and menacing. To the Soviets, the West with its seductive ways of life and its history of Napoleon's and Hitler's aggressions probably looks just as menacing—something to be kept at a distance, like an infectious disease, by the "sanitary cordon" of Warsaw Pact states.

George F. Kennan, originator of the containment concept, wrote in 1947 that such a policy might eventually result in "either the breakup or the gradual mellowing of Soviet power." There has been no breakup, and only a certain amount of mellowing. Despite considerable improvement in the treatment of individuals by the Soviet state (see next section), the official Soviet propaganda line still blames the sinister designs of imperialism for the heavy cost of the Soviet military forces, and thus for the hardships of Soviet life; and the views of the few Soviet citizens who dare to dissent publicly from the official line are still relentlessly suppressed in the controlled Soviet media. But—and this is fundamentally important—every Soviet leader since the death of Stalin has agreed with his American counterpart that nuclear war would mean mutual suicide and that prolonged coexistence of the two systems is unavoidable.

The Superpowers and Nuclear Arms

This cautious realism has not, however, prevented nuclear weapons from playing a major part in the military strategy of both superpowers (see Chapter 4). Most Western authorities agree that Soviet nuclear forces increased substantially faster than those of the United States during the 1970s in several major categories. In strategic weapons, these include multimegaton ICBMs and missile-launching submarines. In the European theater, Soviet SS-20 intermediate-range missiles and Backfire bombers were seen as a new threat to the balance.

Some experts argue that the threat is exaggerated, pointing out that the U.S. nuclear arsenal at every level from battlefield to strategic weapons is extremely formidable. Moreover, U.S. strategic weapons development, notably the Trident submarine, cruise missiles, and the MX missile, has by no means been standing still. And Britain, France, and China all maintain their own nuclear deterrent forces, which are "small" only by comparison with those of the superpowers. The Soviets, this school of thought maintains, would no more dare to take the terrible risk of crossing the nuclear threshold than the West would, and hence cannot credibly threaten to do so. In this view, the Soviet nuclear buildup, both in Europe and at the strategic level, is no wiser or more necessary than that of the West—but neither is it more threatening.

But the governments of the United States and its NATO allies have not evaluated the situation that way. The resolve of the NATO governments in 1979 to emplace new U.S. "theater" nuclear weapons in Europe reflected their belief that the Soviet SS-20s and Backfire bombers were tipping the European balance and must be countered. And a similar sense of alarm about Soviet strategic weapons underlay Washington's determination, under both the Carter and Reagan administrations, to accelerate the further buildup of its strategic-weapons "triad" in all three environments land, sea, and air.

Confusing though it is, the essence of the nuclear debate has not changed since the atomic bomb was invented. It concerns two very different dangers. The first is the danger of utter *physical* disaster in an all-out nuclear war that might well put an end to both superpowers, and some European countries too, as organized societies. The other danger is of *political* disaster if, for example, the Soviet Union, having somehow achieved decisive nuclear superiority, succeeded in dominating Europe or the Middle East after a short conventional war or even without firing a shot—merely by nuclear blackmail.

In this discussion both these dangers can be considered together, for what prevents either of them from happening is the same thing: effective deterrence. The power that is strong enough to deter armed attack is strong enough not to tremble or give way in the face of threats. The overriding question of military policy facing each of the superpowers, therefore, is how to maintain the deterrent strength on which its side of the global power balance depends.

The problem has been complicated by advances in nuclear weapons technology. New delivery vehicles, especially ICBMs, have such accurate guidance systems and other improvements that they could be used in a counterforce attack to destroy opposing ICBMs in their silos. As a result, confidence in the stability of mutual deterrence has been somewhat shaken. Former U.S. strategic arms negotiator Paul C. Warnke put the matter this way: "As your ICBMs become both more dangerous and more vulnerable . . . there is the temptation to strike first because you fear you won't be able to strike second."

Why have both sides—the Americans again in the lead—considered it worthwhile to build such weapons? In part, the stated aim on the American side is to deter a possible Soviet *limited nuclear attack*—or even an overwhelming "conventional" attack by the larger armies of the Warsaw Pact—in some future crisis by building a capacity for *limited nuclear response*, such as a superaccurate "surgical" strike against a Soviet ICBM site or some other military installation. A more urgent aim for both the Carter and Reagan administrations has been to ward off what many regard as a massive Soviet threat. The Soviet ICBM force, it is said, will become powerful and accurate enough by the mid-1980s to destroy all or most of the U.S. ICBM force in a single strike. The main U.S. answer is the proposed MX missile system, presented as a way to make the U.S. ICBM force mobile and less vulnerable. Ironically, there has been much controversy over whether a mobile MX launching system can be devised at bearable cost—but little controversy over plans to make the missile itself more accurate, more powerful, and more heavily "MIRVed" than the Minuteman force it is designed to replace. Yet it is these latter characteristics of the MX that pose an increased counterforce threat to the Soviet strategic arsenal—which, much more than the American one, is concentrated in fixed-base ICBMs.

Despite all such technological advances, some critics have dismissed the talk of counterforce attacks by either side, whether all-out or limited, as largely fantasy—dangerous only to the extent that such talk might be believed and acted on. Against the supposed danger of an *all-out* counterforce attack, they argue that no government in its right mind would gamble its national existence on the mere hope that its first strike, by a weapons system never yet used in combat, might destroy the will or ability of the other side to retaliate with equally devastating effect. What if, for example, the defender's ICBMs were launched almost the minute the attacker's launching was detected, leaving the aggressor missiles to strike empty silos? What about the defender's strategic bombers, able to be airborne minutes after the first alert—and, still more invulnerable, its nuclear-armed submarines, constantly on the move and hard to track?

Similar doubts are expressed about the supposed plausibility of a *limited* counterforce attack—or even the use of "battlefield" nuclear weapons, no matter how small—by either side. Would the United States, for instance, really dare to fire the first nuclear artillery shell into a superior Soviet ground army attacking Western Europe? Or to launch one superaccurate warhead to destroy one Soviet ICBM silo, arms factory, or the like, as a "warning shot" to gain the upper hand in some future European or Middle East war? How could it be sure the Soviets would not counterattack on a larger scale, escalating the nuclear exchanges to who knows what level? This would be all the more likely if the first U.S. attack turned out to be less "surgical" than intended and inflicted heavy devastation on civilian areas nearby.

The uncertainty surrounding such questions must weigh heavily against *any* use of nuclear weapons in war—except in reply to an enemy that has used them first. And the mere possibility of that devastating reply tends to keep deterrence stable. Yet not entirely so—for ever since counterforce attacks became technically possible, there has been a lingering fear that jumpy nerves in the command center on one or both sides might some day produce the hair-trigger state of mind that Warnke described.

Amid such murky imponderables, as much psychological as technical, the strategic doctrines concerning nuclear weapons remain confused. Some bold souls argue that a nuclear war could be fought and won, just like other wars, with heavy but acceptable casualties; and military specialists on both sides have flirted with such ideas—understandably, for what is a soldier to think of a weapon he is forbidden to use? But not for many years has the *government* of either superpower even pretended to believe that a full-scale nuclear exchange could be won by anybody. As for limited nuclear war, whatever theories or doctrines may be aired at times, the actual behavior of both sides strongly suggests that they understand well enough that *any* war between them, armed as they are, must never happen.

Why, then, must the two sides continue the ever-spiraling race in these weapons that must not be used—a race so resistant to control by negotiation? The answer seems to be that each continually suspects the other of planning to break out of the deadlock called mutual deterrence and make a dash for decisive nuclear superiority—whatever that term may mean. Indeed, on the American side at least, it seems to be assumed that any relative increase in the capabilities of Soviet nuclear weapons means a corresponding increase in Soviet world power at the expense of this country—and, of course, vice versa.

Many critics also reject this assumption. They maintain that traditional measures of military superiority or equality—such as numbers or explosive power of weapons—do not mean much as long as each side retains a credible capacity to destroy the other. It is estimated that there are 10,000 or so strategic warheads on the American side, and a somewhat lower but rising number on the Soviet side; yet it is widely agreed that a small fraction of these would suffice (if most reached their targets, and who is to say they would not?) to reduce all of both countries' major cities and their populations to radioactive rubble. What difference, then, does it make whether one side has x times, and the other y times, the capacity to do the job? A human being does not have to be killed twice. According to this view, the only equality between the two sides that really counts strategically is the equal capacity to deter.*

However, prenuclear concepts of military power die hard. In the early years of the SALT debates, American politicians insisted on some visible equality of numbers which the uninformed American-in-the-street could easily grasp. A complaint against the SALT I agreement of 1972 was that it froze the numbers of missile launchers (other than bombers) on the two sides at a moment when the Russians had more of them, even though the Americans were "ahead" in other ways. On the Senate's insistence, the SALT II treaty of 1979 therefore provided for exactly equal numbers in all categories. But then other inequalities cropped up, as already noted, some of them in the Soviets' favor. These have often been pictured as

---

*Concerning "the insignificance of nuclear superiority" in the Cuban missile crisis of 1962, see page 80.

confronting, or at least threatening, the United States with a strategic choice in any future crisis between surrender and annihilation.

The debate between this view and its opponents, with many shadings of difference in between, continues as this is written. As the 1980s began, the NATO governments' official pronouncements about the menace of Soviet theater nuclear weapons and the need to counter them in the West gave rise to a surge of public fear and a vigorous antinuclear movement in Western Europe. It soon spread to the United States, where it drew further stimulus from the menacing nuclear rhetoric sometimes uttered by President Reagan and Caspar W. Weinberger, his Secretary of Defense. The movement's strength was evident both in public demonstrations and in the major attention given to several proposals. Prominent among these were:

- That the United States press for early agreement with the Soviets on that elusive project, a comprehensive, adequately verifiable ban on all testing of nuclear weapons. This would mean a virtual halt in the development of new nuclear weapon systems—an outcome that the technologically superior American side has for many years seemed particularly reluctant to face.
- That the United States join the Soviet Union and, if possible, other nuclear powers in a pledge not to be the first to use nuclear weapons in a future war. This "no first use" concept was rejected in Washington, partly on the premise that nuclear weapons are still NATO's "equalizer" against superior Warsaw Pact ground forces. As long as NATO lacks the will to strengthen its conventional forces, it was argued, such a pledge would create more confusion than confidence.
- That both superpowers, pending agreements on strategic and European intermediate-range weapons, agree at once to freeze their nuclear arsenals at present levels. This nuclear freeze proposal gained wide popular and congressional backing. In August 1982 a resolution favoring it came within two votes of passing the House of Representatives. A considerable White House lobbying effort was required to defeat it.

The Reagan Administration, faced with such antinuclear trends but still committed to redress what it insisted was Soviet nuclear superiority, adopted a dual strategy. It pressed for, and Congress agreed to, a massive strategic—as well as conventional—arms buildup over several years, giving this program top budgetary priority in a period of budget deficits and cuts in domestic spending. But is also opened nuclear arms control talks with the Russians at both the strategic and the European level. In both negotiations, the opening U.S. proposals called for sharp reductions in existing nuclear arsenals, with much deeper cuts on the Soviet side. The opening Soviet proposals, as expected, leaned the opposite way. Long negotiations were in prospect. Whether they would result in an actual reduction in nuclear stockpiles—the first ever—remained highly uncertain.*

In sum, President Reagan seemed intent on proving himself a man of peace—but the peace was to be based on increased U.S. military power. At times the warnings in Washington against Soviet superiority sounded like a call not for equality but for a restoration of the nuclear superiority that the United States itself once possessed. Some argued that in an all-out nuclear arms race with the Soviet Union the United States, budget deficit or no, would come out ahead, and once again be, in some meaningful sense, "number one." As for the Soviet Union, its leaders, despite their economic headaches, have often proclaimed their country's readiness to hold its own in such a race if need be.

Thus, in many minds in Washington—and perhaps in Moscow too—the strategic question of the day still seemed to be, in the famous words of Lewis Carroll's Humpty Dumpty: " . . . which is to be master—that's all." Yet what "master" or "superior" can mean in the nuclear circumstances of the late twentieth century has never been clearly explained.

Third-World Insecurities

As previous chapters have shown, a recurrent problem for the United States in the third world, and to some extent in Latin America, is how to deal with military threats to U.S.-backed governments. Assuming that important U.S. interests are at stake, should U.S. armed forces be sent, or is it enough to give military aid to the threatened friend?

Intervention by U.S. forces in local conflicts, even when widely objected to, has sometimes proved effective in achieving limited aims. In Lebanon in 1958, and again in the Dominican Republic in 1965, the presence of a few thousand U.S. Marines helped to save—or install— pro-American governments without major hostilities, and in both cases the

---

*The outlook was equally uncertain for the decade-old Vienna talks on reducing the two alliances' conventional forces in Europe. The perceived Soviet advantage in conventional forces, it should be remembered, has been the main argument for NATO's dependence on theater nuclear weapons.

Marines were withdrawn soon afterward. But this instrument of policy has been a sticky subject since the Vietnam War. As Vietnam showed, even when intervention is requested by the host government, if political conditions are unfavorable it may simply galvanize nationalist opposition to the foreign intruder. In Central America's current conflicts the U.S. military presence thus far has been small and, on congressional insistence, strictly advisory. In the Middle East it has been mainly naval, and hence out of sight of land most of the time. However, U.S. air and ground uits held small, well-publicized maneuvers in Egypt and Oman late in 1981—a demonstration that some U.S. capability to intervene in the event of trouble does exist.

The Soviet Union's war in Afghanistan is, thus far, its only such venture in the third world. Elsewhere, when pro-Soviet participation in combat was called for, it has relied on proxies or tactical allies, such as Vietnam, Cuba, Libya, and Southern Yemen, whose aims are compatible with Moscow's and whose personnel blend better than Russians can with the political scenery of third-world countries. Similarly, to provide third-world countries with military advice on training, Moscow has often relied on such friends as Cuba, East Germany, and North Korea.

Both superpowers have made increasing use of the second approach, **the supply of weapons**, usually combined in the American case with economic aid. In the period 1979–1981 the Soviet Union accounted for over 36 percent of the world arms traffic; the United States (formerly number 1) for 34 percent; France 10 percent, and Italy, Britain, and West Germany another 10 percent between them. Other significant suppliers include Austria, Brazil, China, Czechoslovakia, Israel, and North Korea. Since the OPEC oil boom of the 1970s, a rising proportion of all international arms sales have gone to developing countries.

The suppliers' interests in this traffic vary. All foreign sales, military or otherwise, are good for the seller's balance of payments, especially when paid for in cash by oil-rich countries (which sometimes happens even when the buyer, such as Egypt, Pakistan, or Sudan, is poor). The official aim, however, and probably the truly dominant aim in most cases, is to strengthen a friendly power that feels threatened. In some cases the friendly ruler may be partly motivated by a desire for prestige and wider influence—in which case, like Iran's ill-fated shah, he may demand more technologically sophisticated and deadly weapons than his forces really need. Even in such cases, Washington may provide the requested weapons rather than see the ambitious friend take his shopping list to Moscow instead—as Egypt did in 1955, and Peru in the late 1960s.

Another frequent U.S. aim in foreign military sales is to provide a steady flow of business to manufacturers who also supply the U.S. armed forces, thus obtaining the lower unit price that goes with higher volume. Finally, as in all government procurement, there is an element of domestic politics, for arms contracts mean jobs and profits, and that means votes—especially when business is slack and unemployment is high. So strong are such purely domestic pressures at times that policy-makers find it virtually impossible to concentrate on the diplomatic and strategic issues which arms sales are supposed to serve.

Presidential policy on U.S. arms sales abroad has ranged from on-and-off discouragement during the Carter Administration to active promotion under President Reagan. Congress has acted from time to time to ban or discourage politically controversial arms transfers, especially to Arab foes of Israel, to Turkey because of its quarrels with Greece, and to repressive right-wing regimes in Central America. Some critics argue that the competition in arms supplies makes third-world wars more deadly and diverts money from socially desirable programs. They also point out—as the record in Egypt, Indonesia, Peru, Iran, and others has shown—that the source of a developing country's weapons cannot determine for very long which way its foreign policy will lean. Still, the competitive traffic goes on apace; and third-world leaders, no strangers to the competition for national power, have seldom shown much interest in attempts to curb it.

More worrisome still is the creeping **proliferation of nuclear weapons** in the developing world. Ever since India's 1974 nuclear explosion, its much weaker rival Pakistan has been striving to follow suit. Israel's nuclear weapons capability, unannounced but never denied, may have stimulated answering attempts by Iraq and possibly other Arab states. South Africa may be close to having its own bomb. Brazil and Argentina may not be far behind.

Are these trends controllable? The outlook does not seem bright. Most of these "threshold" countries have refused to submit to full international inspection safeguards, designed to detect use of peaceful nuclear facilities for weapons manufacture. Even where the safeguards are in effect, the inspection routines of the International Atomic Energy Agency have been widely criticized as inadequate. Henry Kissinger, as President Gerald R. Ford's Secretary of State, strove with only modest success in 1975–1976 to discourage nuclear supplier countries from transferring nuclear technology in ways that might be secretly used to make bombs. A Carter Administration effort along similar lines made little headway. The Reagan Administration has given the item a lower priority and has shown more interest in promoting nuclear energy systems, including the weapons-prone fast-breeder reactor, both domestically and abroad. But it has not ignored the nuclear proliferation problem. Its plan to sell $3.2 billion worth of advanced conventional weapons to Pakistan was explained partly as an attempt to make Pakistan's leaders see these, rather than nuclear weapons, as the best means of self-defense. However, Pakistan, like India, continued to avoid a clear pledge not to go nuclear.

Another brake on the spread of nuclear weapons is the Nonproliferation Treaty of 1970 (see pages 95–96). It pledges its 113 nuclear "have-not" parties never to acquire nuclear weapons and requires them to accept international safeguards. All are believed to have kept the pledge thus far. But this alone does not solve the problem, since most threshold countries have never become parties to the treaty. (Nor is Brazil or Argentina bound by the Treaty of Tlatelolco of 1967, creating a nuclear-weapons-free zone in Latin America.) Moreover, the treaty's "have" members, especially the two superpowers, have not performed well on their treaty pledge to negotiate for a halt to—indeed, a reversal of—their own "vertical" proliferation. So, say the have-nots, why should they themselves be permanently bound to a stricter standard, dividing the world forever into two classes of power?

What seems to be lacking is not the technical capacity but the common will to bring this problem under control. Whether the mobilization of such a common will is still possible, or whether each nation's military development must go hand in hand with its economic and political develoment, remains a profoundly troubling question. Nobody knows whether the risk of a nuclear war starting in the developing world within, say, the next five years is 10 percent, or 0.01 percent, or some other fraction. But clearly such a risk exists; and any increase in the number of possessors of nuclear weapons would seem to increase it.

Underlying all these third-world military issues is a deeper question of U.S. political strategy. To what extent are U.S. interests served by forging **military alliances** with anti-Communist governments? In an earlier chapter we noted two opposing views on this question, the *globalist* and the *regionalist*. The globalist approach is more partial to such alliances, but is vulnerable to upsets if the government in question changes its mind or is overthrown, as has happened to both superpowers at times. The regionalist approach, on the other hand, assumes that both big powers will show restraint toward each other, leaving Washington free to concentrate on the particular problems of each country or region. But no ground rules for such restraint have ever been agreed on, and it is hard to conceive of rules that both adversaries would construe the same way in all situations: nor is there any global umpire to judge between them. Thus far, about the only rule of self-restraint that both superpowers have consistently observed in the third world is not to fight each other directly—a rule enforced by the instinct of self-preservation.

A related question is how to handle the function of **peacemaking** and **peacekeeping** in the developing world's conflicts. Often this work requires not only strenuous diplomatic negotiation but the posting of military contingents in danger spots. In the Middle East as well as Latin America, the United States has been more active in these ways than the Soviet Union—thus hoping to influence the terms of settlement, but also accepting the risks of failure. In some cases former colonial powers have been the main peacemakers and peacekeepers in places where they retain an interest: France, for example, in the conflicts of its former West African empire, and Britain in Rhodesia before that colony became independent as Zimbabwe.

An alternative to direct big-power involvement is to work through **international organizations**—regional bodies, such as the OAS in the Americas or the OAU in Africa; or, at the global level, the United Nations. Two basic methods are available. One is to submit a dispute for a final, binding decision by an impartial third party such as an arbitrator or a court. Widely used by the United States and others as recently as the 1920s (see Chapter 2), arbitration of international political disputes has been much less in favor since World War II. The European Court of Justice has a busy docket, but few important disputes have been submitted for binding settlement by the International Court of Justice, the UN's judicial arm. Much more frequent is settlement by direct negotiation between the disputing governments. This method too makes extensive use of impartial third parties, but as mediators and channels of communication, not as judges. Among the important sources of such help is the United Nations, especially the office of the Secretary-General. As noted earlier, the UN's success in such work depends mainly on the readiness of the powers involved to make the necessary compromises. Where that readiness was present, the UN has often been highly effective in solving, or at least defusing, dangerous disputes in the Middle East, Cyprus, the Congo (now Zaire), Kashmir, Namibia, and elsewhere. In 1982 UN diplomats were seeking a basis for withdrawl of Soviet forces from Afghanistan—an unusual case in UN peacemaking annals in that it directly involved a superpower.

The UN procedure in such conflicts is easily described, but nobody who is without great stamina and infinite patience would be wise to try it. First, if armies are still shooting, arrange a cease-fire. Then recruit and deploy an impartial "presence"—perhaps a UN or other multinational peacekeeping force—to separate the two sides. Then persuade the two sides to keep talking until they reach a compromise, which nobody will like but all will prefer to resuming the war. And back up the settlement with a reliable local balance of power—which may mean limits on outside military aid, or big-power guarantees, or both—so that neither side will be tempted to try war again as a means of getting better terms. Whoever does all that will have an excellent shot at a Nobel Peace Prize.

No power has a greater interest than the United States in building a world order that will make international life less dangerous. The creation of stronger international institutions, able to enforce peace and a common rule of law, seems a remote prospect, although they may be slowly evolving. For the present, we have only the diplomacy of the armed powers themselves, plus weak international institutions that work only when the powers want them to. It is a primitive system, but until a better one becomes possible the nations must do their best with it.

HUMAN RIGHTS

In addition to avoiding war and opposing communism, most Americans seem to want more affirmative values in the nation's foreign policy. Among these, none has had a stronger appeal than the promotion of human rights. Committed from our nation's beginnings to a belief in the "unalienable rights" of every individual, we still identify with those who seek to fulfill these rights in other countries. There are also some less obvious concerns behind the emphasis on human rights—concerns over conflicts of power and threats of war. A Soviet government minus its well-known monopoly of public information, for example, might be less able to mislead its people—and many people abroad—into believing in the necessity of a foreign policy hostile to the United States. Also, policies of repression within a nation, such as Iran, Poland, or South Africa, can stir up international emotions and threaten peace among nations. Thus human rights, peace, and power are all interdependent.

Three questions have to be considered, however, before we can be clear about the place of human rights in foreign policy. First, what *kind* of rights are we talking about? Second, *which countries'* abuses of human rights should be of most concern to the United States? Third, by what *means* should we promote these rights?

What Kind of Rights?

Americans, in the Western tradition, think of rights as belonging to individuals—something with which all persons are "endowed by their Creator," and which the state has a duty to protect.

Most basic of all individual rights are *civil liberties*: the right to say, hear, read, and believe what you choose; the right to privacy; the right to own property; to the equal protection of the laws; to a fair trial; to freedom from torture. In addition, the state must guarantee certain *political* rights: the right to vote in honest, multiparty elections; to belong to organizations; to petition the government; to run for office. All these rights are protected by the U.S. Constitution. Their application has widened greatly since the nation was founded, mainly by the inclusion of nonwhites, the ending of property qualifications for voting, and the granting of the vote to women.

Such individual rights also have international standing. They are spelled out in the famous Universal Declaration of Human Rights adopted by the UN General Assembly in 1948, when the Western political tradition was more influential in the Assembly than it is today. The declaration has had wide influence. Scores of newly independent nations have borrowed from it in writing their constitutions. It is often invoked by dissidents against repressive governments, and by such organizations as the International League for Human Rights and Freedom House.

To translate these proclaimed rights into reality in a country without a strong tradition of individual freedom can be a monumental task. In the more stable one-party states whether Communist or right-wing military dictatorships, the dissident who seeks to exercise such rights is asking for trouble. In other countries of Latin America and the third world where political life is more unsettled, periods of dictatorship and repression have been followed again and again by periods of free elections, multiparty politics, a free press, and public criticism of official policy. We who live in countries where such freedoms are the constitutionally protected norm and where any violation of them is generally considered an outrage, may find it difficult to realize how much courage it takes, for example, to risk the hazards of a free election in a country where the penalty for losing (and sometimes, indeed, for winning, if the losers have the guns on their side) may be silence, jail, exile, or even death.

There are other classes and concepts of human rights for which international support has also developed. A wide array of *economic and social* rights—rights to a decent standard of living, education, health care, etc.—was also included in the UN declaration of 1948, and further elaborated in a more recent UN treaty, or *covenant.* The germ of the idea was in the "freedom from want . . . everywhere in the world" which Franklin D. Roosevelt included among his wartime list of "four freedoms." There has been vigorous objection to this concept. To promote the individual's material well-being to the status of a right—that is, a lawful claim by the citizen against the state—is a mockery of reality, critics argue, because most governments lack the economic capacity to fulfill it. Advocates reply that that universal proclamation of such rights, even though an exaggeration of what is now possible, creates a standard of aspiration, especially in developing countries and thus puts pressure on governments to strive to meet it.

Some of the most widespread violations of human rights have operated not against individuals as such but against large *groups or classes* of people defined by race, religion, or sex. In all three of these categories there have been international efforts, either by treaty or by the force of publicity, to redress the wrongs complained of.

Just how the wrongs—and the rights—should be defined, however, can be a troublesome question. Should a person who is discriminated against for belonging to the "wrong" race, creed, or sex be guaranteed exactly the same rights as everybody else, or should he or she also enjoy special compensatory rights, such as "affirmative action" in employment? And a still more basic question: are the rights that count most those that belong to the individual, or the collective rights of the group itself—such as the claimed right of whole peoples to national self-determination and independence, or the right of a racial or language or religious group to equal power and respect?

Individualists tend to lean one way on such questions; leaders of aggrieved groups the other way. At the UN, ever since the former colonies became a majority there, group rights—especially the right of the *nation* to self-determination and independence, and of nonwhite *peoples* not to be discriminated against because of race—have held a substantial, though far from absolute, priority over issues of individual rights.

The United States does not really go along with the prevailing third-world view of human rights as essentially national or ethnic. For example, true to its own pluralistic tradition, it has opposed South Africa's apartheid policies as an offense against the rights of nonwhite *individuals.* If the offense were committed by nonwhite rulers against nonwhite victims, by

U.S. principles it would be just as grave, even though there might be less international indignation over it. To be sure, the United States has favored (although seldom pressed hard for) self-determination and independence for colonies, but has viewed this chiefly as a political, not a human rights question. Primarily, the U.S. concern in the human rights field is still with advancing the civil and political rights of the individual and with ending repression of those rights by the state.

In What Countries?

There is no denying that the United States—although not quite so blatantly as some other countries—has been somewhat selective about its emphasis on human rights abroad, applying a more rigid scrutiny to its adversaries than to its friends. As noted in earlier chapters, the United States has often backed repressive military regimes in the third world and Latin America when this seemed the best available way to meet a Communist or left-wing threat to U.S. interests. In contrast, the Soviet Union has been our main target—partly to remind world opinion that our strategic adversary has a most unattractive record in this respect, but also for more substantial purposes. A combination of public pressure and quiet diplomacy has been a factor in causing the Kremlin to grant more exit visas to Jews and others seeking to emigrate. And it has helped to restrain the persecution of famous dissidents like the late Boris Pasternak and the physicist Andrei Sakharov.

In 1977 President Carter, taking office on a wave of post-Vietnam idealism, proclaimed a U.S. concern for human rights in all countries. "No member of the United Nations," he said in a UN address, "can claim that mistreatment of its citizens is solely its own business." Human rights achieved a new visibility in the State Department and in U.S. policy. Some changes for the better were reported in such countries in Indonesia, South Korea, and the Dominican Republic. In 1981 the Reagan Administration issued mixed signals, first saying that Communist violations were especially objectionable and would have its main attention, then proposing to speak and act even handedly against violations anywhere. It has continued to obey a congressional mandate, laid down during the Carter Administration, requiring an annual State Department report on the condition of human rights throughout the world.

No matter who is President, human rights often yield to other priorities in U.S. foreign policy. When major negotiations with the Soviet Union were in prospect, Washington's attention to the plight of Soviet dissidents has sometimes been toned down. The Carter Administration had little to say about wholesale repression by our then Middle East ally, the shah of Iran. And the repression of political opponents by successive governments in strategic South Korea has been treated very gingerly in Washington.

Can such a selective approach be justified? Many think not, calling it hypocritical. But the answer may depend on what other U.S. interests are at stake. Sometimes the cooperation of a repressive government is necessary in order to deter aggression, defuse a dangerous crisis, or achieve an arms control pact. "Human rights are not the only item on the American international agenda," wrote the late philosopher Charles Frankel. "A desire to maintain conditions conducive to peace and the prevention of bloodshed is not an immoral desire, and the consequences of protest against human rights violations should rightly be weighed against it."

By What Means?

Many influences have served the human rights cause. Perhaps the most potent influence of all is exerted by the relatively open borders of the United States and other Western democracies. Aside from the freedom thus gained by millions who have resettled in the West, there have been other results. Some dictatorial governments have sought to counter the attraction of Western life not just with the stick of repression and border controls but also with a carrot—a somewhat better life for the average citizen. Moreover, the influence of immigrants from such countries has been reflected in U.S. foreign policy, tending to increase official pressure on governments in Eastern Europe and elsewhere to respect human rights.

Another approach long in favor with some governments, but not that of the United States, is to write a human rights treaty, trusting mainly to world opinion to induce governments to live up to it. The earliest example is the UN Convention on Genocide (1951), inspired by a determination that nobody should ever again do to any people what Hitler and his accomplices did to the Jews. Other notable conventions, or covenants, sponsored by the UN, deal with civil and political rights, economic and social rights, a ban on racial discrimination, and—as an outgrowth of the ground-breaking UN Women's Conference of 1975—a ban on discrimination against women. All these have come into force. Although the United States has signed all of them, it is not a party to any of them since the Senate has not given its consent to ratification. It is, however, a party to three antislavery conventions, one on the rights of refugees, and one on the political rights of women.*

American opponents of such pacts object to the idea of international treaties overriding U.S. domestic law on essentially internal issues. Moreover, many human rights pacts appear ineffective in the countries that do adhere to them. The Soviet Union, for example, is a party to all those just mentioned and has not visibly changed its practices as a result; nor has it been much criticized on that account. Advocates reply that no conflict with U.S. laws could arise, since the latter set a higher human rights standard than the UN texts. As for the pacts' ineffectiveness, they argue that international public opinion is a potent force but takes time to become effective; and that nothing could do so much to strengthen public opinion behind the human rights conventions and covenants, or to symbolize U.S. concern for human rights for all peoples, as for the United States to accede to them at last.

When a particular human rights cause has not yet mustered enough support at the UN to produce a legally binding convention, one way to keep the pressure up is a *declaration* by the General Assembly. The classic case is still the Universal Declaration of 1948. Subsequent declarations on more limited topics, such as the rights of the child, are less famous but have served a useful "consciousness-raising" purpose. Some declarations have led to later conventions on the same subjects. A recent example of this technique is a declaration against "intolerance or . . . discrimination based on religion or belief," adopted by the Assembly in 1981.

The declaration method of promoting human rights is not confined

---

*By signing a *treaty, convention,* or *covenant* (legally, the latter two words mean the same thing as treaty), a government signifies its intent to *ratify* it. Ratification is an additional procedure, governed by each country's laws. (For the procedure in the United States, see page 65.) Each multilateral treaty prescribes how many and in some cases which states must ratify it in order to bring it into force (make it legally binding) for those that have done so; these thereupon become *parties* to the treaty. Additional states may become parties to a treaty already in force by *acceding* to it. As of August 1982 the Genocide Convention had 85 parties; the Convention on the Elimination of All Forms of Racial Discrimination (1965), 116; the International Covenant on Economic, Social and Cultural Rights, 74; and the International Covenant on Civil and Political Rights, 71. The last-named covenant has annexed to it an "optional protocol" under which citizens of states that are parties to it may address complaints of violations to an international human rights committee. As of August 1982, 28 states had ratified this protocol—a unique expression of willingness to have their performance in regard to civil and political rights monitored by the international community.

to the UN. The human rights portion of the Helsinki Final Act of 1975 (see page 93) is another celebrated example. Although lacking the legal force of a treaty, the document was signed amid great ceremony by leaders of 35 states including the Soviet leader himself, Leonid Brezhnev, plus the heads of all the Communist governments of Eastern Europe. Helsinki "watch committees" have been set up in the United States, Western Europe, and—until suppressed by the authorities—in Moscow and other East European capitals, in order to monitor compliance with the Helsinki pledges. The compliance in Eastern Europe has been meager at best. Clearly, Moscow does not regard the Helsinki rules as requiring it to tolerate Western-style human rights in its strategic domain—and will pay a price in international public opinion sooner than do so.

If public opinon doesn't get through, how about stronger methods? At times Washington has tried various other kinds of leverage. In 1974 the Senate agreed to a major trade agreement with the Soviet Union only after adopting the Jackson-Vanik Amendment requiring that Soviet curbs on emigration, especially of Jews, be eased. Moscow rejected the agreement on such terms, and the number of exit visas it granted the following year went down, not up. Similarly, as noted in Chapter 7, the Carter Administration failed in 1977 in its attempt to foster human rights in three South American countries by suspending small programs of military aid.

Such pressures can sometimes work, however, when the penalty for noncompliance is high enough. In 1981 the military dictator of South Korea spared the life of the jailed opposition leader Kim Dae Jung rather than endanger his political support in Washington. And in 1981 Moscow, under strong public pressure, gave an exit visa to the stepdaughter of Andrei Sakharov rather than risk its goodwill among antinuclear activists in the West.

Sometimes, too, it is better to dangle a carrot than to brandish a stick. in 1955, when China was threatening to try 15 captured U.S. airmen on criminal charges, Washington's efforts to free them got nowhere. Then UN Secretary-General Dag Hammarskjold flew to Peking and met with Premier Zhou Enlai. America got its fliers back; China got a top-level contact at the UN from which it was otherwise ostracized.

Human rights will always be hard to fit into the foreign policies of governments preoccupied with issues of war and peace and the pull and haul of powerful interests. Often quiet diplomacy can get results when public pressure would only arouse the offender's angry pride. Often, too, the pressure of private organizations and famous individuals can succeed where governments fail.

That human rights should be an international issue at all tells us something about the limits of national sovereignty. When foreigners can intercede for an oppressed citizen with the government that is oppressing him, and do so in the name of a universal principle, the notion of world civilization—still a frail growth in this world of nation-states—takes on a little more reality.

9

Global Issues II:
Economics, Ecology, and
World Order

ECONOMIC RELATIONS

The nature of the papers that come to the desk of the Assistant Secretary of State for Economic and Business Affairs is not normally announced to the world, but it is a fair guess that a list of questions confronting that official on an average day in the early 1980s would have read something like this:

- European complaints about high U.S. interest rates: effect on NATO economies and military budgets.
- Japan trade: can U.S. industry compete with Japanese products? Will Japan agree to relax import curbs on U.S. products?
- Charges of dumping European steel in U.S. market.
- Poland: U.S. food aid; stretchout of Western bank loans: what leverage do these give us on the human rights situation?
- Mexico: its oil exports, food imports, and heavy foreign debts; possible U.S. cooperation in its rural development; population boom and illegal migration to the United States.
- International development: followup to the Cancún conference, U.S. aid, food, trade, and investment policy.
- Canada: fisheries dispute; "Canadianizing" of U.S.-owned oil companies.
- Trade with the Soviet Union: how to harmonize U.S. policies with those of the other industrial democracies.
- Oil: OPEC's power is seemingly on the wane, but how prudent is continued heavy U.S. dependence on imported oil?

This imaginary listing will suffice to remind us of two facts. First, the United States—although its share of the world's economic product fell from 39 percent in 1950 to 23 percent in 1979—is still by far the world's biggest national economy, profoundly affecting—and affected by—the economies of the rest of the world. Second, committed though it is to private enterprise, the U.S. government cannot help but be deeply involved in economic decisions affecting the nation's interests. And, like every government, it tends to see economic power as part of national power and to view all issues, economic or otherwise, through its political lens. In some countries, such as Egypt or the Philippines, its economic aid is linked to military and political cooperation. It promotes trade with a friend, such as South Korea, while obstructing trade with an unyielding foe such as Cuba or Vietnam. In many such ways it uses its economic power— as do other governments—as a lever to advance its political interests against rival states.

But the United States also strives to maximize the *common* interests of states in mutually profitable trade and investment, raising of living standards, relief of suffering—all those positive-sum games that make up the great bulk of international economic relations. In fact, it was with this in mind—and made wiser by the world economic chaos of the interwar years—that Washington took the lead after World War II in creating major international economic institutions, notably the World Bank, the International Monetary Fund (IMF), and the General Agreement on Tariffs and Trade (GATT).

Let us look a little further into some of the main economic issues affecting relations with different parts of the world.

The Industrial Democracies

Although Canada, Japan, Australia, New Zealand, and all but one (Ireland) of the countries of the European Common Market are our military allies, their economic interests do not always blend smoothly with ours. Together, these countries and the United States account for the great bulk of world trade and investment. All are mixed economies, private enterprise and government sharing the big decisions. The economic health of each is heavily dependent on that of the others, and they pay close attention to each other's decisions on trade, investment, government spending, monetary policy, wages, prices—just about every big economic issue.

In the years just after World War II, this interdependence was institutionalized in the so-called *Bretton Woods system*, in which the IMF was to play a key role in smoothly adjusting currency exchange rates so as to promote trade and development. In practice, however, the system was extremely lopsided, for the U.S. economy was vastly stronger than the others. America, with its giant appetite for imported goods and its booming investments abroad, was the locomotive that pulled the world economic freight train. The dollar—almost free of inflation in those years—became the main world trading and reserve currency. It was redeemable in gold at $35 an ounce and became the standard by which all other convertible currencies were valued.

But later it became apparent that under this system the United States was even less master in its own national economic house than its increasingly prosperous trading partners were in theirs. An international dollar-based private money market evolved, the so-called *Eurodollar market*, outside the jurisdiction of any government. American banks were leading participants in this market. In it, money tended to move freely to whatever country was paying the best return; thus all governments found it next to impossible to control their domestic interest rates and money supply. The United States was doubly vulnerable because, under the dollar-standard rules then prevailing, it alone could not devalue its currency to correct a deficit in its balance of payments. Such deficits occurred regularly in the 1960s.

This vulnerability became fully apparent only during the Vietnam War. Heavy budget deficits to finance both the war and the nation's social welfare programs saddled the United States with a higher inflation rate than those of its main trading partners. So American goods became overpriced in the world market, and the deficit in the U.S. balance of payments became wider than ever. At the same time the Federal Reserve, in an attempt to stimulate the sagging U.S. economy, was holding U.S. interest rates below the levels investors could earn abroad.

As a result of all this, dollars moved abroad in a rising flood. The crunch came in 1971 when the Nixon Administration, determined to stop the dollar hemorrhage, broke up the dollar-exchange system by forcing other governments to raise the value of their currencies against the dollar. This soon led to the present system, or nonsystem, of free-floating exchange rates and gold prices.

On top of the "Nixon shock" of 1971 came the OPEC shock of 1973–1974, when the prices paid for vitally needed oil imports began their dizzy climb from about $3 a barrel (1972) to $34 a barrel (1981), causing an enormous transfer of wealth from the oil-importing to the oil-exporting countries.

Of the many far-reaching results of these events, two are important to note here. First, the industrial world as a whole caught a baffling new disease with a new name, stagflation, in which business stagnated while prices kept rising so that the average citizen's standard of living stood still or even declined. Second, it became clear that no country could recover from this disease by itself. This awareness led in 1975 to a new fixture on the international calendar: the annual "economic summit." Every summer since then, the heads of the seven most economically productive non-Communist countries in the world (in rank order according to GNP: the United States, Japan, West Germany, France, Britain, Italy, and Canada), together with a top official of the Common Market, have met for two or three days in an attempt to sort out their common economic problems and discuss ways to start a new cycle of growth.

The discussions of the "summit seven" range widely: inflation, growth rates, unemployment, productivity, investment, and policies affecting all those things. But the subject on which all discussion tends to converge is trade—the desire of all the great trading countries to increase their sales to each other and to the rest of the world.

In principle, all the governments in the group—and, for that matter, in the 86-nation GATT—are for lower trade barriers as a key to expanding trade; for all agree that prosperity for all is increased when efficient producers everywhere are free to sell in the widest possible markets. All are committed to the periodic rounds of world trade negotiations that have taken place under GATT auspices at intervals ever since the late 1940s, resulting in wide-ranging agreements lowering tariffs, quotas, and other governmental barriers to imports.

In practice, though, it isn't that simple. In every industrial democracy, government is under constant pressure to protect its least efficient and most vulnerable producers from foreign competition. Such protection is hard on the consumer (all of us) but good news for the producer and his employees, at least for a while. But then comes retaliation: "You exclude my country's wheat, I'll exclude your country's steel." Or else a government may devalue its currency, or grant tax breaks or other subsidies to its domestic producers—steps that enable them to sell their goods at more attractive prices both at home and abroad. Such devices can be good politics domestically—and seemingly compassionate, since jobs in a threatened industry may be at stake. But the compassion may be misplaced, for the wider result is often a trade war in which inefficiency is rewarded, trade is choked, living standards suffer, and everybody loses. In short, a negative-sum game.

The political-economic problem of trade is one of the severest economic issues facing the industrial world. But no less severe are a host of closely interacting problems including inflation, unemployment, wildly gyrating interest rates and currency values, and the often haphazard deployment of human, physical, and financial resources. Government strongly affects all these things but, especially in such a decentralized system as the United States, cannot control them. At the international level the institutions of coordination and control are much weaker still. In this field, where the seeming interest of each participant can so often add up to the ruin of all, the maker of foreign policy confronts challenges fully as difficult, and potentially as grave, as those in the more headline-catching realm of war and peace.

The Developing "South"

Some 124 countries, from huge China and India down to microstates like Kiribati or Tuvalu, are listed by the UN as *less developed countries* (LDCs). Their population comes to about 3.3 billion, or three-quarters of the human race. They produce a little less than three-eighths of the world's economic product. Almost all of them are in Asia, the Middle East, Africa, Latin America, and the Caribbean. Politically, they coincide fairly closely with the third world. In economic discussion, they are often called the "South," and they are united by a common interest in extracting more help for their development from the industrial "North." Their caucus at the UN is still called the "Group of 77," for that was their number when the group was formed at the first UN Conference on Trade and Development in 1964.

Lumping all these countries together under such labels conceals tremendous differences. Saudi Arabia and other big oil-exporters are still classed as LDCs, and their national development has a long way to go; but they are awash in oil money and long ago became donors, not recipients, of development aid. A handful of *newly industrializing countries* (NICs) such as Brazil, Taiwan, South Korea, and Singapore—all of them hospitable to foreign private investment—are far along the development road. The poorest countries, mainly located in Black Africa and South Asia, face desperate poverty with few resources and fewer skills.

The idea that the industrial North should aid the developing South got started in the United States in 1949 with President Truman's "Point Four" proposal for technical assistance. Other countries espoused the same idea. From the outset, the motives were mixed. Many people felt a generous concern for the world's poor. Business sought new markets, investment opportunities, and raw materials, often in countries that lacked good roads, schools, medical care, and other infrastructure without which business cannot thrive but which no private investor could profitably supply. And Northern governments felt a political interest in combatting Communist influence by helping poor nations to grow stronger and fulfill their aspirations for a better life.

It was the accelerating tide of decolonization beginning in the late 1950s that got development aid started on a substantial scale. Bilateral aid programs became a fixture in the foreign policies of the United States and most other industrial democracies. In addition, the Eisenhower Administration encouraged the expansion of UN development aid programs. In 1961 President Kennedy initiated the UN's first Decade of Development and, in Latin America, the Alliance for Progress. In 1960 the industrial democracies formed the Organization for Economic Cooperation and Development (OECD), a main task of which was, and still is, to promote and coordinate development assistance. In addition to financial aid, OECD governments also undertook to open their huge markets wider to the exports of developing countries. Meanwhile the Soviet bloc, on a much smaller scale, developed trade-and-aid relationships with a few politically favored third-world countries.

But the development policies of the industrial world soon ran into heavy weather. The U.S. Congress was less and less willing to underwrite a policy that called for billions a year in foreign aid over a time span measured in decades, addressed to countries in which most Americans showed little interest and in which progress, against communism or poverty or anything else, was often almost impossible to measure. While UN resolutions repeated a demand for raising development assistance to new highs—0.7 percent of each donor country's Gross National Product (GNP) became the official benchmark—the actual share of GNP transferred to LDCs by the U.S. government fell from above 0.5 percent in the early 1960s to 0.27 percent in 1980—one of the lowest shares among the 17 aid-giving countries of the OECD. Moreover, the great bulk of U.S. economic aid in recent years has been concentrated in Egypt, Israel, South Korea, and a few other countries deemed to be important to U.S. security. Development assistance to the rest of the world has been hedged about with requirements that it concentrate on simple, low-technology, village-type "basic human needs" rather than on expensive, relatively high-technology infrastructure projects. And there is a lenthening list of countries to which, on various political grounds, Congress has decreed that there be no aid at all.

Other sore points have appeared. The LDCs want special tariff preferences for their manufactured exports to Northern markets; Northern governments have responded warily in most cases. The LDCs have demanded commodity agreements, supported by a "common fund," to stabilize—and presumably raise—the prices of their staple agricultural exports; the results, still being worked out, are likely to fall short of what they had in mind. They want the North to agree to strict codes of conduct to regulate the activities of multinational companies operating in the LDCs—a prickly issue that is still under debate. Food-importing LDCs want the North to help them grow more of their own food—an ambitious goal for which foreign aid is important (and has increased), but for which the policies of developing countries themselves are even more important. And in the decade-old UN Conference on the Law of the Sea (see page 205), LDCs pressed hard for a guaranteed share of the wealth from future mining of mineral nodules that lie on the deep seabed. In 1982 a treaty negotiated among over 150 countries, embodying a compromise on this issue along with many other provisions modernizing maritime law, was rejected by the Reagan Administration and drew a cool response from most other industrial nations. The question of when, by whom, and for whose benefit the seabed will be mined remains unresolved.

The North-South dialogue on such issues reached its most acrimonious point in 1974, just after OPEC's first big oil price rise. Most LDCs are oil importers and were hard hit by that move; but instead of venting their anger on OPEC they joined forces with its more militant members in the UN and aimed their demands exclusively at the industrial North. The demands, under the title "New International Economic Order" (NIEO), were written in strident, accusatory tones. They called for a redistribution of wealth and productive capacity from North to South, and increased voting power in the World Bank and the IMF. They also claimed a right of every country to decide by itself what compensation, if any, it will pay when it nationalizes a foreign-owned business. The United States and other industrial powers responded with such moderate concessions as their legislatures were willing to make. Even today the dialogue continues—for example, it was the subject of a 22-nation North-South summit meeting in Cancún, Mexico, in October 1981, attended by President Reagan. Like the issues it addresses, it is expected to go on for many years.

Certain broad trends, significant for U.S. policy, are visible in this picture:

- The role of private business and banking in the LDCs, both as trader and as direct investor, has increased. The LDCs now account for about 35 percent of U.S. foreign trade, 48 percent of foreign lending by U.S. banks, and $52 billion in U.S. direct investments.
- Despite the antibusiness rhetoric, LDCs are well aware that development has been most rapid in countries that welcome foreign capital. Many impose conditions on the foreign investor, but if the conditions are too stiff he can take his money elsewhere. Case-by-case bargaining, rather than the writing of worldwide codes of conduct, seems likely to be the decisive factor in this relationship.
- The worldwide recession that began in the 1970s dealt a heavy blow to many LDCs whose ambitious development plans were based on expected high earnings from oil or other commodity exports—much of which did not materialize as demand sagged in the huge markets of the North. Some, like Mexico, went dangerously into debt to cover the shortfall. An economic adage says "a rising tide lifts all the boats," but since the world's economic tides usually originate in the great trading economies, much of the future of the LDC "boats" is beyond LDC control. By the same token, ending the recession has become a first-rank goal of U.S. foreign— not only domestic—policy.
- One ominous feature of the recession was the lending crisis of 1982. For years, Northern governments had left it to private banks to make hundreds of billions of dollars worth of loans to overextended governments, mostly LDCs such as Brazil, Argentina, Mexico, and Zaire. The loans were largely unregulated and, it turned out, not always prudent. By 1982, governments and the IMF were struggling to tide the borrowers over and stave off massive defaults which could shake the whole international banking system. Some commentators concluded that such high-risk lending to governments must henceforth be a function of governments—either singly or cooperating through the IMF—not the job of private banks.
- Some of the poorest LDCs are barely developing at all, and their peoples face a grim future. For the NICs, on the other hand, development is rapid but frequently uneven, favoring the economic and political power of the state and of the governing class but doing little for the majority. Brazil, a prime example, shows rising national power alongside deep mass poverty. Such situations contain serious threats to future political stability.
- Migration of the poor to richer countries is one of the main results of underdevelopment. The industries of Western Europe employ millions of "guest workers" from poorer areas of the Mediterranean. In 1979,

according to official figures, immigration to the United States from Latin America and the West Indies came to 177,000 and from Asia, to 183,000—compared to 64,000 from Europe, a striking contrast to the pattern of the early 1900s. And these figures greatly understate the trend, for they omit a still larger annual flow (estimated by some authorities at up to 1 million from Mexico alone) of illegal migrants, temporary or permanent, who come mostly from Mexico and the Caribbean region in search of jobs. How much of this migration the United States should try to absorb, and whether to control it by border patrols and criminal penalties or by development and population policies that help make life more tolerable in the migrants' homelands—these are already perennial questions for U.S. policy makers.

- With the stagnation of aid from the troubled industrial North, some of the burden of development finance has shifted to the most affluent of the developing countries themselves, chiefly the OPEC countries. This "cooperation among LDCs" is a new phase in the process. Along with it goes a redistribution of the influence that goes with aid. Thus, U.S. influence on the development process, although still great, has declined and may decline further.

- Trade is a chronic sore point as LDCs' manufactured exports increasingly compete with the technologically less complex Northern industries such as textiles and light machinery. Whether to yield to political pressure to protect the affected industry, or let it painfully "adjust" into some less vulnerable high-technology or service line, will be a problem for the United States and other Northern governments for a long time to come.

With U.S. policy on North-South issues in low gear, relations with the LDCs are a weak spot in the range of U.S. foreign policy. Except in a handful of countries, the early anti-Communist argument for development aid has become almost irrelevant. Other, newer threats—uncontrollable immigration from Latin America; civil chaos and political breakdown in hard-pressed regions like South Asia and East Africa—have not yet been fully recognized in U.S. policy. These may be among the key foreign policy issues of the future.

The Communist States

Decades ago, almost the only economic issue in U.S. relations with the Communist nations was purely negative: preventing exports of strategically useful items. That is still a major concern; the Western powers' committee called COCOM, which coordinates lists of strategic goods and technology whose sale to the Soviet bloc is banned or controlled, is over three decades old and still going.

But this policy of denial is not the overriding concern it used to be. As has often happened between enemies in times past, the mutual economic benefits of trade have grown—and have put a damper on the use of economic sanctions as a political weapon. This is especially true in Europe, where East-West trade goes back to the czarist era in Russia and has grown substantially since the flowering of détente a decade or more ago. The trade consists mainly of Soviet oil, natural gas, and minerals for West European manufactures, with gold from Soviet mines making up the deficit. The main U.S. export to the region is grain, of which the United States is the world's leading exporter and the Soviet Union the leading importer. But the trade bulks far larger for Western Europe than for the United States: in 1979, for example, the Common Market's trade with the entire Soviet bloc was valued at $33 billion compared to $8.5 billion for the United States.

In Henry Kissinger's version of détente, East-West trade was reckoned as a net benefit for the Soviets. Accordingly, Washington expected them to pay for it in political coin by restrained behavior toward the rest of the world, or else suffer the economic consequences. However, this "positive linkage" did not work well when put to the test by later administrations in two crises: the Soviet invasion of Afghanistan and, just afterward, the troubles in Poland. In the Afghan case, the main economic reprisal—most European governments took little action—was President Carter's partial embargo on U.S. grain exports to the Soviet Union. Soon even America's resolve melted in the heat of the 1980 presidential campaign, when Ronald Reagan wooed the farm vote by promising to rescind the embargo—which he did in 1981.

The economic reaction to the Polish crisis was more complex, involving relations both with Poland and with the Soviet Union. In the Polish case there was a further complication: Poland's $27 billion debt to Western banks, which Warsaw incurred in the 1970s with Soviet consent. Poland's hope was to lift its limping economy by its own bootstraps and thereby produce enough to meet its people's demand for a better life. The gamble was lost, and by 1981 Poland. could not even meet its interest payments.

Should Poland, already in dire straits, be declared in default? Western governments and Western banks all agreed it should not: the cost would be too great both for the financial community and for the Western powers' remaining economic influence in Eastern Europe. Instead, even after the crackdown against Solidarity in December 1981, the Polish repayment schedule continued to be stretched out—as was that of Rumania, also heavily in debt to the West—while modest amounts of Western food flowed to Poland to ease the people's plight. Some curbs were imposed on Western commercial exports to Poland, but a problem remained: how to impose economic penalties on the hard-line Jaruzelski leadership without hurting the Polish people even more.

But how about penalizing the Soviet Union, whose threats of invasion had virtually forced the Warsaw government's crackdown? The Reagan White House strongly favored this course, but Western Europe did not. In 1982 the issue came to a head over a long-planned project to build a big pipeline to carry Soviet natural gas from Siberia to Western Europe. By 1985 the added sale of gas would substantially increase the Soviet share of the West European energy market and would bring the Russians an extra $10 billion a year with which to buy the grain and high-technology items they need.

The main American participation in the pipeline scheme was technology, chiefly specialized pumping components made by Western European companies under license from U.S. patent-holders. The Reagan Administration concluded that this involvement gave it enough leverage to obstruct the deal and decided to try. Its aim was not only to show displeasure over Soviet behavior toward Poland but also to keep Moscow from gaining new influence over Western Europe and a new source of hard currency. Implicit in the decision was a much darker view of U.S.-Soviet relations across the board than had prevailed in the heyday of détente.

The President's decision overrode strong dissent from Secretary of State Haig and his staff, who argued that the pipeline contracts were already signed and it would be extremely costly in transatlantic relations, and perhaps impossible, to bring the Europeans into line. Haig resigned partly over this issue, and his prediction proved to be correct. All the main participants in the project—first France, then Britain, West Germany, and Italy—told their companies to honor the contracts despite the threat of penalties under U.S. law. After months of mutual transatlantic defiance, Washington lifted the sanctions in apparent exchange for a broad allied statement of intent to improve COCOM's East-West trade controls.

What of the other side of the economic coin—attempting to moderate Soviet behavior by increasing its economic dependence on the West? Such positive linkage may make economic sense in some cases, but its political results have yet to be demonstrated. And, as the pipeline case shows, it is hard to turn the coin over and cut off trade when Soviet behavior is no longer judged to be acceptably moderate.

What has been said here about the Soviet bloc could also apply, on a smaller scale and with variations, to economic relations with that other Communist giant, China. Even more than the relatively advanced Soviet Union, China's fast-growing foreign trade under the post-Mao government emphasizes imports of foreign technology. U.S. exports of militarily sensitive technology are strictly controlled, but since the 1970s improved political relations between this country and China have created an encouraging atmosphere for U.S. trade and investment in—and the export of technology to—China's oil, coal, and other industries. Serious conflict between economic and political relations could yet arise, but the more obvious limits are set by the modest rate at which China's still largely antiquated economy can absorb new capital and new ways.

This whole subject of Western economic relations with Communist countries must be seen in perspective. Measured against total foreign trade, the amounts involved are minor—about 4 percent for the United States, although substantially higher for Western Europe. Politics, not economics, is still the main determinant of the governmental relationship, at least for the United States. But the economic factor has increased in importance over the decades and may increase further—and not to the West's disadvantage. Although life for most Soviet citizens has greatly improved in the past generation, the Soviet economy still cannot begin to compete with the West in consumer goods. No barrier has been able to blind Eastern Europe to the potent attractions of the easier life lived in the West, nor the mainland Chinese to the allurements of Hong Kong, Taiwan, and Japan. Craving for the good life could prove to be a stronger force than ideology. Hungary has managed to cater to it without losing political control; Poland has failed to do so. Whether the Soviet Union, East Germany, and China can do so over the long run, and how their attempts to do so may affect their political systems and foreign relations, nobody knows.

But the West cannot be complacent. The ability of the United States and its allies to maintain the common defense and to continue to offer a more attractive alternative to peoples of the Communist-ruled countries will depend on how well they cope with their own economic and human problems, and how well they manage their highly productive but discordant economic relations with one another.

MAINTAINING OUR PLANETARY HOME

During the 1960s, after two decades of uninterrupted postwar growth in population, technology, and living standards, governments in the industrial world began to heed the long-neglected warnings of scholars about a new problem that, though far from new, had finally grown to international dimensions: the deterioration of the natural environment. In the spring of 1970 "Earth Day" was celebrated by environmental enthusiasts across the United States, and sweeping new environmental laws were enacted by Congress. Other industrial countries were doing likewise. In 1972 a UN conference on the human environment met in Stockholm, Sweden, to alert governments—in the developing as well as industrialized countries— to the threat that environmental damage can pose to the interests of all nations, and, indeed, of all humanity.

Delegates to the Stockholm sessions discussed a disturbing catalogue: erosion of agricultural soil; destruction of fisheries and forests; extinction or endangerment of whales, other large mammals of land and sea, and many other valued living species; threats to human health from urban and industrial pollution of air, water, and soil. Many developing-country delegates, who had come to Stockholm suspecting the environmental movement as an excuse to block their development, concluded that the environmental threat was real and that sound development must deal with it. A small permanent UN Environment Program was established, and follow-up UN conferences were held on such problems as water supply, the encroachment of deserts, and the urban environment.

Meanwhile, after the OPEC oil price revolution, awareness grew that mankind's fossil fuels—chiefly oil, natural gas, and coal—are subject to a long-term threat much more fundamental than North-South politics: ultimate physical exhaustion. Stored up over hundreds of millions of years and being consumed in ever-rising volume, they are sure to rise in price as the more accessible deposits are depleted. It also became apparent that nuclear reactors, although already providing a significant share of the industrial world's electric power, have serious cost and safety problems and possibly insuperable problems of preventing diversion into nuclear weapons, and cannot be counted on to fulfill their early promise.

As these new facts and new anxieties sank in, the industrial economies began to conserve fuels by more efficient use, and also—on a small but increasing scale—to turn to renewable energy sources including hydroelectric and geothermal power, alcohol from crops, and that ultimate source, the sun. Oil-importing developing countries also began to look harder for alternative energy sources. And, for similar reasons, more attention began to be given to conservation and recycling of metals, paper, and other materials as scarcities appeared and prices rose.

By 1982, however, U.S. oil imports had been greatly reduced by conservation (including more fuel-efficient cars), by a moderate shift from oil to coal, and by a method nobody favors, economic recession. A world oil glut appeared; OPEC prices softened and OPEC unity was in doubt. In the United States, jobs and recovery took top priority, and the trend was back to bigger cars and higher oil consumption. Some critics warned that U.S. dependence on imported oil was still dangerously high and that another world oil crisis could strain the U.S. economic and political system far more seriously than those of the 1970s.

The Surge in World Population

In 1974 the UN held the first world conference of governments on a problem closely related to that of the environment, and equally fundamental: population. Our century is unlike any previous time in human history in the rapid acceleration of population growth in nearly every region of the world. Of the 4 billion increase that experts estimate has occurred in the size of the human population in the past 2,000 years, *two-thirds* has occurred in this century. This happened because unprecedented advances in health care, such as control of insect-borne diseases, rapidly cut down death rates while birth rates remained high.

Thus far, equally great advances in technology and management have enabled a large part of this skyrocketing population to enjoy a rising standard of living. But this is by no means universally true, and will probably be still less so in the long future—for two reasons:

1. The most rapid population growth takes place in poor countries—or in poor areas of rich countries. More than 80 percent of the population growth in 1900–1975 occurred in Asia, Africa, and Latin America. Their share of current world population growth is over 90 percent. The difficulty those regions have experienced in raising living standards can be traced in large part to the very rapid increase in the number of mouths they must

feed—and to the rising percentage of their populations who are children, too young to be producers and in need of costly care and schooling. (In France, for example, 23 percent of the people are under age 15; in East Germany, 21 percent; in the United States, 24 percent—but in Mexico, 46 percent.)

2. The more prosperously we live, the fewer of us the planet can support without gradually destroying its forests, agricultural soils, and living and mineral resources. Spokesmen of developing countries, when urged by Northern critics to slow their population growth, often reply that one baby born in a prosperous American suburb will put a heavier burden on the planetary environment than a dozen babies born in a Mexican or Nigerian village or in the slums of Cairo, Bombay, or Recife.

Nevertheless, a growing number of low-income countries have begun in the past decade to promote family planning as a means of slowing their population growth. China, numbering more than one-fifth of humanity, appears to have one of the most effective programs, officially (and optimistically) aimed at zero population growth by the year 2000. India's effort has been vigorous but erratic and plagued by poor management and political controversy. Other LDCs' programs in this field vary from highly effective in Singapore and Indonesia to nonexistent in most countries of Black Africa.

Developing countries are receiving some help on their population programs from the industrial North. It comes through governmental and private programs and through UN agencies. The UN Fund for Population Activities, now a decade old, spends about $150 million a year on this work; the U.S. foreign aid program about $185 million.

Birth control is still highly controversial in many countries and, besides, is aimed at a condition that not all developing-country governments have yet perceived as being a problem. The tradition of large families is backed in many areas by religious tradition, by the low status of women, and by customs formed when infant and child mortality was far higher than it is today. Moreover, many political leaders still believe that growing population means growing national or ethnic power.

When will world population level off, and at what size? Most demographers expect it to rise from the 4.3 billion mark passed in 1980 to about 6 billion by 2000. How fast and how long it will rise beyond that point is mostly a matter of guesswork; but the huge proportion of children—the parents of future decades—in the world's present population has created such a powerful "demographic momentum" that continued rapid growth far into the twenty-first century, barring some global catastrophe, is virtually certain. Whether human population will ultimately stop growing at 8 billion, or 10 billion, or some higher number—and whether the leveling off will be caused mainly by the sum of individual decisions, or by governmental policies, or by the disasters of war, flood, and famine—all these questions will depend for their answers, in great measure, on the effectiveness of national development and family planning programs in the developing world between now and the end of this century. These answers, in turn, will go far to determine the future character of human civilization.

The debate on the human environment and human population goes on, but there is still no clear consensus. Nor have economists figured out how to combine environmental protection with economic growth and the conquest of poverty. Some experts sound an almost desperate cry of alarm; others exude optimism. The Reagan Administration, both domestically and internationally, has given these issues a lower priority than they have had since before 1970. If its view proves right, the alarmists will be laughed at some day. If the alarmists happen to be right, our descendants in the twenty-first century may pass a severe judgment on the generation now in power.

A BETTER WORLD ORDER?

Underlying all the big programs discussed in this and the preceding chapter is a question of a different kind: *Who is to solve them?* The answer may seem obvious: the sovereign states that wield power in this world. But quite a few critics maintain that the nation-state system which has evolved over the centuries is now obsolete; that it cannot solve the great problems it has helped to create, and that some new and more effective system must replace it.

That kind of talk is seldom heard from the rulers of states themselves, but it is not unusual to hear it from highly reputed scholars and even some public servants. And they can make an impressive case. Just consider how modern states behave. They all pay lip service to the rules of national conduct laid down in the UN Charter, yet the rules are widely violated and usually with impunity. They all claim to be interested in peace; yet they quarrel interminably over the terms of peace, pile up armaments, threaten war and even make war to get their way, and write their own versions of history to lay the blame on each other. They talk of prudently maintaining a balance of power, while each works incessantly to tilt the balance in its own favor. They all agree on the need for cooperation to bring their peoples a better life, yet many shamefully neglect their people's needs, and their cooperation on such matters is fitful at best. Again and again, their readiness to deal with their common interests is overriden by their relentless competition for influence, prestige, and power.

When such a system is confronted with a great global problem like the escalation and spread of nuclear weapons, or the degrading effects of world poverty and denial of elementary human rights, what can you expect? Clearly—so the argument runs—human survival imperatively demands a new and more effective world order.

Governments, of course, can point to their many efforts for international peace and their extensive cooperation for human benefit. But the critics are not so easily dismissed. Even if we grant only a slight probability that the defects of the present system will lead to global catastrophe, that should be enough to start us thinking about something better. Let us look briefly at a few possible approaches.

1. A *world empire*, in theory at least, is one possibility. Suppose one or both of the superpowers collapsed and a surviving power became something like the imperial Rome of the Caesars—but on a global scale. Given the spectacular advances of our century in the technologies of transportation, communications, and data processing, effective control— even more or less beneficent control—of a world empire is by no means unimaginable. But how could such a colossal change in power relations come about, except perhaps as the result of a new global war—the very tragedy we seek to avoid? Such a cure would be far worse than the disease.

2. A more benign approach, although no less drastic in its way, is to chart an entirely new course toward disarmament, peace, and world order. This order would not be based on power balances and rivalries as of old, nor on a world empire, nor even on great-power cooperation to enforce peace, such as the UN's founders vainly hoped for. Instead, it would educate all the world's peoples toward *new, more humane values and* patterns of cooperation. National armaments would be progressively reduced and eventually outlawed. The nation-state system we know would cease to exist. Global and regional authorities would be created, empowered to settle disputes peacefully, to promote human rights and respect for law, and to devote greatly increased resources to science, the arts, the benign uses of technology, the conquest of poverty, and education in peaceful human values.

To many, perhaps most, experts on world affairs, the numerous solutions of this kind that have been proposed are little more than utopian dreams, irrelevant to the harsh realities of the world. "You can't get there from here," say the critics. "How do you know, since you haven't tried?" retort the advocates. The heart of the argument is not really over organization charts, but over human nature. Can successive generations of human beings be taught to stop fighting and scheming against each other, and learn—as the preamble of the UN Charter puts it—"to practice tolerance and live together in peace with one another as good neighbors"? Or are group antagonism and the striving for dominance so rooted in our souls, or our genes, that the best humanity can ever hope for is essentially what now exists—limited cooperation among powerfully armed rivals, restrained in some degree only by mutual need and by fear of nuclear suicide? What you think of this approach to world order will depend mainly on how you answer such speculative questions as those.

3.   There are more modest approaches. One of these stresses the value of *regional organization*. Regional bodies in Europe and the Atlantic area have done a great deal to promote cooperation and peace in what was once the most blood-drenched region of the globe. Regional organizations elsewhere have done significant work in settling disputes, promoting trade and development, and—in the case of the Latin American Nuclear-Free Zone—putting a brake on the spread of nuclear weapons. There are limits to this approach, however, since some conflicts, notably those of the Middle East, cross regional lines. Regional organization surely has to be a major element in any design for world order, but could hardly be the main structure.

4.   Finally, many proposals call for strengthening *world organizations of states*, especially the United Nations system. This is a gradualist approach, since it would leave political and military power pretty much where it is, in the hands of independent states. But it could be far-reaching if, as its advocates hope, nations and peoples become increasingly aware of their common interests.

Most proposals of this kind call for improving existing institutions rather than creating new ones. Some examples:

- Since 1956 the UN, in most cases the Security Council, has sent more than a dozen small, lightly armed UN peacekeeping forces composed of units made available by various medium and small powers—Sweden, Canada, India, Finland, Brazil, Colombia, Ethiopia, Ireland, Fiji, Austria, to name only a few—into cease-fire zones to guard against a renewal of fighting. The service of these "blue helmet" soldiers in Egypt, the Congo,

Cyprus, Syria, Lebanon, and elsewhere has often been dangerous and sometimes fatal. Their value in muffling international conflicts is widely acknowledged. There has been much controversy over how such peace forces should be controlled and financed, with the West favoring a fairly broad grant of authority to the Secretary-General and the Soviet Union insisting on tight control by the Security Council where each big power has a veto. Years of U.S.-Soviet talks on this issue have brought little agreement. Are agreed guidelines possible? Or it is enough to build on past practice, improvising to meet each emergency? Are these improvised forces possible forerunners of a permanent international police force of the future?

- The World Bank and the International Monetary Fund provide important aid to developing countries. Their funds are contributed mainly by member governments. Might they one day have their own "automatic" sources of revenue, such as a small tax on all transactions in international trade?

- The International Monetary Fund originated more than a decade ago a device called *special drawing rights* (SDRs) which countries with balance-of-payments deficits can use to help balance their accounts. Only governments may buy and sell SDRs. Might this barrier some day be removed, making the SDR the first world currency? If so, what authority would stand behind its value?

- For nearly a decade UN members have been struggling to write a comprehensive world treaty on the Law of the Sea, covering everything from territorial and fishing rights to antipollution measures. If approved, the treaty will create an international authority with a 50 percent share in the mining and marketing of nodules rich in manganese, nickel, cobalt, and copper, lying on the ocean bed, a region outside any state's jurisdiction. In 1982 the treaty's fate was cast into doubt by the Reagan Administration's decision not to sign it because of objections to the seabed authority provision. But the treaty project is not dead. If the United States and other industrial powers with seabed-mining capabilities should later decide to join it, what powers should the seabed authority have? Should it have power to decide how to spend or invest income from its seabed mining? Should it share in decisions on allocating metal production between the seabed and competing producers on land? Should it be able to make such decisions over the objections of a state with a commercial interest in the outcome?

- In 1961 the United States, the Soviet Union, and ten other nations joined in a Treaty on Antarctica, promising not to militarize that vast frozen continent, not to press territorial claims to pieces of it, and to cooperation in Antarctic research. The treaty says nothing about tapping oil, gas, or mineral resources, but now there is lively interest in doing so. In 1991 the treaty will expire unless renewed. What will be done? Will

Antarctica, its wealth, and its fragile ecosystems be divided into national territories, or be governed by some international regime?

● Soon, perhaps early in the twenty-first century, the first human communities may be established in outer space. The UN-sponsored Outer Space Treaty of 1967 rules out all national claims to territorial rights in outer space or on the moon or other celestial bodies. It also bans the placing of nuclear weapons on the moon or in earth orbit. An additional "agreement governing . . . the Moon and Other Celestial Bodies," opened for signature December 1979, also provides that the moon shall be used exclusively for peaceful purposes. A few questions: Who will see to it that future space colonies remain free of nuclear weapons? What flag will fly over them? What passports will their citizens carry? Who will enforce their laws? Might the first emigrants to outer space be, in the full legal sense, the first citizens of the world?

● It is hard to imagine a decisive solution of the problem of nuclear weapons without some world authority to oversee, inspect, and, if need be, enforce the nuclear disarmament of nations. Such an authority, with a world monopoly of nuclear weapons, was proposed by the United States in 1946, when it had a few of these weapons and no other state had any. As proposed, the U.S. plan called for veto-proof punishment of any country caught violating the world monopoly. The Soviet Union, whose veto power was its weapon against the Western majority in the UN of that day, reacted coldly—apparently concluding that the United States meant to dominate the proposed world agency, use it to prevent the Soviet Union from developing its own bomb, and continue the U.S. atomic monopoly in disguise. So the U.S. plan got nowhere in 1946. Now, however, with nuclear weapons increasingly perceived as being too risky to use in war, might agreement on the nuclear disarmament of nations, and on creation of such a world authority, begin to look politically possible?

Such are a few approaches to the problem of building a better world order. Is it possible to persuade sovereign governments to act along these or similar lines? Sometimes it seems as if nothing will persuade them, short of a vast catastrophe, which is precisely what we seek to avoid. What to do?

There is no simple answer, but some points may be set down which make these problems look a bit less impossible.

1. World order does not consist solely of great organizations and vast programs. Every new bond of international friendship and cooperation that benefits all concerned—every contact, large or small, that enables

strangers or enemies to perceive each other as human beings—is a small bit of order in the world. In that sense every one of us has a contribution to make.

2.   Crises, large or small, help to focus top-level attention on needed reforms. Some crises are inevitable. Astute planners have sometimes, in moments of crisis, gained acceptance for far-reaching proposals that had been gathering dust for years. The important thing is to be ready.

3. Institutions that have disappointed early hopes are not necessarily ready for discard. The United Nations, however much its quarreling members frustrate its possibilities, remains the great symbol and custodian of certain universal values. On its better days it has served those values well. And it has developed civilized procedures—of debate, of parliamentary courtesy, of negotiating technique—that in the future, *if* the necessary desire arises among the members, will stand the world in good stead. A wise UN diplomat, Max Jakobson of Finland, once advised that the most important thing to do with the UN is to keep it alive until its members learn how to use it. Flawed though it is, the UN, and the complex of institutions at whose center it stands, may yet become the centerpiece of a stronger and better world order.

10

Thinking About Foreign Policy

Read not to contradict nor to believe, but to weigh and consider.

Francis Bacon
Essays (1597)

Albert Einstein once said that the task of physics is to draw a picture of the universe that is "as simple as possible—and not one bit simpler." Even to his powerful mind, material reality withheld its ultimate secrets and displayed an irreducible complexity. And yet Einstein himself also observed that politics is more difficult than physics!

What hope is there, then, of anybody ever really understanding politics, whether domestic or international? If "understanding" is taken to mean the scientific ability to predict and control future events, most authorities would agree there is no hope at all. But there is plenty of hope if what we seek is the kind of knowledge and insight that can be useful to makers of policy.

There have been many attempts through the ages to state such insights about politics as general rules. Philosophers and scholars, from Aristotle to leading political scientists of the present day, have made their contributions, as have many practitioners. Even the folk wisdom of proverbs can be suggestive.

But great difficulty can arise when we try to apply general rules to particular cases, especially in the realm of foreign policy. "Look before you leap," says one proverb. Good advice. "He who hesitates is lost," says another. Good advice again. Which of these opposite truths is the right one for the harried policy-maker facing a particular diplomatic headache on any given Tuesday morning?

There are, alas, no foolproof answers. Indeed, one obstacle to understanding is our natural hankering after some way to make all foreign policy questions lie down on some theorist's bed of Procrustes—globalism, regionalism, Marxism, democratic idealism, or whatever—and rise up solved. A better approach—or so it seems to this writer—is to draw general conclusions from our own study and experience of particular cases; then test, refine, or reject these generalizations as our knowledge increases. The few reflections that follow are offered in that pragmatic spirit.

Finding the Truth

1. **The complexity of motives**. Motives of nations and their leaders are not easy to pin down. Analysts often assume, for simplicity's sake, that leaders make foreign policy decisions by logical reasoning. So they do, but not always and not entirely. For one thing, a government may be poorly informed on the problem confronting it. Second, leaders are seldom in full control, since they face many conflicting and powerful interests within their governments and societies. Third, logical reasoning must compete with strong personal or group emotions—private loyalty, ambition, greed, fear, injured pride, vengefulness—a familiar list.

2. **Special pleading**. Accounts of important foreign policy issues, along with ideas for solving them, are always in plentiful supply; but it is important to be on guard against special pleading. Governments and other institutions are skilled at explaining problems in terms that suggest the solutions they want. Seemingly impartial proposals can be ingeniously crafted to favor a particular interest. Ambiguous phrases can make a promise less watertight than it seems. Loaded words like "freedom" and "peace" (good) or "aggression" and "terrorism" (bad) can be used to put a controversy in the desired light. Arguments can be won by debating tricks, such as answering a charge with a countercharge (the "look who's talking" method) or demolishing a weak argument that has not been made (the "straw man" method) or singling out the worst features of an opponent's position as proof that negotiation with such a scoundrel is out of the question. Faced with so many ways of distorting the truth, whoever studies international politics must cultivate a healthy skepticism about evidence and a taste for logical thought.

3. **Sources**. The truth in human affairs is usually complex, and a half-truth can be worse than a lie; so the advice of a wise Harvard law professor, Paul A. Freund, is worth bearing in mind: "When you perceive a truth, look for the balancing truth." A good way to find balancing truths is to get information and ideas from diverse, even opposing, sources. Even though each government or other source stresses those parts of the truth most convenient to it, the sum of them may yield something close to the

whole truth. News reports that carefully identify sources are invaluable in this respect.

4. "The facts." Getting and interpreting the facts, even if reliable sources are available, is not a straightforward matter. Knowing what facts to look for, and how to interpret them—that is the hard part. We all tend to select (or let somebody else select for us) those facts that fit a familiar pattern and confirm our opinions and hunches. Especially in a field as full of ambiguity as foreign policy, it is important to leave room in our minds for surprising facts and ideas—those that upset our preconceptions and make us think in new ways about familiar problems, or open our minds to unfamiliar ones.

5. Different kinds of knowledge. Much of the study of international relations boils down to a study of power politics—military power, wars, peace terms, diplomatic strategy, and statecraft. This is the emphasis of most traditional histories, and biographies of great leaders often take a similar approach. These are indeed basic aspects of international reality, but there are others just as important. Many modern writers— historians, political scientists, economists, sociologists, journalists, and others—have probed deeply into nations' economic and social life, technology, population, migration, human ecology, depletion of resources, cultural interactions, and changing attitudes, values, and institutions. For the observer of international affairs, all these kinds of knowledge contain clues to the present and future conduct of nations. Nor are all the insights confined to nonfiction. The best works of fiction, drama, and poetry, from Homer down to the present day, have an unrivaled power to illuminate universal truths about the varieties of human character and conduct.

Values and Interests

1. Setting the agenda. On an average day, the nation's main attention in foreign policy is fixed on a currently urgent issue—often one that has exploded into violence or threatens to do so at any moment. Intent on getting the right answers, policy-makers find too little time for asking the right questions. Important questions that take a long time to solve, such as those involving population and resources, tend to be pushed to the bottom of the agenda until they, too, become glaringly urgent—by which time it will be too late for a good solution. Questions involving intangible values, such as education and cultural exchange, also tend to get lost in the policy shuffle. Keeping such questions on the policy agenda is one of the difficult—and neglected—aspects of the policy-maker's art.

2. How many goals? The demands on the policy-maker's attention are almost without limit. Yet even the greatest mind—or the greatest power—cannot cope simultaneously with every problem. The wise leader will leave most problems for lower-level handling and occasional high-level review, and pare the top agenda ruthlessly to a manageable number of problems that demand timely decision at the top level. Some "urgent" issues go away if treated with benign neglect; still others, of long-term importance, can be dealt with on a slower track—but not forgotten or neglected—until time and circumstance ripen them for solution. The leader's decisions about selection and timing are crucial, and history may prove them wrong; but without selection there is no policy.

3. Special and national interests. The interest of the whole nation—for example, in military defense or in controlling arms races—is obviously superior to any special interest within the nation, such as that of an industry that makes weapons or of a military establishment that procures them. The leader who makes concessions to such special interests is often charged with "sacrificing principle to expediency." There may be justice in such charges; but a great national goal can seldom be attained without paying some price to special interests for their support. The statesman's problem is not whether to pay a price, but how to keep the price in reasonable proportion to the higher interest that must be served.

4. National and world interests. Assuming that special domestic interests are kept subordinate, is it enough for the state to serve the national interest of its own people? Or should it also serve—perhaps even give priority to—the needs and interests of all the world? There are strong arguments on both sides. The nation that promotes its narrow interests too single-mindedly—and successfully—is likely to be seen by others as a threat, and to end up with more enemies than friends. On the other hand, the statesman who sets out to serve a great world interest—such as peace through collective security, or the conquest of poverty—may find that the problem is more baffling than had been thought and that it demands long-term commitments and sacrifices that the people are unwilling to endure. Or a nation may convince itself that its way of life or ideology must be exported for the world's happiness—a notion that, if pressed too far, is more likely to produce war than happiness. What mix of national and world interests a nation should serve is thus a matter not only of ethics but also of practical wisdom.

5.   Great goals or modest ones?   In its long-term goals, a nation may aim high or low, tackling great difficulties or small ones. Should the United States strive to abolish world poverty and oppression, or only to relieve the worst sufferings they cause? Should we seek to foster a more peace-loving human civilization through education, or aim somewhat more modestly at a world of increasing tolerance, civility, and cooperation, and of decreasing conflict? Such questions seem pertinent for our own country in particular, both because of its great power and influence and because of its national character—quickly roused in times of crisis by the appeal of a simple and noble enterprise, but just as quickly discouraged and bored by difficulty. How to propose great and challenging foreign policy goals and maintain support for them over many years and even many presidential terms in spite of repeated failure and frustration—that is a question the American system has yet to answer.

Means and Tactics

1.   Linkage.   Persuasion, as was noted in earlier chapters, is often achieved through linkage. The desired action may be linked either to a promised reward or to a threatened reprisal. Rewards are pleasanter but not always wise. Rewarding another country for refraining from some unfriendly act can become an invitation to extortion. On the other hand, harsh reprisals may poison a valued relationship or widen a conflict until it is out of control. Certain rules can, however, be set down for all cases of linkage, whether of the positive or the negative kind. For example: (a) the promised action should bear some reasonable proportion to the action sought; (b) it should not unduly harm domestic interests or the interests of third parties; and (c) where possible, the link should be attached outside the glare of publicity lest it be taken as an insult to national pride and produce an action opposite to that desired.

2.   Timing.   Where an agreement hinges on the consent of several governments with different interests and domestic pressures to consider, timing is often the negotiator's most difficult problem. Like a farmer scanning the sky and wondering whether to plant today or later, the negotiator must guess whether the deal that can certainly be made today is as good as what *may* become possible next week or next year. The success of foreign policy depends on such intricate tactical judgments just as much as on the right grand strategy or ultimate values.

3.   "Bad" means and "good" ends.   Nations—sometimes even those on officially friendly terms—often do things clandestinely on each other's territory that would be punishable offenses under domestic law: espionage, forgery, bribery, sabotage, even political assassination—and, in extreme cases, aggressive war. Governments normally either deny using such means (even aggressive wars can be dressed up to look defensive) or insist that the means, though regrettable, are necessary to achieve a just end. Yet even when the end is just, violent or degrading methods are no better than a necessary evil. Moreover, governmental agencies that specialize in such activities tend to take on a life of their own, evading the control of higher authority. Thus the matching of means to ends in foreign policy raises questions that are both ethical and pragmatic.

4.   Friends, enemies, neutrals.   Some old maxims of politics say: "Reward your friends and punish your enemies." "He who is not with us is against us." "The enemy of my enemy is my friend, the enemy of my friend is my enemy . . . ," etc. In foreign policy such maxims are seldom helpful. A special fidelity is certainly due to allies and old friends, or we would soon not have any. But to reserve all the nation's favor for present friends, or to adopt their enemies as one's own, could lead to unfriendly relations with most of the world. The wiser course may be to keep faith with friends and expect the same of them, while searching for common ground with neutrals and even with the most implacable foes—even if existing friendships are sometimes disturbed as a consequence. Friendship based on traditional ties has its undeniable place in foreign policy, but clear-minded assessment of substantial common interests, and of the facts of power, makes a sounder basis for policy.

5.   Results, not motives.   Governments, like business firms, often cooperate for quite separate reasons. The two superpowers, for example, negotiate on arms control not only because of their common interest in preventing war but because each hopes to gain some strategic advantage from the negotiation—and some favor with world opinion—at the other's expense. Moral: Motives are less important than results. If governments do the "right" thing for the "wrong" reason, that, in diplomatic life, is a success. A further moral: It makes little sense to say "you can't trust the Russians," or the Americans, or some other power. You can trust any power to serve what it believes, wisely or unwisely, to be its own interest.

6.   Wrong and right uses of history.   Makers of foreign policy often warn against falling into famous pitfalls of the past, only to stumble into new and unfamiliar ones instead. The word "Munich" is enough to remind us of the folly of appeasing an overpowering and implacable foe; while the word "Vietnam" warns against being sucked into a distant, poorly understood, and perhaps unwinnable war. As the Harvard historian Ernest R. May has pointed out, such warnings are often issued by people who know too little about the real Munich crisis of 1938, or about the history of the Vietnam War—let alone about the current situations with which these are glibly compared—to make valid comparisons. Moreover, these two famous disasters are cited so often mainly because they are recent enough for today's policy-makers to remember them vividly (though not always accurately)—whereas incidents from remoter history might well offer more relevant insights but are not even looked up.

The study of history, both remote and recent, can often suggest to a thoughtful reader some practical insight on a contemporary problem. Much more important, it makes us aware of the inherited memories, values, attitudes, and beliefs that powerfully affect, for better or worse, the behavior of every nation and people. But history never repeats itself exactly, and knowledge of it can never be a substitute for intensive study of the actual problems of the day.

There is no claim to special wisdom in these observations. They are offered here only to indicate that it is possible to think about foreign policy—about all the issues and disputes, indeed, that are touched on in this book—in a more or less coherent and orderly way, even while allowing for the baffling complexity of the subject and the need to be ready for surprises.

To sharpen our thinking about these things is interesting in itself, but there is more to it than that. Americans are, after all, citizens of a very great power, which is, nevertheless, not all-powerful. It needs knowledge and intelligence if it is to define its interests wisely and pursue them effectively.

And it will not do to confine the needed knowledge to the few whose daily business it is to govern, for in this democracy the decisions are not entirely in their hands. Private citizens and groups press in on them every day, urging particular changes in the mosaic of U.S. foreign policy. Some changes may be clearly helpful to the national interest, others debatable or clearly harmful; but whatever the outcome, those of us who take no part in such proceedings have small ground for complaint. If the foreign policy product is to be improved, there will have to be greater participation in the process by Americans who have applied their intelligence not only to the intricate art of diplomacy but to the wider questions and values with which foreign policy is, or ought to be, concerned.

Glossary

The definitions and descriptions below are given in order to clarify the meanings of terms used frequently in the text of this book or in other writings on foreign policy. They are not intended to be complete.

ANZUS—A security pact signed in 1951 by Australia, New Zealand, and the United States to guard the parties from attack in the Pacific area.

Arab League—An association of Arab states, created in 1945 to strengthen inter-Arab relations by coordinating its members' political, cultural, social, and economic policies. There are 21 member states. The PLO is also a member.

ASEAN (Association of Southeast Asian Nations)—Formed in 1967 by Indonesia, Malaysia, the Philippines, Singapore, and Thailand, it promotes cooperation among its members on economic and, since 1975, political questions.

autonomy—A degree of self-government that falls short of independence.

balance of payments—The difference in the value of the nation's exports and imports. Included are goods, services, dividends, interest, tourism, and all other international economic transactions. A "favorable" balance is said to exist when exports exceed imports.

balance of power—A system involving two or more competing states or alliances of states, in which the power of each is balanced by that of the others. *See* **deterrence**.

bilateral—Involving two governments: as, a bilateral agreement, treaty, or program. Distinguished from **multilateral**, which see.

cold war—Conflict, short of military hostilities, between the United States and the Soviet Union, beginning after World War II.

colonialism—Synonym for **imperialism**, which see.

colony—1. Originally, a body of settlers who occupied and developed a distant territory under the sovereignty of the mother country. 2. A country whose land and people are governed by a distant "metropolitan" power as part of the latter's empire.

217

communism—1. In Marxist theory, the ultimate stage of human society in which the state withers away and goods are distributed "to each according to his need." 2. Historically, the doctrine of some Russian and other socialist parties that split from European democratic socialism after 1917, advocated a one-party state, and called themselves "Communist."

containment—The global policy, pursued by the United States since World War II, opposing the expansion of Communist—especially Soviet—power.

convention—In international law, a treaty, usually multilateral, dealing with economic, technical, or humanitarian matters.

conventional weapons—Weapons other than nuclear weapons.

covenant—A synonym for **treaty**, which see.

credibility—The ability of a state to inspire general belief in its promises, threats, and other pronouncements; specifically, in military affairs, to inspire belief in the claimed strength and capabilities of its armed forces.

customs union—A trading system, such as the EEC, in which several countries abolish tariff barriers among themselves and maintain common tariffs against imports from outside countries.

détente—In international affairs, a lessening of tensions between two countries. In current usage the term usually refers to the period of improved U.S.-Soviet relations in the 1970s.

deterrence—The use of power, especially military power, to deter an adversary state from attack.

EC (European Communities)—Three organizations, all with the same membership; currently ten states of Western Europe. The most important is the European Economic Community (EEC), also known as the Common Market, established in 1957. The others are the Coal and Steel Community (1951) and the European Atomic Energy Community (1957). The original members were France, West Germany, Italy, Belgium, the Netherlands, and Luxembourg. Britain, Denmark, and Ireland joined in 1973, and Greece in 1981. As of 1982 Spain and Portugal were negotiating for membership.

free trade—A policy opposed to **protectionism**, which see.

free trade area—A trading system such as the European Free Trade Association (EFTA) in which several countries abolish tariffs among themselves but each controls its own tariffs on imports from the rest of the world. Compare **customs union**.

globalism—A concept of U.S. policy toward countries of the third world and Latin America that places primary emphasis on competition with the Soviet Union for political influence in these areas. It is contrasted with **regionalism**, which holds that U.S. interests in such areas are best served by helping to solve local or regional problems of poverty, injustice, political instability, etc. U.S. policy has combined elements of both views.

Group of 77—A caucus of developing countries on economic matters which has grown from 77 members in 1964 to 124.

guerrilla—A soldier in an armed insurgency or other "irregular" army, as contrasted with those in the uniformed forces of recognized states.

hegemony—Domination by a stronger power, to the exclusion of other strong powers, over one or more weaker powers which nevertheless remain legally independent. *See* **sphere of influence**.

IMF (International Monetary Fund)—A specialized agency of the UN created in 1945 to maintain international monetary stability.

imperialism—The system of overseas colonial empires maintained by major European powers, the United States, and Japan until after World War II; also, the doctrine supporting that system. See **colony**; **protectorate**

intelligence—Information, whether acquired openly or secretly, concerning trends and developments abroad, used as a basis for policy decisions.

interest—In international affairs, any benefit or privilege that a state wishes to gain or maintain.

International Court of Justice (ICJ)—The judicial arm of the United Nations, located at The Hague in the Netherlands and consisting of 15 judges from different countries.

intervention—Foreign intrusion, military or otherwise, into the domestic affairs of a sovereign state. Considered unlawful by contemporary international standards, but whether a given action constitutes intervention or not is often a highly disputed question.

LDCs (Less developed countries)—Also called developing countries or, collectively, the "South" as contrasted with the industrialized "North." The UN list of LDCs includes all countries with per capita GNP under $2,000.

linkage—In diplomacy, a bargaining technique in which one side joins two or more issues together so that progress on one requires progress on the others.

massive retaliation—A term often applied to a U.S. policy, first enunciated in the early 1950s, of deterring Soviet attack by threatening nuclear retaliation against the Soviet homeland.

multilateral—Involving many governments: as, a multilateral treaty, organization, or program.

NATO (North Atlantic Treaty Organization)—An organization of governments established in 1949 to integrate the military defenses of the parties to the North Atlantic Treaty. The treaty is a security alliance joining the United States with 15 other countries: Belgium, Britain, Canada, Denmark, France, West Germany, Greece, Iceland, Italy, Luxembourg, Netherlands, Norway, Portugal, Spain, and Turkey.

NICs (Newly industrializing countries)—A term applied to developing countries that have achieved rapid economic growth.

nation—1. Strictly defined, a community of people bound together by strongly felt ties such as common language, religion, tradition, etc. In many cases the people of a nation, so defined, live in two or more countries. 2. In common American usage, synonymous with **state**, which see.

nationalism—The sense of belonging to, and loyalty to, a nation. In its extreme form, often called chauvinism, loyalty to the nation is the supreme value.

neutral—Not favoring either side in a war. In international law, the term *neutral rights* refers to the right of a neutral state to conduct trade and other relations with either side in a war—a subject of much controversy in past wars.

nonaligned—A term adopted by nations that are not, or profess not to be, politically or militarily aligned with either the West or the Communist bloc. The Conference of Nonaligned Countries has 97 members.

OAS (Organization of American States)—Created in 1948 by the United States and the republics of Latin America and the Caribbean to maintain peace and justice and increase hemisphere solidarity. There are now 28 member states.

OAU (Organization of African Unity)—Established by the independent states of Africa in 1963 to help promote unity and solidarity. There are 50 members.

OECD (Organization for Economic Cooperation and Development)—Created in 1961 by nations of the non-Communist industrial "North" to promote mutual economic well-being and progress in the developing countries and to expand world trade. The members are Australia, Austria, Belgium, Britain, Canada, Denmark, Finland, France, West Germany, Greece, Iceland, Ireland, Italy, Japan, Luxembourg, the Netherlands, New Zealand, Norway, Portugal, Spain, Sweden, Switzerland, Turkey, and the United States.

OPEC (Organization of Petroleum Exporting Countries)—A producers' cartel created in 1960 to coordinate oil price and production policies of the world's main oil-exporting countries. The members are Algeria, Ecuador, Gabon, Indonesia, Iran, Iraq, Kuwait, Libya, Nigeria, Qatar, Saudi Arabia, United Arab Emirates, and Venezuela.

Ostpolitik—West Germany's policy of reconciliation with the Soviet Union and Eastern Europe.

PLO (Palestine Liberation Organization)—The umbrella group for a number of Palestinian factions whose common aim is to create a Palestinian state on lands occupied by Israel.

peaceful settlement—Collective term for methods of settling international disputes without war, including negotiation, mediation, conciliation, arbitration, and judicial settlement.

protectionism—An economic policy that uses tariffs, quotas, etc. to limit importation of foreign goods that compete with goods produced domestically. Contrast with **free trade**.

protectorate—A state whose foreign relations and defense are controlled by a another power, but which is largely self-governing domestically and retains its formal identity as a state. Compare **colony** (definition 2).

regionalism—A foreign policy concept contrasted with **globalism**, which see.

SALT (Strategic Arms Limitation Talks)—U.S.-Soviet negotiations, begun in 1969, resulted in the two SALT I agreements of 1972 and the more comprehensive SALT II treaty of 1979. The latter was not ratified by the U.S. Senate but has been adhered to by tacit agreement of both parties. The negotiating process was resumed by the Reagan Administration under a new name, Strategic Arms Reduction Talks (START).

self-determination—The act of a nation or people, hitherto under foreign or colonial rule, in choosing their political future from among such options as independence, merger with a neighboring state, or autonomy under the existing sovereign.

socialism—Any of various political movements that arose in reaction to the industrial revolution, advocating social justice for the poor and greater state control of economic life. Some are democratic, others are not. Most influential in Europe were the movements inspired by the writing of Karl Marx (1818–1883). See **communism**.

sovereignty—The supremacy of the state (originally, of the monarch) as the law-giving and law-enforcing authority within its territory. Sovereignty implies independence from control by any outside power, but not freedom from external constraints where domestic and foreign interests conflict.

specialized agency—Any of 14 agencies associated with the United Nations, with worldwide membership, each devoted to international cooperation in a special field of human activity (health, agriculture, science, labor, etc.).

sphere of influence—A region in which a stronger power exercises hegemony over weaker states beyond its borders, with the acquiescence of other powers. See **hegemony**.

state—In international affairs, a political entity comprising a country or territory, its inhabitants, and a government whose sovereign authority to rule over them (with or without their consent) and represent them internationally is recognized by other states. Compare **nation**.

strategy—In a nation's foreign policy, the large-scale ordering of priorities among different aims and interests, and of means necessary to achieve them. Compare **tactics**.

strategic weapon—In the nuclear arsenal of the United States and the Soviet Union, a weapon designed to attack the adversary's homeland.

superpower—A term coined after World War II to refer to a class of states whose power far exceeds that of all others. The only superpowers are the United States and the Soviet Union.

tactics—The detailed actions that a government takes in its foreign relations in order to carry out strategy. See **strategy**.

terrorism—The practice of committing or threatening spectacular acts of violence, frequently against innocent persons, in order to demoralize a political enemy or gain public attention for a political grievance. Although the term usually refers to actions by insurgent groups, it can also be applied to actions by governments or by factions within governments.

theater weapon—A weapon, especially nuclear, designed for deployment in a particular military theater of operations, such as Europe.

third world—A collective term for countries of Asia, Africa, and the Middle East, most of which have recently attained independence and are not allied to either superpower. *See* Chapter 6; also, **non-aligned**.

totalitarianism—An extreme form of dictatorship in which the people are mobilized by, and required to profess positive loyalty to, the leaders, doctrines, and policies of the state. Nazism, fascism, and communism are the major examples.

veto—The ability or right of one member of a body to prevent a decision favored by the majority; specifically, the veto power of each of the five permanent members of the UN Security Council.

Warsaw Pact—A security alliance formed in 1955, led by the Soviet Union and including six Communist-ruled countries of Eastern Europe: Bulgaria, Czechoslovakia, the German Democratic Republic, Hungary, Poland, and Rumania. Albania, an original member, withdrew in 1961.

World Bank—A UN specialized agency that makes loans to developing countries for educational, agricultural, and other infrastructure development projects. It and the IMF (which see) are the main financial institutions of the UN system. Its original name was International Bank for Reconstruction and Development (IBRD).

Reading Suggestions

Listed below is a small sample of recent books and pamphlets on important regions, countries, and problems discussed in this book. Most contain bibliographies or notes on further reading.

History and Politics—The United States and the World

Bailey, Thomas A., *A Diplomatic History of the American People*, 9th edition. Englewood Cliffs, N.J.: Prentice-Hall, 1974.

McNeill, William, *The Rise of the West: A History of the Human Community*. Chicago: University of Chicago Press, 1970.

May, Ernest R., *"Lessons" of the Past*. New York: Oxford University Press, 1973.

Merli, Frank J., and Wilson, Theodore A., editors, *Makers of American Diplomacy*. New York: Charles Scribner's Sons, 1974. Two volumes.

Morgenthau, Hans J., *Politics Among Nations: The Struggle for Power and Peace*, 5th edition, revised. New York: Alfred A. Knopf, 1978.

Paterson, Thomas G., and others, *American Foreign Policy: A History*. Lexington, Mass.: D. C. Heath, 1977.

The U.S. Foreign Policy Process

Bloomfield, Lincoln P., *The Foreign Policy Process: A Modern Primer*. Englewood Cliffs, N.J.: Prentice-Hall, 1982.

Halperin, Morton H., *Bureaucratic Politics and Foreign Policy*. Washington, D.C.: The Brookings Institution, 1974.

Levering, Ralph B., *The Public and American Foreign Policy, 1918 1978*. New York: William Morrow, 1978.

Europe and the Superpowers

DePorte, A. W., *Europe and the Superpower Balance*. New York: Foreign Policy Association, December 1979. Headline Series 247.

Gaddis, John Lewis, *Strategies of Containment*. New York: Oxford University Press, 1982.

Levering, Ralph B., *The Cold War: 1945–1972*. Arlington Heights, Ill.: Harlan Davidson, 1982.

Schaufele, William E., Jr., *Polish Paradox: Communism and National Renewal*. New York: Foreign Policy Association, 1981. Headline Series 256.

Smith, Hedrick, *The Russians*. New York: Quadrangle Books, 1976.

Ulam, Adam B., *Expansion and Coexistence: Soviet Foreign Policy, 1917 to 1973*, 2nd edition. New York: Holt, Rinehart & Winston, 1974.

Northeast Asia

Fairbank, John K., *The United States and China*, 4th edition. Cambridge, Mass.: Harvard University Press, 1979.

Feintech, Lynn Diane, *China's Four Modernizations and the U.S.* New York: Foreign Policy Association, June 1981. Headline Series 255.

Barnds, William J., *Japan and the United States: Challenges and Opportunities*. New York: New York University Press, 1979.

Reischauer, Edwin O., *The Japanese*. Cambridge, Mass.: The Belknap Press of Harvard University, 1977.

The Third World

Ajami, Fouad, *The Arab Predicament*. New York: Cambridge University Press, 1981.

Gelb, Leslie H., and Betts, Richard K., *The Irony of Vietnam: The System Worked*. Washington, D.C.: The Brookings Institution, 1979.

Harrison, David, *The White Tribe of Africa: South Africa in Perspective*. Berkeley: University of California Press, 1982.

Hurewitz, J. C., *"The Persian Gulf After Iran's Revolution."* New York: Foreign Policy Association, 1979. Headline Series 244.

"Israel and the U.S.: Friendship and Discord." By the Editors of the Foreign Policy Association, New York, 1982.

Kitchen, Helen, editor, *Africa from Mystery to Maze*. Lexington, Mass.: Lexington Books, 1976.

Lippman, Thomas W., *Islam: Politics and Religion in the Muslim World*. New York: Foreign Policy Association, 1982. Headline Series 258.

Newell, Nancy Peabody, and Newell, Richard S., *The Struggle for Afghanistan*. Ithaca, N.Y.: Cornell University Press, 1981.

Pauker, Guy H., and others, *Diversity and Development in Southeast Asia: The Coming Decade.* New York: McGraw-Hill, 1977.

Reese, Trevor, *Australia, New Zealand and the United States: A Survey of International Relations, 1941–1968.* London: Oxford University Press, 1969.

Talbot, Phillips, *India As a Middle Power.* New York: Foreign Policy Association, 1983. Headline Series 262.

Wolpert, Stanley, *A New History of India.* New York: Oxford University Press, 1977.

The Western Hemisphere

Craig, Gerald M., *The United States and Canada.* Cambridge, Mass.: Harvard University Press, 1968.

Feinberg, Richard E., editor, *Central America: International Dimensions of the Crisis.* New York: Holmes & Meier, 1982.

Lowenthal, Abraham F., and Fishlow, Albert, *Latin America's Emergence: Toward a U.S. Response.* New York: Foreign Policy Association, 1979. Headline Series 243.

The Issues

Peace, Security, and the Military

Etzold, Thomas H., *Defense or Delusion: America's Military in the 1980s.* New York: Harper & Row, 1982.

Henkin, Louis, *How Nations Behave: Law and Foreign Policy,* 2nd edition. New York: Columbia University Press, 1979.

Mandelbaum, Michael, *The Nuclear Revolution: International Politics Before and After Hiroshima.* New York: Cambridge University Press, 1981.

Yost, Charles W., *The Insecurity of Nations.* New York: Praeger, 1968.

Human Rights

Baumann, Fred E., editor, *Human Rights and American Foreign Policy,* Gambier, Ohio: Kenyon College, 1982.

Boulding, Elise, *Women: The Fifth World.* New York: Foreign Policy Association, 1980. Headline Series 248.

Frankel, Charles, *Human Rights and Foreign Policy.* New York: Foreign Policy Association, 1978. Headline Series 241.

Economic and Social

Kindleberger, Charles P., *America in the World Economy*. New York: Foreign Policy Association, 1977. Headline Series 237.

North–South: A Program for Survival. Report of the Independent Commission on International Development Issues (Brandt Commission). Cambridge, Mass.: MIT Press, 1980.

Spero, Joan Edelman, *The Politics of International Economic Relations*. New York: St. Martin's Press, 1977.

World Resources and Population

Brown, Lester R., *Building a Sustainable Society*. New York: W. W. Norton, 1981.

Piotrow, Phyllis T., *World Population: The Present and Future Crisis*. New York: Foreign Policy Association, 1980. Headline Series 251.

Simon, Julian L., *The Ultimate Resource*. Princeton: Princeton University Press, 1981.

World Order

Bloomfield, Lincoln P., and Bloomfield, Irirangi C., *The U.S., Interdependence and World Order*. New York: Foreign Policy Association, 1975. Headline Series 228.

Hoffmann, Stanley, *Primacy or World Order*. New York: McGraw-Hill, 1978.

Index

Acheson, Dean, 72
Adams, John Quincy, 27
Afghanistan: history, 126–27; and
    India, 127; and Islamic nations,
    20, 117; and Pakistan, 4,
    126–27; and Soviet Union, 9,
    116, 126–27, 129, 140, 175; and
    U.S., 116, 126, 196–97
Africa, 141–50; and Afro-Americans,
    35; economy and trade, 14, 114;
    and Europe, 14, 36–37; and
    France, 114–15; population,
    200–1; and Soviet military
    power, 116. See also Black
    Africa; colonies; North Africa;
    names of individual countries
African National Congress, 149
Afrikaners, 147, 149
agriculture. See food and agriculture
Alaska, 28, 30
Albania, 4, 39, 55
Alberta (Canada), 153
Algeria, 141–42; disputes in Maghreb,
    4, 129, 142; and independence
    war, 20, 114; and third world,
    115, 142; and U.S., 142; and
    Zionism, 142
Allende, Salvador, 157, 162
Alliance for Progress, 61, 157, 192
alliances, military: and balance of
    power, 11; in Europe, 80–81,
    87–88, 91–92; Sino-Soviet,
    104–7; Soviet-Vietnam, 121–22;
    by U.S. in Asia and Middle East,
    third world, 177–78; by U.S. in
    Asia and Middle East, 108–10,

118–20, 122–23; by U.S. in
    Latin America, 155–56. See also
    treaties
ambassadorships, U.S., 53, 65
America First Committee, 45
Amin Dada, Idi, 145
Amnesty International, 18
Angola: Cubans in, 9, 147–48;
    independence fight, 20, 146; and
    Namibia, 147–48; Shaba invasion
    from, 145; and South Africa,
    147, 149; and Soviet Union,
    116; and U.S., 55, 60, 116
Antarctica, 205–6
ANZUS Pact, 123
apartheid: in Namibia, 147; in South
    Africa, 148–49, 181–82
Aqaba, Gulf of, 133
Arab-Israel conflict, 4, 128, 130,
    132–42; European positions on,
    14–15; and Persian Gulf policy,
    131; and U.S. arms exports, 176
Arab League, 12, 115, 128–29, 136,
    141
Arab states: and Black Africa, 143;
    military budgets, 10; and nuclear
    weapons, 176; oil embargo by,
    197; and U.S. arms exports, 176.
    See also Arab-Israel conflict
Arabian Gulf. See also Persian Gulf
Arabs, history of, 128–29, 132, 141,
    143
Arafat, Yasir, 134, 137, 140
arbitration, international, 30–31, 178
Argentina, 162–63; bank loans to,
    194; in Central America, 162;

About the Author

Born into a family of writers and journalists, Wallace Irwin, Jr. has been writing for most of his life, mostly on foreign policy subjects, in a succession of posts both in and out of government. He served from 1976 to 1980 as editor of the Foreign Policy Association, publishers of the annual *Great Decisions* and of the *Headline Series* pamphlets.

He graduated in 1940 with high honors from Princeton University, majoring in humanities and modern languages. After a brief stint in *Newsweek*'s foreign news department and three years of army service in North Africa and Europe during World War II, he decided on a career in international affairs and returned to Princeton to earn a master's degree in politics. In the quarter century that followed he served, successively, as a legislative aid in the U.S. Senate; evaluation officer in the Truman Administration's Psychological Strategy Board; public affairs advisor and speech writer for UN ambassadors Henry Cabot Lodge and Adlai E. Stevenson; speech writer at the Standard Oil Company of New Jersey (now Exxon); and speech writer and occasional policy planner for UN ambassadors Arthur J. Goldberg, Charles W. Yost, and George Bush. He was an advisor on the U.S. delegation to the U.N. Conference on Human Environment in 1972.

On leaving the government in 1972 he became a free-lance writer, edited the United Nations Association's annual *Issues Before the General Assembly*, and contributed frequently to the UNA monthly *The Inter Dependent*. The FPA editorship followed. He has lectured widely on the United Nations and other foreign policy topics.

Mr. Irwin and his wife, the former Barbara Sprott, live in Larchmont, N.Y. They are the parents of a son and a daughter.